The Critical Response to Robert Musil's
The Man without Qualities

The Austrian writer Robert Musil ranks among the foremost novelists of the twentieth century. Despite a series of lesser but well regarded shorter works, his literary reputation rests almost entirely on his novel *Der Mann ohne Eigenschaften* (The Man without Qualities), a life-work in the truest sense, which became the focus of all his energies and thinking from 1924 until his death in 1942. This study analyzes the principal trends in scholarship on the novel from the 1950s to the present. It contrasts earlier criticism, which foregrounded the eponymous central character's search for identity against the background of existentialist assumptions, with more recent criticism, which has focused on aesthetic and ethical approaches to the novel within the broader context of theories of value. A focal question in the study centers on the persistent difficulty critics have encountered with the idea of "Eigenschaftslosigkeit," the state of being without qualities named in the novel's title. Earlier criticism viewed the absence of qualities positively as a stage before union with the divine. Recent approaches have found difficulty in making commitment-free versions of subjectivity accord with social theories of value, particularly in the light of the conclusion of the novel, where war was to be seen as the logical outcome of the social descriptions sustained over the earlier sections. This difficulty is compounded by the controversy that raged for many years over the order of the unpublished later chapters. While this controversy has waned of late, the positions it marked out are still central to deciding what is involved in the notion of "Eigenschaftslosigkeit" and whether it has the capacity to further our understanding of modern subjectivity.

Tim Mehigan is Associate Professor of German and Deputy Head of the School of Languages at the University of Melbourne.

Studies in German Literature, Linguistics, and Culture:
Literary Criticism in Perspective

Literary Criticism in Perspective

Edited by James Walker

About *Literary Criticism in Perspective*

Books in the series *Literary Criticism in Perspective* trace literary scholarship and criticism on major and neglected writers alike, or on a single major work, a group of writers, a literary school or movement. In so doing the authors — authorities on the topic in question who are also well-versed in the principles and history of literary criticism — address a readership consisting of scholars, students of literature at the graduate and undergraduate level, and the general reader. One of the primary purposes of the series is to illuminate the nature of literary criticism itself, to gauge the influence of social and historic currents on aesthetic judgments once thought objective and normative.

The Critical Response to Robert Musil's
The Man without Qualities

Tim Mehigan

CAMDEN HOUSE

First published 2003
by Camden House

Camden House is an imprint of Boydell & Brewer Inc.
668 Mt. Hope Avenue, Rochester, NY 14620 USA
and of Boydell & Brewer Limited
PO Box 9, Woodbridge, Suffolk IP12 3DF, UK

ISBN: 1–57113–117–5

Library of Congress Cataloging-in-Publication Data

Mehigan, Timothy J.
    The critical response to Robert Musil's The man without qualities:
parallel actions / Tim Mehigan.
        p. cm. — (Studies in German literature, linguistics, and culture.
Literary criticism in perspective)
Includes bibliographical references and index.
ISBN 1–57113–117–5 (alk. paper)
    1. Musil, Robert, 1880–1942. Mann ohne Eigenschaften.   I. Title.
II. Series: Studies in German literature, linguistics, and culture (Un-
numbered). Literary criticism in perspective.

PT2625.U8M396 2003
833'.912—dc21

                                                             2003006385

A catalogue record for this title is available from the British Library.

This publication is printed on acid-free paper.
Printed in the United States of America.

For Amanda

Contents

Acknowledgments

I AM INDEBTED TO the German Academic Exchange Service, the Alexander von Humboldt Foundation, the University of Melbourne, and the School of Languages at the University of Melbourne for their generous support of this project. I also thank James Walker at Camden House for his patient and unflagging assistance in preparing this manuscript for publication, and Jim Hardin for his continuing interest in my work on Musil.

Tim Mehigan
The University of Melbourne

Abbreviations

QUOTATION FROM MUSIL'S NOVEL *The Man Without Qualities* is referenced to the following German edition of Musil's novel: Robert Musil: *Der Mann ohne Eigenschaften*. Sonderausgabe. 2 vols. Edited by Adolf Frisé. Reinbek bei Hamburg: Rowohlt 1981. Quotes from the novel are rendered by the customary short form *MoE* and the page number.

Quotes from Musil's diaries are rendered by the short form *TB,* the appropriate Roman numeral for the volume number, and page number, and refer to the following edition: Robert Musil: *Tagebücher*. 2 vols. Edited by Adolf Frisé. Reinbek bei Hamburg: Rowohlt 1976.

The short form *B,* followed by the appropriate Roman numeral for the volume number, and the page number, is taken from *Robert Musil. Briefe 1901–1942*. 2 vols. Edited by Adolf Frisé, with the collaboration of Murray G. Hall. Reinbek bei Hamburg: Rowohlt 1981.

GW with number and page reference refers to the collected works of Musil in nine volumes: *Robert Musil: Gesammelte Werke in neun Bänden*. Edited by Adolf Frisé. Reinbek bei Hamburg: Rowohlt 1978.

Other works of Musil are individually cited, as appropriate.

Introduction: Parallel Actions

Ich glaube nicht einmal, daß ein Künstler sein eigenes Werk versteht, wenn es fertig ist. Es kommt vielleicht für die menschliche Entwicklung auch gar nicht darauf an, was der wirkliche Inhalt eines Kunstwerks ist, sondern nur auf das, was dafür gehalten wird; jeder Einzelne, jede Epoche tritt mit anderen Schlüsseln heran und erschließt sich etwas anderes, das Kunstwerk ist in dieser Hinsicht ein Ästhetikum an sich, das es so wenig gibt wie das Ding an sich in der Welt der Wirklichkeit. Entkleidet man dies der Paradoxie, so erscheint das Verstehen des Kunstwerks einfach nicht als ein unendlicher Prozeß, der sich mit immer kleineren Abweichungen einem adäquaten Erfassen nähert, sondern als eine Mehrheit solcher Prozesse mit ganz verschiedenem Ergebnis
— Robert Musil

THE APPEARANCE OF THE first part of Robert Musil's *Der Mann ohne Eigenschaften* in 1930 with the Rowohlt-Verlag in Berlin was something of a sensation. The novel immediately aroused great excitement in literary circles, and was extensively reviewed in the press and in journals in Musil's native Austria and in Germany. With this major new work of fiction Musil finally appeared to deliver upon the promise that had struck the literary critic Alfred Kerr upon reading drafts of Musil's first novel *Die Verwirrungen des Zöglings Törleß* in 1906. Rowohlt brought out a second part to the new work at the end of 1932, only months before Hitler's ascension to power in Germany. The response to this second volume, however, was noticeably less enthusiastic. Its title — "Ins tausendjährige Reich (Die Verbrecher)" (Into the Thousand-Year Reich [The Criminals]) — struck a satirical note toward political events that were unfolding in Germany, while the story itself seemed to drift more and more into an intellectual utopia few readers could understand, much less share. Moreover, the novel still remained unfinished. Nothing more of it was to appear in Musil's lifetime, although Musil continued working on chapter drafts right up to the last days of his life. In 1938, following the annexation of Austria by Hitler's Germany, what had appeared of the novel was placed on a list of banned books, thus putting the entire project of *Der Mann ohne Eigenschaften* in jeopardy. In the same year, Musil headed into exile with his wife Martha Marcovaldi, taking only those materials with him he considered essential for completing work on the novel. The Musils finally settled in the city of Geneva in neighboring Switzerland in 1939. Musil died there in the middle of the Second World War in 1942, the year in which the "final solution," the extermination of the Jewish people, had become Nazi policy.

Musil's novel, initially so exuberantly received, had therefore steadily receded from public view over the course of the 1930s, and along with it the name of its author. With Musil's sudden death from a stroke in his sixty-second year, the novel appeared on the point of sinking into oblivion altogether. In 1943, a year after Musil's death, his widow attempted to revive the novel and the literary reputation of her husband by bringing out a third volume at her own expense. This limited edition — twenty-four chapters based on notes that Musil had been working on before his death, including all but two of the chapters he had initially authorized, but then withdrawn from publication in 1938 (the so-called "Druckfah-nenkapitel") — drew little public or critical response in the last years of the war. Furthermore, this edition of the novel did not complete Musil's project in any final sense. Subsequent attempts to divine the outline of the novel and to reason out its conclusion, though they continue to the present day, have remained inconclusive.

There was scarcely any interest in Musil or *Der Mann ohne Eigen-schaften* in the years immediately following the Second World War. To a small number of scholars — among them, most notably, Hermann Pongs, who was working on an ambitious historical study of German fiction at this time — Musil remained a writer of importance. Outside Germany, Musil entirely escaped attention. The widespread indifference toward Musil and his novel in the years immediately after the war moved Eithne Wilkins and Ernst Kaiser — subsequently to become Musil's English translators — to draw attention to Musil in an anonymous review in 1949 in the *Times Literary Supplement* "as one of the least known writers of the age" who was nevertheless "the most important novelist writing in German in this half century" (1949, 689).[1] This claim must have appeared preposterous to an English-speaking public who had never heard the name of Musil before, much less learned to appreciate him as one of the great authors of the twentieth century. Despite Wilkins and Kaiser's article, interest in his major novel was to remain muted in the English-speaking world for some time to come. J. B. Priestley, a highly regarded English critic and author, for example, saw fit to exclude the name of Musil from his major study of world fiction *Literature and Western Man,* published in 1960.[2] (Priestley considered Thomas Mann, Musil's main literary rival, "Germany's greatest novelist.") Even in the academy there were few stirrings. The first work of criticism on Musil in English — an essay by Hugh Puckett in the American journal *Monats-*

hefte — did not appear until 1952.[3] In fact, Musil cannot be said to have entered the scholarly mainstream in English-speaking countries until the mid 1950s. The appearance in 1954 of the first volume of *The Year's Work in Modern Language Studies,* a bibliographical reference work based at Cambridge University, in which an entry was made against the name of Robert Musil, may be taken as a convenient point for measuring the upswing of interest in the author in the anglophone world. The entry refers to three essays on Musil — by Karl Michel, Walter Boehlich, and Ingeborg Bachmann — that had appeared in the first issue of the German literary journal *Akzente* in 1954.

A compelling reason for the heightened interest in Musil and his novel in the 1950s was the appearance in 1952 of a new edition of the *Der Mann ohne Eigenschaften* with additional materials from Musil's posthumous papers, edited by Adolf Frisé and published by Musil's old publishing house Rowohlt — the first reissue of Musil's novel since 1930/32. Although Frisé's edition of the novel was not entirely beyond reproach — his decision to incorporate the posthumous papers in a "finished" version of the novel was energetically debated in subsequent years — it brought Musil's novel to the attention of a literary public beyond the confines of the academy. The new 1952 edition of *Der Mann ohne Eigenschaften* was hailed as a significant event and immediately aroused a great deal of critical interest. By 1956 it led to a new study in German according Musil prominent status in discussions of the German novel.[4] The first dissertations on Musil completed in Germany appeared in the same year.[5] Back in England in 1957, *The Year's Work in Modern Language Studies* recorded the 1955 publication, also with the Rowohlt-Verlag, of Musil's *Tagebücher, Aphorismen, Essays und Reden* (the diaries, aphorisms and essays) with the words "a publication of first importance." It also made mention of the 1957 publication of the *Prosa, Dramen, späte Briefe,* the third and last volume of Rowohlt's collected works of Musil (the *Gesammelte Werke in Einzelausgaben*) in its yearly edition of 1958. French and Italian translations of the novel appeared in 1957 and 1958; the first installment of the English translation by Wilkins and Kaiser had appeared as early as 1953. It can be confidently stated, therefore, that Musil, virtually forgotten in his own country by the outbreak of the Second World War, had attracted a following by the late fifties in both Germanys,[6] his native Austria as well as in England, France, and Italy.

Two more decades were to pass, however, before the name of Musil and his epic novel were to attract widespread attention. As the decade of the sixties began, the work of several scholars whose names have since come to be closely identified with Musil began to appear in academic journals and publications. Among these scholars were Walter Sokel in the United States, Helmut Arntzen and Wolfdietrich Rasch in Germany, and Karl Dinklage in Austria. In 1964, as the scholarly enterprise of hermeneutics was in full swing, Wilhelm Bausinger published a historical-critical analysis of the genesis of *Der Mann ohne Eigenschaften* with Rowohlt in Germany — the first stage in what he hoped might become a definitive historical account of the emergence of the novel. This ambition was quickly overtaken by Frisé's later editions of the novel, and was finally superseded by the appearance of a critical addition of Musil's notes to his novel on CD-ROM on the fiftieth anniversary of his death in 1992. In 1965 the first bibliography devoted to scholarship on Robert Musil appeared — already some measure of the amount of critical attention Musil had attracted in the years since Frisé's edition of his works in 1952.

The publication of an annotated edition of Musil's diaries in 1976 and a revised and improved Rowohlt edition of the collected works (the *Gesammelte Werke in neun Bänden*) two years later, both edited by Adolf Frisé, transformed Musil scholarship. The diaries and the new edition of the works were a revelation for Musil scholarship and fundamentally altered the understanding of Musil as a writer. The diaries were valuable on their own because they showed the immense amount of learning in which all Musil's writings were steeped. They revealed Musil as a conscientious reader of physics, chemistry, engineering, and mathematics and showed his deeply nuanced understanding of philosophy, psychology, and the emerging discipline of psychoanalysis. They also revealed that Musil kept up with new literature, particularly of German and Austrian origin, and had more than a passing familiarity with English and French literature (which he appears to have read in German translation). The diaries revealed influences on Musil that had not been widely appreciated, notably the American poet and essayist Ralph Waldo Emerson (1803–82) and the French philosopher Henri Bergson (1859–1941). They also brought to light Musil's familiarity with Goethe, Lessing, and Shakespeare, and his ambivalence toward Thomas Mann. Musil's sound judgment in appraising controversial ideas of his day also became apparent in the diaries. For instance, after reading the first volume of Oswald Spengler's *Untergang des Abendlandes* in 1918, Musil, a great believer in the humane project of civilization, immediately foresaw the danger in weakening and racializing the idea of culture (cf. *TB I*, 406). The diaries therefore added weight to what studies of Musil from the early sixties in Germany had been emphasizing, namely Musil's declared aim in his works to undertake a grand "conceptual dealing with the ideas of his time."[7] The diaries made clear that Musil made himself familiar with these ideas in a fair and non-polemical way.

Frisé's 1978 edition of Musil's works, which contained in a separate volume roughly one third of Musil's formerly unpublished notes from *Der Mann ohne Eigenschaften,* threw light on Musil's approach to his craft. Responding to earlier criticism of his attempts to provide a conclusion to the narrative, Frisé now eschewed any attempt to do so, instead reprinting not only the chapters Musil had finished before his death, but also chapter variations, drafts of chapters, and notes containing questions pertinent to plot and character development. The new arrangement of the *Nachlaß* volume confirmed what had only been partially understood in the 1950s and 1960s — that Musil worked "experimentally" with his own texts, exhaustively laboring over sections and chapters of his works until a final form emerged. Francesca Pennisi is one of many critics who have interpreted Musil's approach to writing as part of the "problem situation" of his novel. These notes showed that for Musil — more than almost any other writer — writing was a laborious process in which textual variants jostled with each other for attention and, in the final analysis, for the right to occupy center stage. Accordingly, they brought about a new understanding of the status of Musil's published texts, which could be seen for the first time as but one "authorized" version among competing versions of ideas, motifs, and plot variations. Since the *Nachlaß* had also shown Musil to have published no more than the "torso" of his major novel during his lifetime, Musil scholarship in the late seventies and eighties had no difficulty following trends contesting the dominance of "authorship" in the wake of Roland Barthes's announcement of the "death of the author."

The absence of a finished version of *Der Mann ohne Eigenschaften* and of an "authoritative" Musil was to do Musil's literary legacy no permanent injury. By slow degrees before 1978 and quickly thereafter, Musil was established in the critical literature as one of the foremost German-speaking writers of the twentieth century. Important milestones on Musil's road to literary fame were the foundation of the international Robert-Musil-Gesellschaft in Vienna and the publication of the first issue of its journal in 1975, the *Musil-Forum,* based in Saarbrücken at the University of Saarland. In 1982 a collection of influential essays on Musil appeared in the well-known *Wege der Forschung* series, edited by Renate von Heydebrand. A new English translation of Musil's novel by Sophie Wilkins appeared in 1995, attracting positive reviews, notably by Nicholas Spice in the *London Review of Books* in 1997.[8] Today Musil's reputation rivals, and in some respects even exceeds, those of Thomas Mann and Franz Kafka. However, unlike these writers, who still command a substantial readership outside academic circles, Musil's reputation was largely constructed by scholars and academics working at German, Austrian, English, French, Italian, and American universities in the postwar period. In an important sense the reputation of this fiercely independent and idiosyncratic writer still depends on these same scholarly institutions and is sustained by them.

An overview of the publication history of *Der Mann ohne Eigenschaften* provides valuable insights into its reception in the postwar period. Six thousand copies of the first edition of *Der Mann ohne Eigenschaften* were published by Rowohlt in 1952. From 1956 to 1960 another 23,000 copies were published in four new editions of the novel — an indication of the level of interest in Musil that had been building over the second half of the fifties. Over the next ten years, a further 33,000 copies were published in five new reprintings, bringing the total number of copies published between 1952 and 1969 to 62,000. From 1970 on, a new pattern emerged: Rowohlt began to issue significantly higher print-runs of its new editions. Fifty thousand copies of a special edition of the novel brought out in September 1970 sold so quickly that second and third printings of 10,000 copies each became necessary in 1972 and 1974. The statistics show that the novel had attracted more readers during this four-year period in the early seventies than in the seventeen years prior to that time — a clear indication of a heightened level of interest. The 1978 edition of the nine-volume collected works, of which *Der Mann ohne Eigenschaften* constituted volumes one and two, and a simultaneously released paperback edition with identical pagination of *Der Mann ohne Eigenschaften,* also sold well: taken together, a further 50,000 copies were issued between 1978 and 1981. To date, more than 172,000 copies of volume one of this paperback edition of the novel containing Book One and thirty-eight chapters of Book Two, and more than 103,000 copies of volume two, which contains additional materials that did not appear in Musil's lifetime, have been published. The 1978 and 1981 publications provided Musil's readers with reliable editions that have become the basis for research and scholarship on the author.

Although useful for its account of the passage of Musil's novel to public attention, the edition history throws little light on how Musil's novel has been received and understood by successive generations of readers. Such a task — the undertaking of the present volume — can only be gleaned from a study of the critical literature on Musil. Which works of criticism may be considered to constitute critical literature for the purposes of the present study? Rogowski, for example, whose critical commentary on the secondary literature on Musil's works was published in 1994, excepted from consideration most doctoral dissertations and master's theses and based his reception history on what he calls "mainstream literature" on Musil. Part of the justification for this modus operandi lies with the fact that the vast majority of doctoral and master's theses are not readily available to the general public and are sometimes difficult to track down even for the specialist. Against this view must be set the fact that much of the most interesting work that has been done on Musil has been done as or emerged from doctoral research. There is great value, therefore, in highlighting the valuable contribution that the best doctoral research has made in drawing an overall picture of Musil, even if Rogowski's point about the uneven and repetitive nature of much of this research must still be borne in mind. The present study aims to provide an insight into both the more accessible secondary literature that has appeared in the mainstream academic press, and the more specialized studies that have resulted from university research.

In discussing such work, I do not pretend to present an exhaustive study of the entire critical output on *Der Mann ohne Eigenschaften*. The enormous proliferation of studies on Musil's major novel in the postwar period precludes such an undertaking. Nevertheless, I do seek to discuss the most interesting and important work on Musil's novel that has been written, especially in German and English, and to make evident how these views have changed over time. In following this goal, it quickly became evident that Musil's work has been considered by a variety of critical approaches that cannot be brought under a neat periodization. While many of the works on Musil in the 1950s and 1960s, for example, were rooted in existentialist assumptions and a sense of melancholy about humanity and society typical of the immediate postwar period, existential critique has persisted in Musil studies despite being displaced in the main by more socially and aesthetically focused approaches that still form the most popular avenues to the novel. Any attempt to divine trends in postwar scholarship on Musil must therefore take account of the fact that the appearance of new critical approaches has not meant that older approaches have ceased to have application to their subject or to command interest among scholars. Rather, one witnesses today a rich variety of approaches. Social and cultural critique commands attention alongside old-style textual hermeneutics. Biographically informed approaches seek a new accommodation with poststructural approaches to writing and the text, or remain aloof from them. Furthermore, the widely proclaimed "death of the author" (Roland Barthes) has not meant the death of the text, but, if anything, its resurgence amid a new chorus of different voices and approaches. A guide to the secondary literature on *Der Mann ohne Eigenschaften* must meet the challenge of interpreting this startling variety of critical approaches without succumbing to undue simplification. At the same time, this consideration of trends in Musil criticism seeks to take account of the immediate cultural and political context in which scholarship in the last fifty years has sought to maintain its relevance both within the academy and within the wider community.

The present survey of the critical literature on *Der Mann ohne Eigenschaften* addresses itself both to new readers of Musil and more established readers and critics working within the field of Musil scholarship. While only the significant works of secondary literature — pre-eminently those in book form — have been dealt with at length, shorter studies such as articles and essays have been considered where these offer a fruitful or novel point of entry to interpreting the author and his work. Finally, a work of reception history might be considered to be an especially apt way of approaching an author who saw his own generation as being distinct in its nature and ambitions from the one that had gone before. Musil, addressing the demise of an age at the end of what E. J. Hobsbawm has called "the long 19th century," wrote in an immediate sense for the generation that came to prominence at the end of the First World War,[9] but also for a future age — one that he imagined would be more liberal, tolerant, and optimistic than his own. The story of scholarship on *Der Mann ohne Eigenschaften* indicates not only that Musil has spoken to a succession of generations since the appearance of his first novel, *Die Verwirrungen des Zöglings Törleß,* in 1906, but continues to speak to them, perhaps more clearly and persuasively than ever before.

The modern scholar investigating the works of Robert Musil encounters a vastly different critical situation than that which prevailed in the two decades following the Second World War. Whereas the scholar of the fifties and early sixties relied on a small number of influential critical works on the author, the full compass of individually cited books, essays, articles, and book reviews on Musil nowadays numbers in the thousands. Even if the scope of this immense output is reduced to include only the significant criticism on the author, today's scholar would still spend years absorbing the two or three hundred important critical works on the novel that have appeared over the last fifty years. For this reason, modern scholars of Musil have long given up the pretense of consulting the critical works on the author in any comprehensive way. More usual is a highly selective treatment of individual works of scholarship that appear either sympathetic to their chosen critical methodology, or at sharp variance with it. Even in such cases, Musil scholars struggle to demonstrate even a basic mastery of the vast criticism on the author.

Despite the overwhelming number of critical responses Musil and *Der Mann ohne Eigenschaften* have attracted since the 1950s, certain works of criticism and certain topics of critical debate stand out. The most influential of the early works of criticism was Helmut Arntzen's study on satire, first published in 1960, subsequently revised and republished in 1970, and reissued again in 1982 in a third edition. Arntzen's study drew attention to Musil's satirical portrait of the Austrian state, which Musil had dubbed "Kakanien" (Kakania), and inspired a generation of socially critical approaches from the late 1960s onward. Among the most prominent of these is Hartmut Böhme's study of Musil that appeared under the title of *Anomie und Entfremdung* in 1974. Böhme's approach mixed Frankfurt School Marxism, Weberian sociology, and psychoanalysis in seeking to account for the heavily ironical portrait of Kakania as well as the somewhat dysfunctional individualism of the novel's antihero Ulrich. Böhme's was the first of the critical approaches to generate interpretative categories that could satisfactorily address both Musil's view of a society in steep social and historical decline and the type of individualism he contrasted with it.

Böhme's approach was built on the assumption that Musil's unfinished novel, had he brought it to an end, would have dissipated into war and chaos and the protagonist's unconventional pursuit of individual happiness would have foundered in a degraded focus on the self. Böhme, in reaching such conclusions, was very much following the dominant view of the day about the novel's outcome. This view, issuing largely from the influential opinion of Wolfdietrich Rasch, who had written extensively on Musil in the early 1960s and had known Musil personally, argued that Musil could not sustain his utopian vision against the forces of social dissolution which were increasingly prevalent in his time. War and chaos, Rasch held, were to represent the final outcome of the novel. Rasch's view had won out over a contrary position maintained by Eithne Wilkins and Ernst Kaiser in their study of 1962. Wilkins and Kaiser had argued that Musil's picture of encroaching war and social dissolution would not overwhelm the private utopia of sibling love pursued in the name of "der andere Zustand" (the Other Condition). Wilkins and Kaiser instead believed that the unusual love between Ulrich and his sister Agathe was to be sustained against the collapsing social order they found around them. Wilhelm Bausinger's monumental historical-critical study of Musil's novel of 1964 — certainly one of the stellar achievements of early Musil scholarship — also came out in broad support of the Wilkins-

Kaiser line of interpretation. Wilkins and Kaiser vigorously defended their view, and were now opposed with great vigor and even vituperation, most notably by Ulrich Karthaus, who undertook the first survey of Musil criticism in 1965. The result of this early controversy, which is ultimately traceable to conflicting views about Frisé's ordering of the posthumous material to Musil's novel in the first postwar edition of the novel which he published in 1952, was settled in these early years not in favor of Musil's utopia, but of the dystopian elements that were increasingly read into Musil's portrait of Austrian society from the sixties on.

Nevertheless, the debate about Musil's intentions in the final part of the novel has not found resolution. While many critics incline toward the view that the question of the possible conclusion to the novel is passé in a postmodern age where the dynamics of the text exercises its own fascination over readers and where the text either undermines authorial intention or reaches an uneasy accommodation with it, speculation about the final shape of the novel still remains central to much of Musil scholarship, albeit in more indirect ways. Zingel (1999), for example, is one of several recent scholars who rely on a positive reading of the outcome of the novel as a basis for concluding that the Other Condition reconciles men and women in a wider, morally progressive, social utopia. Among more historically focused approaches, Jonsson (2000) has even enlisted the idyll of the sibling lovers in support of an idealized conception of global supranationality. Jonsson's postcolonial reading of the novel, however, can only be endorsed if Musil's utopia can be said to resist the historical reality whose tilt into war so manifestly assails it. Alexander Honold (1995) is one of many recent scholars whose conviction about the finality of war as the narrative "solution" to the novel speaks against such a conclusion. Clearly, then, the Wilkins-Kaiser-Bausinger/Rasch-Karthaus debate of the 1960s has laid no Musilian ghost to rest, nor can it hope to do so for the foreseeable future.

Two important new directions nevertheless grew out of the early Musil scholarship led by Arntzen and Böhme. The first of these directions was social criticism, which was energetically pursued from the 1970s onward and focused on Musil's description of the diseased Austrian state and the protagonist's involvement in the "Parallelaktion" (Parallel Campaign), an ambitious project seeking to align the seventieth anniversary of the Austrian monarch's rule with that of the German Emperor's thirtieth anniversary planned for the same year (1918). In Musil scholarship, social criticism has increasingly been accompanied by and has to some extent been expressed as cultural critique, that is, criticism that assigns importance to the immediate socio-cultural environment in which a work of art or literature is produced. While social criticism was indebted to the pre- and postwar Marxism of the Frankfurt School philosophers, particularly in the approaches of Schelling (1968), Reinhardt (1969), Laermann (1970), and Böhme (1974), cultural criticism has forged connections with multicultural and postcolonial discourses about identity and social action of a more recent provenance. In Musil scholarship, cultural criticism can be dated from Claudio Magris's pioneering historical study of Habsburg Vienna of 1966. Although not a contribution to Musil criticism in the first instance, Magris's study may nevertheless be considered the first of several approaches to have accorded Musil's cultural outlook on his society singular importance. This new cultural focus shows that Musil commands the attention not just of scholars of literature seeking to further an understanding of Robert Musil, but also of scholars of history who wish to develop an understanding of Viennese society in the last years of the Habsburg Empire. Both social and cultural criticism, therefore, assume the priority of historical assumptions, even as both approaches attempt to bridge the gap between aesthetic and historical understanding.[10]

At about the same time as the publication of Hartmut Böhme's *Anomie und Entfremdung* in 1974, Karl Corino published a psychosexual interpretation of Musil's early work *Vereinigungen*. Although quite dissimilar in outlook — Corino's detailed study of *Vereinigungen* was written with close attention to Musil's biography and the textual genesis of the two novellas, whereas Böhme's sociological study rested on a thorough knowledge of philosophy — both approaches show how Musil scholarship in the early to mid 1970s suddenly discovered a vital interest in the psychological disposition of Musil's protagonists, to some extent in opposition to Musil's explicit disavowal of Freud and early psychoanalysis.[11] In the eyes of some scholars, however, Musil's attempts to distance himself from the psychoanalytical approach did not invalidate the connection with Freud, but only served to make it more apparent. Henninger (1980) is one among several scholars who, while following Corino's focus on *Vereinigungen,* saw a clear relation between the psychosexual concerns of this early work and *Der Mann ohne Eigenschaften.* These psychological approaches are connected in their emphasis on pathological aspects of identity formation in Musil's works. Henninger, in an unacknowledged reference to Freud's case study of the "Wolf Man,"[12] even goes so far as to postulate connections between dysfunctional subjectivity in *Vereinigungen* and *Der Mann ohne Eigenschaften* and Musil's apparent witnessing of his parents' coitus recorded in the fragment *Grauauges nebligster Herbst.*

By the early 1980s, therefore, psychological and psychosexual readings of Musil's novel took their place alongside socially and culturally based approaches. Social and cultural criticism, in turn, had developed from the importance attached to Musil's picture of alienated individuality in the early postwar period. It was this sense of alienation coupled with a profound sense of isolation and existential despair that had supplied the first point of focus for critical writing on Musil in the 1950s. By introducing the question of Musil's use of satire in the novel, Arntzen directed attention away from the image of the displaced individual and toward a sense of moral concern over the nature and extent of social decline. This concern loomed large in German society, which was then in the throes of an uncertain process of postwar reconstruction. Musil's descriptions of the decline of prewar Austria therefore resonated in postwar Germany amid widespread concern about the sort of social progress being pursued in that country. Böhme, following Arntzen, then struck a discordant and skeptical note about attempts to resist social decay, particularly since Musil's protagonist was held to suffer from as many afflictions of identity as the society to which he remained so implacably opposed. Klaus Laermann (1970) was even less sympathetic to the main character Ulrich than Böhme. In a polemical study directed as much against postwar German society as against Musil's novel, Laermann viewed the protagonist of *Der Mann ohne Eigenschaften* as ethically corrupted as well as corrupting of others. He found nothing of value in the state of being without qualities, and even turned his analysis into a wider attack against all ethically compromised bourgeois writing.

Such trenchant social criticism sprang up in ground made fertile for a spirit of social transformation by such avowed critics of capitalism as the Hungarian Georg Lukács. His widely reported debate with the Frankfurt School philosopher Theodor Adorno between 1957 and 1961 about realism in the novel had important repercussions for Musil scholarship. In some ways this was a debate about Marxism, with Lukács supporting a stringently dogmatic, "applied" Marxism and Adorno upholding a more compassionate and theoretically oriented interpretation.[13] But it was also a debate about what the highly subjective prose of such modernists as Joyce, Kafka, and Musil could be taken to mean and how much it engaged with social reality and the need to change it. In Musil scholarship, there were many — like Schelling (1968), Laermann (1970), and Böhme (1974) — who, adopting Lukács's understanding of realism, felt obliged to attack Musil for contributing to the moral and cultural decline that he had captured so compellingly in his description of the bankrupt Kakanian state. These scholars accused Musil of burying the spirit of postwar collectivism along with the Habsburg state. It was only through the willingness to make common cause with others, they implied, that society could hope to arrest the forces that were corroding it. (Musil, it is noted in passing, had indeed been skeptical about the prospects for collectivism in his own time, drawing a distinction between the ideal of humanity in the late eighteenth century and the new "anti-individualistic" appearance of the collectivist dream of his present age.[14])

Those scholars who defended Musil's intentions against Lukács's antibourgeois dogmatism in the late 1970s and early 1980s, argued for a positive conception of Musil's utopia. Two of these scholars — David Luft (1980) and Cornelia Blasberg (1984) — focused on the position of the intellectual in Austrian and German society in the early twentieth century. Blasberg's analysis revealed the depth of the cultural atrophy afflicting not only bourgeois writers, but Musil's entire generation. That social decay and the mental crisis of intellectuals were so pervasive in European society before the outbreak of the First World War lent weight to Adorno's view about the nature of divided subjectivity in the modernist novel. While Musil's utopia had found few adherents in the 1970s and 1980s, it took even longer for his complicated political stance to draw any support. Musil's politics, so frequently opposed by the 1968 generation of scholars, did not receive a persuasive defense until Cay Hehner's study in 1994. Hehner purported to uncover an underlying "conservative anarchism" in Musil's work.

By the early 1980s, therefore, several different portraits of Musil had come into view. The existentially displaced Musil of the fifties had given way to the socially aggrieved and to some extent socially disagreeable Musil of the seventies. By the mid 1970s, psychologically based approaches to Musil's oeuvre were also in evidence, as if in response to the pathological individualism that social criticism had diagnosed in Musil's uncertain and decidedly unheroic protagonist Ulrich. By the late seventies, however, Adolf Frisé's new edition of the novel and his expanded, annotated edition of Musil's diaries threw more light on Musil's thinking on philosophical, psychological, and scientific topics and increasingly held old views about the conclusion of Musil's novel up to question. About this time, the word "project" was used to characterize Musil's literary intentions, which were increasingly seen as far more open-ended and unresolved than even the Wilkins-Kaiser/Rasch debate had suggested. For this reason, yet another portrait of Musil was emerging clearly by the early 1980s. This portrait, which sought to renew the dialogue on Musil's aesthetic outlook — a prominent concern of scholarship in the 1950s and 1960s — now updated the picture of the writerly

Musil in the light of radical new postmodern ideas about the nature of textual production.[15]

One of the most notable attempts to accord this aesthetically focused Musil prominence was undertaken by Roger Willemsen in two studies published in the mid 1980s. The earlier of these two studies appeared under the title of *Das Existenzrecht der Dichtung* (1984) and reflected the wider interest of German criticism of the seventies and eighties in aestheticism.[16] In this work Willemsen engaged with the utopian aspects of Musil's literary vision — aspects that had attracted comparatively little attention in the socially minded criticism of the 1970s — in order to defend the province of art as a legitimate form of individual expression and truly lived experience. It was in the realm of art, Willemsen found, that Musil's scenarios of possibility took root. Art would also make them real. Since this approach also began to show up points of contact with other related discourses, Willemsen's research appeared to lead the rationally minded Musil not just to the center of new aesthetic thinking, but also into areas adjacent to aesthetics such as mythology, mysticism, and anthropology. Willemsen's radical aestheticism also brought him into protracted public conflict with a more traditionally minded colleague, Helmut Arntzen, whose new two-volume study of Musil's works had appeared in 1980 and 1982. Ironically, Arntzen was the scholar who had arguably done the most to launch Musil scholarship on its long path towards radical aestheticism in the first place. Arntzen's new study, which showed a sensitivity to the expressive categories of language and what, in the manner of Wittgenstein, could or could not be uttered through the medium of language, therefore brought him much closer to Willemsen's aesthetically based view than either critic would perhaps have wished to acknowledge.

Insistent probing of Musil's epistemological position since the inception of Musil scholarship, and particularly since the appearance of the diaries in 1976, precipitated a rush of new studies in the 1980s and 1990s that engaged with the ethical dimensions of Musil's work. To be sure, Musil's ethical outlook had long been seen as important. Renate von Heydebrand (1966), Ingrid Drevermann (1966), and Marie-Louise Roth (1972) were among several scholars who had been attracted to Musil's "philosophy of feeling" and had connected feeling with the ethical disposition of the Other Condition. What seemed new in the eighties and nineties, however, was the depth of the analysis to which Musil's ethical project was now subjected. Instead of simple questions about influence, scholarship now forged profound connections with thinkers who helped shape Musil's ethical outlook, in particular Nietzsche (Venturelli 1980, Dressler-Brumme 1987), Kant (Luserke 1987), Husserl (Cellbrot 1988), the Vienna Circle (Döring 1999), and Friedrich Schelling (Bohn 1988). Most of these ethical approaches engaged passionately with Musil's category of "Möglichkeitssinn" ("sense of possibility") which was seen as an ethical modality of foundational importance. While situating Musil squarely within discursive modernity, these and other studies were increasingly drawn to the discursive nature of Musil's ethics, rather than to the aspect of modernity favored in approaches of the early postwar era (emphasizing, therefore, Musil's discursive practice rather than his modernity). For this reason, the unfinished nature of Musil's novel no longer typified the failed project of modernity, but rather represented the discursive precondition for any future ethics. To this extent, the interest in the ethical component of Musil's novel arose out of a new postmodern outlook on the novel. The ethically progressive *project* of modernism was no longer held to fall irredeemably away with the waning of the modern period, but could be separated from it more or less intact, as the German philosopher Jürgen Habermas had famously suggested[17] and as Venturelli (1980) and Finlay (1990) attempted to show in their studies of Musil's modernism. With a shift of perspective, therefore, Musil's novel not only shored up Habermas's argument about the "unfinished" modern project; its fragmentary nature also suggested the very embodiment of such a project.

The predilection for partial views at the expense of holistic ones in the postmodern critique of culture had followed, among other things, Adorno's anti-Hegelian dictum that "das Ganze ist das Falsche." Adorno's overall purpose was to underscore the danger inherent in the totalizing philosophies that could be traced back as far as German idealism and which in his view had helped bring about the rise of fascism.[18] The influence of Adorno and, more generally, the philosophy of the Frankfurt School in the postwar period even moved Hartmut Böhme, in a 1986 essay, to consider fascist tendencies in Musil's holistically oriented thinking. The insight that comprehensive views of the world should not be confused with totalizing ones, however, was not to gain ground in any serious way in Musil criticism until the early 1990s. This more differentiated understanding of Musil's attraction to holistic thinking coincided with a new line of approach to *Der Mann ohne Eigenschaften* from the late 1980s onward.

In this line of inquiry, Musil's reception of "Gestalt" theory[19] and his lifelong digestion of the functionalist philosophy of Ernst Mach,[20] on whose epistemology Musil wrote his doctoral dissertation, were accorded new significance. Mach had confronted the early Musil with powerful arguments against the fixed space-time continuum and the idea of direct causality. Musil had immediately seen value in Mach's functionalist view of reality, despite his critical reading of Mach's epistemology in his dissertation. As Arvon had made clear as early as 1970, Musil's interest in Mach was to exact a price, since the functionalist view could not be adopted without abandoning the principle of causation which itself presupposed a substance-based view of reality. From the beginning, functionalism had attracted a number of implacable opponents in Musil scholarship, most notably Reinhardt (1969), who had held that the functionalist outlook, so evident in the idea of "Eigenschaftslosigkeit" and in the radical openness of the Other Condition, completely fails and was actually renounced by Musil in the latter part of his novel. Arvon (1970) then put forward a more differentiated account, arguing that Musil, while greatly attracted to the functionalist view, was nevertheless unable to abandon substantial reality altogether. Later scholars such as Hoffmann (1997) and Kümmel (2001) have moved Musil steadily closer to the functionalist outlook, where reality is not conceived dualistically as the tension between mind and body, or nature and culture, but more in procedural terms as the interplay of formal and functional units. The circulation of functional units of information, in turn, has allowed these critics to make sense of both the formalized nature of the Kakanian state — defined as the primacy of information over substance implicit in the descriptor "Seinesgleichen geschieht" — and the underlying communicative self-reflexivity of the novel. The most far reaching of the studies to have engaged with the functionalist aspect of Musil's novel was undertaken by Albert Kümmel and published under the title *Das MoE-Programm* in 2001. His study was significant for directing attention back toward Musil's picture of Kakania, and specifically to Kakania as a model of communication for the postmodern age. In Kümmel's approach, the iterative aspects of "Seinesgleichen geschieht" in the Kakanian state are not rejected, as in the past, for a lack of authentic substance, but actually define how communication is generated discursively as literature. In Kümmel's view, "Eigenschaftslosigkeit" should not be discarded on the grounds of any incipient lack (of substantial or authentic qualities), but stands for the underlying absence of fully articulable "meaning" that characterizes all informational and communicational states. In Kümmel's view, following the lead given in the pioneering work of Friedrich Kittler in the mid 1980s,[21] absence of qualities is a structural dynamic that generates discourse in connection with prevailing "discourse networks."

In this area of literary production, questions may now be asked about the relation of criticism to the work of art. In Kümmel's reading, the activity of scholarship appears as a second order observation of a system of textual communication that generates a new discursive formation related to, but nevertheless separate from, the original text from which it gains its point of departure. This iterative formation implies no reproduction of an original content, but doubles it discursively in nonsubstantial and procedural ways. This loss of the original — in Derrida's formulation, the loss of "originary presence" — was already suggested by Benjamin in a key formulation about the nature of the critical enterprise in the early part of the twentieth century:

> Kommentar und Übersetzung verhalten sich zum Text wie Stil und Mimesis zur Natur: dasselbe Phänomen unter verschiedenen Betrachtungsweisen. Am Baum des heiligen Textes sind beide nur die ewig rauschenden Blätter, am Baume des profanen die rechtzeitig fallenden Früchte.[22]

Criticism relates to the work of art as the profane relates to the sacred — there is no capacity to retrieve the lost original presence. Commentary and translation in Benjamin's understanding are therefore constituted as "ewig rauschende[n] Blätter" — leaves that imitate nature's rustling, but which amount to no more than the "Rauschen" (noise) of circulating profane discourse in the age of information. In this sense, the iterative doubling of the text that is the critical enterprise is a parallel procedure that emerges from a lost original and yet is powerless to recover it. Critical commentaries, in this sense, are "parallel actions" that multiply a text and connect it in endless iterative performances with other texts. The inflation of discursive readings of a text cannot recapture the meaning of its antecedent, even as these readings generate ever-greater discursive complexity. Musil seems to have thought as much himself in characterizing criticism as "Ausdeutung der Literatur, die in Ausdeutung des Lebens übergeht":

> Kritik in diesem Sinn ist nichts über der Dichtung, sondern etwas mit ihr Verwobenes. Sie ergänzt die ideologischen Ergebnisse zu einer Überlieferung — wobei ideologisch in einer weiten Weise zu nehmen ist, die auch die Ausdruckswerte der "Formen" umfaßt — und erlaubt nicht die Wiederholung des gleichen ohne neuen Sinn. Sie ist Ausdeutung der Literatur, die in Ausdeutung des Lebens übergeht, und eifersüchtige Wahrung des erreichten Standes. Eine solche Übersetzung des Irrationalen ins Rationale gelingt nie völlig [. . .].[23]

By this process, the literary text is "led out" into the world where it connects with the fullness of life: The connection of literature with life does not concentrate meaning; rather, life dissipates meaning as literature connects with other discourses. As a rational enterprise, therefore, criticism never achieves the mastery of the rational over the irrational that may be considered its greatest ambition.

Notes

[1] "Empire in Time and Space," in *Times Literary Supplement* 48 (October 28, 1949): 689–90.

[2] J. B. Priestley, *Literature and Western Man* (London: William Heinemann, 1960).

[3] Hugh W. Puckett, "Robert Musil," in *Monatshefte* 44 (1952): 409–19.

[4] Beda Allemann, *Romanschaffen im Umbruch der Zeit* (Tübingen: Verlag der deutschen Hochschullehrerzeitung, 1956).

[5] Wilfried Berghahn, "Die essayistische Erzähltechnik Robert Musils. Eine morphologische Untersuchung zur Organisation und Integration des Romans Der Mann ohne Eigenschaften," diss. Bonn, 1956; Helmut Arntzen, "Satirischer Stil. Zur Satire Robert Musils im *Mann ohne Eigenschaften*," diss. Bonn, 1960. The first postwar dissertation on Musil was completed at the University of Vienna in 1948 (Karl Riskamm: "Robert Musils Leben und Werk," diss. Vienna, 1948).

[6] The East German writer Rolf Schneider points out that in the 1950s in the German Democratic Republic a thousand copies of the first edition of Frisé's *MoE* were available for DM 38 — at the conversion rate of 1:1. Cf. Rolf Schneider: "Referat auf dem Musil-Symposium in Berlin im Herbst 1989." *Musil-Forum* 16 (1–2) 1990: 113–17, here: 113.

[7] In an interview with Oskar Maurus Fontana in 1926. Cf. Oskar Maurus Fontana, "Erinnerungen an Robert Musil," in Karl Dinklage, *Robert Musil: Leben, Werk, Wirkung* (Reinbek bei Hamburg: Rowohlt, 1960), 325–44. A useful discussion of this interview with Fontana can be found in Wilfried Berghahn, *Robert Musil* (Reinbek bei Hamburg: Rowohlt, 1991), 12–13, 104–5.

[8] Nicolas Spice, "A Very Low Birth Rate in Kakania," in *London Review of Books* 19/20 (October 16, 1997): 16–19.

[9] Cf. *MoE*, 1819: "Ich widme diesen Roman der deutschen Jugend. Nicht der von heute [. . .] sondern der, welche in einiger Zeit kommen wird u. genau dort wird anfangen müssen, wo wir vor dem Krieg aufgehört haben udgl. (Darauf beruht auch die Berechtigung, heute einen Vorkriegsroman zu schreiben!!)"

[10] An example of the simultaneous application of both points of departure is Alexander Honold's study of 1995, *Die Stadt und der Krieg: Raum- und Zeitkonstruktion in Robert Musils Roman "Der Mann ohne Eigenschaften"* (Munich: Fink, 1995).

[11] Von Büren's study of 1970 was the first comprehensive attempt to assay the psychological dimensions of Musil's writing. *Zur Bedeutung der Psychologie Im Werk Robert Musils* (Zurich, Freiburg i. Br.: Atlantis, 1970).

[12] Freud published his case study of the "Wolf Man" in 1918: Sigmund Freud, "From the History of an Infantile Neurosis ('Wolf Man')," in *The Freud Reader,* ed. Peter Gay (London: Random House, 1995), 400–426.

[13] Adorno argued in his *Noten zur Literatur I* (Frankfurt am Main: Suhrkamp, 1961) that Lukács's position, although attenuated in his book *Wider den mißverstandenen Realismus* (1958), remained tenaciously dogmatic and dismissive of all modern literature: Cf. Theodor W. Adorno, "Erpreßte Versöhnung. Zu Georg Lukács: *Wider den mißverstandenen Realismus*," in *Begriffsbestimmung des literarischen Realismus*, edited by Richard Brinkmann (Darmstadt: Wissenschaftliche Buchgesellschaft, 1987), 197.

[14] Cf. Robert Musil, *Tagebücher, Aphorismen, Essays und Reden*, edited by Adolf Frisé (Hamburg: Rowohlt, 1955), 908: "es kann wohl nicht verschwiegen werden, daß er [= der Kollektivismus] sich in der Zeit unserer Klassik auf die 'Humanität' und auf die 'Persönlichkeit' verlassen hat, wogegen er heute antiindividualistisch [. . .] auftritt und nicht gerade ein leidenschaftlicher Verehrer der Humanität ist."

[15] One of the most far-reaching analyses of the "writerly" Musil was undertaken by Kuhn in relation to *Vereinigungen* — Heribert Kuhn, *Das Bibliomenon. Topologische Analyse des Schreibprozesses von Robert Musils Vereinigungen* (Frankfurt am Main: Peter Lang, 1994).

[16] One of the chief proponents of new aestheticism in German letters was the noted critic Karl Heinz Bohrer; cf. e.g. *Plötzlichkeit. Zum Augenblick des ästhetischen Scheins* (Frankfurt am Main: Suhrkamp, 1981), and most recently, *Ästhetische Negativität* (Munich/Vienna: Carl Hanser, 2002).

[17] Cf. Jürgen Habermas, *Der philosophische Diskurs der Moderne. Zwölf Vorlesungen* (Frankfurt am Main: Suhrkamp, 1985).

[18] A like-minded colleague, Karl Popper, even dedicated his work, *The Poverty of Historicism,* which appeared in English in 1957, to the "countless men, women and children of all creeds and nations who fell victims to the fascist and communist belief in Exorable Laws of Historical Identity." Cf. Karl Popper, *The Poverty of Historicism,* (London: Routledge, 2002).

[19] Silvia Bonacchi even concludes that Musil's entire novel could be conceived of as a "gestalttheoretisches Konstrukt." *Die Gestalt der Dichtung: Der Einfluß der Gestalttheorie auf das Werk Robert Musils* (Bern: Peter Lang, 1998), 309.

[20] Yvon Desportes (1974) and Wolfgang Freese (1983) are two scholars who have viewed Musil's reception of Mach's thought as central to his literary project. Desportes, "Études comparative d'un style et d'une philosophie: une oeuvre de Musil à la lumière de Mach," *Revue d'Allemagne et de pays de langue allemande* VI: 79–90; Freese, "Zur neueren Musil-Forschung. Ausgaben und Gesamtdarstellungen," *Text + Kritik* 21/22: 86–148.

[21] Friedrich Kittler, *Aufschreibesysteme 1800/1900* (Munich: Fink, 1985); *Discourse Networks 1800/1900,* trans. by Michael Metteer, with Chris Cullens (Stanford: Stanford UP, 1990).

[22] Walter Benjamin, *Gesammelte Schriften*, vol. 4/1, edited by R. Tiedemann and H. Schweppenhäuser (Frankfurt am Main: Suhrkamp, 1972–89), 92.

[23] Robert Musil, *Tagebücher, Aphorismen, Essays und Reden,* edited by Adolf Frisé (Hamburg: Rowohlt, 1955), 697.

1: Early Philology and Existentialist Readings

Es ist wohl der Typus einer Verfallszeit, einer
Zivilisationsepoche. Wobei als Ursache des
Verfalls anzusehen wäre, daß die Zeit nicht
mehr einheitlich umspannt werden kann.
(*TB I,* 354)

MUSIL'S WORKS WERE rediscovered after the Second World War in an atmosphere of profound despair about the nature and direction of European society. Musil's picture of "Kakania" had already foretold not only the decline of old European society, but also the decay of the values on which that society had been built. For this reason, the substructure on which Musil's portrait of the last days of the Austro-Hungarian Empire had been based — Nietzsche's analysis of a retrograde cultural development called nihilism — also shone through in the early postwar period when skepticism about the prospects for Europe was at its greatest extent. If Kakania delivered proof of a nihilistic strain in old Europe that reached back at least as far as the last decades of the nineteenth century, and possibly, as Nietzsche thought, much further, it was also the attitude struck by the individual in response to such nihilism that spoke directly to the first postwar generation of Musil readers and scholars. This attitude — a kind of ironic aloofness toward the monumentalist project of old Europe — was expressed by the desire of the eponymous hero of the novel to subsist "without qualities," where "qualities" meant the values preordained by the Kakanian collective, which, by definition, were already thoroughly compromised. The epithet "man without qualities," which registered Musil's rejection of the cultural direction embraced by Austrian society before the First World War, thus also stood for a more general sense of being cast adrift from European society and values in the immediate aftermath of the Second World War.

Subsisting without qualities also meant subsisting without society — a state of being that accorded with intellectual positions that were emerging in the early postwar period. Of these intellectual positions, the most dominant was existentialism, a movement that made a direct appeal to the individual confronting the finality of life. Works such as Heidegger's *Sein und Zeit* (1927), Sartre's *L'Etre et le néant* (1943), Camus's

La Peste (1948) and Hemingway's *The Old Man and the Sea* (1952) indicated that the tribulations of life were to be suffered on their own terms, without the tempering influence of spiritual or ethical certainty and with the sure knowledge that death will eventually overwhelm the human struggle, no matter how defiantly heroic such a struggle might prove to be. In a similar way, attention was drawn in Musil criticism of this period to the finality of war as the vanishing point of *Der Mann ohne Eigenschaften*. For existential critique, war could all the more represent the narrative "solution" to the novel since it turned the state of being without qualities into a stoical, if ultimately senseless, struggle against insuperable forces.

Hermann Pongs and Beda Allemann were the most prominent advocates of existentialist perspectives among early critical approaches to Musil's novel. As early as 1939 in the second volume of his major study *Das Bild in der Dichtung,* Pongs had considered Ulrich's existential troubles expressive of an overriding sense of ambivalence toward the world. Moreover, such ambivalence impeded action and presupposed a tragic view of existence: "Indem die Entscheidungen so aus dem Ganzen der Existenz verstanden werden," Pongs contended, setting out the methodology of his study of modern German poets, "läßt sich das Phänomen des Tragischen erweitert begreifen als ein 'wesentliches Element im Universum selbst'" (1963, 299). In later remarks on Musil's novel, Pongs held that Ulrich's "Dauerschwebe zwischen den Möglichkeiten" had little to recommend it, since it suggested "die Struktur des 'Neurotikers,'" rather than any idea of artistic freedom. Moreover, it had been Musil's intention precisely not to confer on Ulrich the liberating status of the artist (435).

Allemann put forward a less anguished view of the problem of existence based on Musil's use of irony in two studies that appeared in 1956 and 1970. In the first study, Allemann viewed irony as a structural principle in the novel. Irony reflected a deep skepticism toward the bankrupt practices of the Austrian state. At the same time, it expressed the hope that these practices could be overcome and the continuity of historical experience restored: "Wie in der Leere der eigenen Seele sich das Utopische des eigenen Daseins mit der Ironie als Grundstruktur von Welt verbindet, so ist auch das Festgestellte der Welt selbst die Voraussetzung der ihr innewohnenden Ironie und Utopie" (1956: 206). In his later essay, Allemann took this utopian aspect of irony a step further by suggesting that irony could dispense with authorial perspective altogether in its construction of an ideal: "Der ideale ironische Text wird der sein, dessen Ironie völlig signallos vorausgesetzt werden kann. Nichts ist dem ironischen Stil so schädlich wie die — sei es auch noch so verschlüsselte — Ankündigung: Achtung, jetzt werde ich ironisch. Die qualifizierte Ironie muß tatsächlich, wie es der große Ironiker Musil einmal formulierte, nackt aus dem Zusammenhang der Dinge selbst hervorgehen" (1970, 24–25). From this standpoint, irony represented a special feature of literature that attempted to establish direct communication with the world. Under favorable conditions, such as those that obtained in Musil's fiction, it was not just a device of self-conscious narrators, but, as Allemann argued, approximated a particular "condition of the world."

This outwardly progressive conception of irony was in fact deeply conservative, if not regressive, since it grafted old notions of authorial will onto the text, but in ways that attempted to beat back any idea that the author was still present in the text. From this angle, true irony was either an impossible condition of the text (in which case it was all the more to be idealized), or it was nothing other than an old notion in new garb. In announcing an exclusive concern with the text and eschewing any outward political focus, Allemann's study of irony actually contained a provocative political gesture in the early postwar period at a time when European society still lay in ruins.

In establishing this approach to Musil, Allemann — like Pongs before him — was clearly influenced by the philosophy of Martin Heidegger. The existentialist proposition Allemann inherited from Heidegger was the notion that the individual's journey in life proceeded from a sense of nothingness, and might end with nothingness. As Heidegger had argued in *Sein und Zeit,* the aspect of being in the world (*Dasein*) had no essence, except as an unfolding of that being's particular existence (*Existenz*). Whether such existence ennobled human beings or demeaned them remained unclear. Jean-Paul Sartre had even asked, on the presumption that life is shaped more by the nothingness of death than the "somethingness" of life: "If I emerge in nothingness beyond the world, how can this extra-mundane nothingness furnish a foundation for those little pools of non-being which we encounter each instant in the depth of being."[1] Allemann found a response to this problem in Musil's description of the Other Condition, a utopian state of being that represented an attempt to combat the uncertain nature of life through artistic means. Musil's goal, accordingly, was an ideal of art whose palpability was underwritten by its capacity to become a particular "condition of the world," which is to say, to become a concrete historical artifact. The historical nature of art as the language of concrete experience therefore took over the problem of returning essence to life, and a consequence of this was that the status of artists could be rehabilitated. The casualty of this argument about art, however, was history. If the artist could be rehabilitated by reversion to art as a self-articulating historical entity, then history must appear as something other than the history whose unfolding had led to the catastrophe of the Second World War. The view that art still spoke out against the problems of existence thus depended on a conciliatory notion of history that avoided the immediate truths of the past by eschewing a direct social and political focus. Such a conciliatory view of history, which was suggested in Allemann's treatment of irony, for this reason, quickly attracted criticism, notably from Walter Sokel (1960/61), who argued for a more complex appreciation of Musil's understanding of the problems of his time. Despite such criticism, Sokel himself was later to propagate existential critique in two studies of Musil in the early eighties (1981, 1983). It was not until the emergence of social criticism and particularly the studies of Laermann (1970) and Böhme (1974) that the presuppositions of existential critique, in particular its reliance on an outwardly apolitical conception of history, were challenged and ultimately overthrown. Nevertheless, Allemann's study helped establish existential critique as one of the major points of departure for understanding Musil's novel and influenced approaches to Musil throughout the sixties.

Against this background, the debate about how Musil wished to conclude the novel — a debate that dominated the first fifteen years of Musil scholarship in the postwar period — appears much more than a philological dispute over the correct way to read Musil's intentions from the surviving posthumous materials to the novel. What was at stake in a dispute that involved the most influential Musil scholars of the day — Adolf Frisé, Wolfdietrich Rasch, and Ulrich Karthaus, on the one hand, and Eithne Wilkins, Ernst Kaiser, and, less directly, Wilhelm Bausinger, on the other — was, above all, the question of Musil's existentialism. If, as Frisé's early edition of Musil's works had suggested, Musil saw no path beyond the overwhelming nihilism of the collapsing Austro-Hungarian Empire, then he was clearly to be understood as one of the most prominent of the early European existentialists. If, on the other hand, war did not end the attempt to envision an alternative to the flawed project of European rationalism, as Wilkins and Kaiser argued in 1962, but rather represented the basis on which the search for alternative values was premised, then Musil's novel was informed by much more than a soberly existentialist account of life. It is perhaps symptomatic of the dominance of despair over hope, of pessimism over a more sanguine attitude toward the prospects of European society in the early postwar period that the existentialist positions defended by Rasch and Karthaus proved more resilient at this time. In an essay that first appeared in 1963 and was reprinted in a collection of essays in 1967, Rasch, for example, drew attention, with reference to the Other Condition, to what he called the "unbegreifliche, unmittelbare Seinserfahrung" (1967, 90). For him, existence and narrative form were inextricably linked: "Das Existenzproblem Ulrichs wird unmittelbar zum Formproblem des Romans" (79). Karthaus, whose analysis of the temporal framework of the novel was directed at evaluating the meaning of the Other Condition, made the existentialist question about the nature of time the major issue of the novel (cf. "Works Consulted," 1965). He held that "die Frage nach der Zeit ist nicht die Frage nach ihrem Charakter, sondern die Frage nach der Möglichkeit ihrer Überwindung" (158). Moreover, this question of time's nature and whether it can be overcome under the influence of some abstracted state of consciousness or "other condition," was not finally answerable — at least not in terms of the conditions that held for earthly existence. To this extent, Karthaus argued, the question of the temporal framework of the Other Condition had ultimately to be pursued as a theological problem.

The theological outlook that Karthaus supported in approaching the final section of Musil's novel, however, did not draw support from Wilkins and Kaiser. The potency of Musil's utopia, they contended, depended precisely on its remaining within the purview of human experience in the here-and-now. To this extent, Musil's utopia contained real choices, but also real dangers. At the same time, they emphasized how Musil's progress on the novel in the 1930s had been overtaken by concrete historical events such as Hitler's ascension to power in Germany and problems Musil encountered in locating a publisher for the novel amid declining health and increasing financial difficulties. As a result of such outward pressures, and because of artistic considerations, Musil began to alter his conception of the novel's development from 1930 onwards. He abandoned the earlier plan to have it end in war, instead choosing to round out the story with a vision of the Platonic ecstasy of brother and sister depicted in the chapter that he was working on when he died, the "Atemzüge eines Sommertags." This view about Musil's new point of emphasis in the novel was supported by Wilhelm Bausinger's historical-critical study of the novel (1964), but contradicted by Wolfdietrich Rasch (1963), who focused attention on the inner coherence of the novel's structure which he evinced along poetological lines. Basing his study on the central importance of "Möglichkeitssinn" — to whose significance Albrecht Schöne had already pointed in his essay of 1961 — Rasch showed how Musil held to his original solution for the novel's conclusion, that is, the unfolding of events before the increasingly insistent backdrop of war, despite the disruptions experienced throughout the thirties: "Der Schluß stellt fest [. . .], das Ganze mündet in den Ausbruch des Krieges. Er rechtfertigt Ulrichs Nichthandeln" (1967, 13). Later critics, such as Albertsen (1968), Böhme (1974), and, most recently, Honold (1995), were to fall in behind this view, seeing the outbreak of war, rather than the sibling's alternative utopia, as the logical end to which all events of the narrative would lead.

Wilhelm Bausinger's historical-critical study of Musil, published in 1964, was adapted from his Tübingen dissertation of 1961. Friedrich Beißner, the chair of the doctoral committee at Tübingen and Bausinger's thesis supervisor, had been one of the pioneers of historical-critical principles in his much admired analysis of Friedrich Hölderlin. Discussing the historical emergence of the novel in Beißner's manner, Bausinger attempted to divine the trajectory of Musil's fragment from a study of the textual variants of the novel. The need to reappraise these variants had become urgent as a result of Adolf Frisé's first postwar edition of the novel in 1952. Instead of presenting the textual variants in an even-handed manner, Bausinger argued, Frisé's edition had arranged certain of these hitherto unpublished materials in a way that made war not only appear a likely outcome, but indeed the only outcome of the novel. Moreover, the inevitability of war had the effect of canceling out all other considerations in the novel, including the utopian visions Musil had set against it. Bausinger's study, whose first 130 pages were devoted to criticisms and suggested improvements to this first postwar edition of the novel, rejected these attempts to provide Musil's novel with a conclusion. They turned the novel's conception back on itself, militating against the idea of a development in Musil's thinking and compromising the value of his later and last chapter variants and, indeed, the writing process itself. By contrast, Bausinger argued, Martha Musil's 1943 edition of Musil's works, with a separately published third volume and an arrangement of chapters based partly on the "Druckfahnenkapitel" (chapters that Musil had authorized for publication in 1937–38 and then withdrawn) was more in accord with Musil's intentions. Bausinger's study, therefore, was a significant milestone on the way toward a comprehensive understanding of the novel at a time when the shape of Musil's thinking still remained unclear.

Ulrich Karthaus re-entered the philological debate about the 1952 Frisé edition in his survey of the critical literature on Musil in 1965. He argued that the historical-critical principles Bausinger applied were open to question, as was Bausinger's notion of authorial "intention" (cf. "Musil Bibliographies," 1965, 443–44). He polemically held against Kaiser and Wilkins that their criticisms of Frisé rested on "pseudoscientific methods" and betrayed signs of a personal attack on Frisé. Elsewhere, Karthaus criticized their study of Musil for transforming the author into a conjurer of magic and symbols. He also denied that Musil's training in logic and mathematics had left significant traces in his work. One of his most serious allegations was that Kaiser and Wilkins had failed to appreciate how irony operates in Musil's novel: "Das Buch von Kaiser/Wilkins verkennt gänzlich die ironische Atmosphäre des Romans und die utopisch-zweifelnde Haltung auch Ulrichs" (1965, 450). By contrast, Karthaus praised Wilfried Berghahn's 1963 biography of Musil for its illumination of the connection between biography and the work of art. More recently, in 1997, Enrico de Angelis's systematic attempt to reevaluate the materials that appeared on CD-ROM in 1992 through the work of Aspetsberger, Eibl, and Frisé indicates that the debate about the way Musil intended to complete the novel — despite the advantages of technology in the digital age — is even today far from settled.

Albrecht Schöne's essay of 1961, which also appeared in 1982 in a collection of essays edited by Renate von Heydebrand, has taken on importance in Musil scholarship because it redirected this early debate about the posthumous materials and the nature of Musil's project. Schöne showed how the subjunctive mood was consciously deployed by the author in order to fashion alternatives to the dominant reality depicted in the novel. Schöne argued that the story of the siblings' love in fact had two "Versuchsrichtungen" (1982, 28): a satirical-ironical and an experimental-utopian direction. The former was meant to end unsatisfactorily amid war and destruction, much as Frisé's 1952 edition had suggested. The latter ran an altogether different course, leading to a spiritual union of the lovers in a state of "Conjunctivus potentialis," "als wäre dieses Experiment nicht mehr zum Scheitern verurteilt, sondern berge eine gleichnishafte Verheißung" (30). Schöne further found that the fragmentary form of this utopian section was exactly appropriate to the spiritual ideal of openness to possibility that it upheld. From this perspective, the dispute over the conclusion to Musil's novel suddenly appeared to have missed the point. Musil's preference for the subjunctive mood, Schöne showed, was a rhetorical gesture of the artist designed to promote understanding of plural perspectives, not to flatten them out in one direction or another. There was, accordingly, no definitive conclusion to Musil's novel. Moreover, Schöne was also able to demonstrate that Musil, in structuring his narrative in experimental ways according to the category of possibility, was working within a tradition that reached back to the eighteenth century, in particular to Lichtenberg, Gottsched, and Breitinger, where God appeared as the creator of worlds of possible experience. The novel thus evinced the "grammatische Struktur eines von der Leidenschaft zum Experiment erfüllten Möglichkeitsdichtens, das nach den 'noch nicht erwachten Absichten Gottes' sucht" (47).

Gerolf Jäßl's dissertation of 1963, although betraying a keen interest in isolating aspects of mystical thought in the manner of existential critique, also maintained a critical line against modernism in ways that were to become characteristic of the social criticism of the 1970s and 1980s. Jäßl's analysis was also consistent with the postwar skepticism about instrumental reason that had come to light in the work of Horkheimer and Adorno in their *Dialektik der Aufklärung* (1944). Jäßl analyzed two main ideas in the novel: first, the collapse of culture and the Western notion of rational culture embodied in the abortive "Parallelaktion"; second, the consequences of this collapse for the individual, who, in the shape of the peculiarly "intellectual" man Ulrich, attempts to distance himself from the chaos of his age and to seek a profound accommodation with it without abandoning the project of reason altogether. It was this second aspect attaching to Ulrich, the mystically minded mathematician, Jäßl contended, that encapsulated the "problem situation" of the novel — the attempt to make reason less metaphysical and more concrete for individual human beings. Anticipating later studies, such as that of Reniers-Servranckx (1972), which also elevated Ulrich's attempt to address the problem of living in the world to the status of a conscious platform, Jäßl showed that Ulrich's new project of reason involved the cultivation of antimetaphysical positivism as well as a psychological phenomenalism that would eschew the mechanistic causality of the material sciences. In this passage between artistic sensibility and scientific understanding Jäßl saw the shape of a new mysticism — one that would be experienced concretely and intuitively without any necessary theological implications. Analyzing Musil's diaries, Jäßl dated the emergence of this line of thinking in Musil to the "breakthrough year" 1913 (1963, 131). Jäßl further averred that Musil coined the term "anderer Zustand," which epitomized this line of thought, after reading Ludwig Klages's *Vom kosmologischen Eros* — a finding subsequently affirmed by Werner Fuld in 1976. Jäßl held that the Other Condition, which set out the new mystical approach to life, was not culled from mystical or religious sources in the first instance, but was inspired by the neo-Romantics of the late nineteenth and early twentieth century. In the concluding sections of the dissertation Jäßl examined what he called the "functionalistic morality" of the Other Condition, linking mysticism to a new type of morality based on aspects of mathematical understanding. Later scholars, such as Hüppauf (1971) and Schmidt (1975), by revising some of Jäßl's judgments, particularly those concerning the source of Musil's mysticism, were to take this debate about Musil's connection with mystical writing a step further.

Helga Honold (1963) and Heribert Brosthaus (1964) were also attracted to the mystical dimensions in Musil's thought — dimensions that had grown out of a preoccupation with the nature of time in existentialist approaches. Whereas Honold viewed paradox as a key ingredient in the mystical outlook on the world, Brosthaus focused on the identity of the artist as "vivisector," a term that appears in Musil's diaries from the period around the beginning of the twentieth century. In Honold's study, Musil's had used paradox in two ways, describing this use as "intellectual-rhetorical," on the one hand, and "ecstatic-intuitive," on the other. Whereas the former type of paradox was elicited by discursive and logical means and was susceptible of resolution, the latter type, which could not be resolved through discursive practice alone, was communicated in direct connection with mystical experience of the cosmos following holistic principles. Honold traced such mysticism to Zen Buddhism and, in the European tradition, to ideas that had emanated from the thought of the medieval mystic thinker Meister Eckhart. Brosthaus, for his part, saw the isolation of the "vivisector" not in negative terms as rationalistically instrumental, but as a particular way of understanding the world that anticipated a spiritual outlook on life.

Renate von Heydebrand's study of 1966 — the published version of a dissertation she completed at the University of Münster in 1962 — was one of the major early contributions to understanding the intellectual influences at work in Musil's novel. Her view that Musil largely conveyed these diverse influences through the device of quotation, however, did not allow for any transformation of these ideas in the process of being absorbed into the narrative. To some extent, therefore, von Heydebrand's analysis of influences ran counter to Musil's declared aim (in an interview with Fontana in 1926) of providing a "geistige Bewältigung" of his own time, if "Bewältigung" was taken to imply a profound grappling with ideas and not merely a soaking up of influences. For this reason, later critics such as Götz Müller (1972) resisted von Heydebrand's analysis of intellectual influences, upbraiding her for underestimating the true depth of Musil's dealing with ideas in the novel. While Müller ascribed social intent to Musil's treatment of ideas, linking Musil's literary project to Horkheimer's notion of "Ideologiekritik," von Heydebrand's reluctance to appraise fully the conceptual level of the novel could be seen as a strategic choice of existential critique. This was a decision to stay "below" the text and to maintain an ideal conception of the author. While social criticism was to see in the preferences of existential critique a flight from the real meaning of ideas, and, implicitly, a flight from the world, the contrast between Musil's finely-nuanced intellectuality and his engagement with the ideas that enliven the problem of living in the world has remained in steady tension in Musil scholarship and cannot yet be considered resolved.

The main influences on Musil, von Heydebrand found, surprisingly, came from outside the German tradition of ideas as much as from within it. Accordingly, while Nietzsche, Ernst Mach, Georg Simmel, and Martin Buber were significant influences on the novel, William James and Ralph Waldo Emerson were also understood to have exercised considerable influence over Musil's thinking. A notable absentee from the list of influences in von Heydebrand's account, however, was Edmund Husserl — perhaps because Musil's indebtedness to Husserl was not to become fully apparent until the appearance of Frisé's new edition of the diaries in 1976.[2] The existential focus of von Heydebrand's study was registered in the prominence accorded to the problem of time, and, concomitantly, a sense of the coexistence of two separate levels of experience flowing from mundane reality and sensually intuited experience respectively (intuitive experience emerges as a theme in Musil's first work of fiction *Die Verwirrungen des Zöglings Törleß* in Törleß's references to "second sight"). While Musil's first novel, clearly written under the strong influence of Musil's early encounter with the thought of Nietzsche, conveys a strong sense of existential crisis, von Heydebrand extended the theme of "second sight" to encompass the utopian final section of *Der Mann ohne Eigenschaften,* thereby underscoring the importance of existentialist assumptions when approaching Musil's oeuvre as a whole. The other implication of this approach — that a sense of thematic continuity obtained from *Törleß* to *The Man Without Qualities* — was taken further by later critics, in particular Reniers-Servranckx (1972). In a lengthy discussion, von Heydebrand saw in the union of the siblings, following the thought of the nineteenth century American philosopher and writer Emerson, "eine zweite Wirklichkeit" — a revelatory condition of the world that appears only to those who have the capacity to see to it: "Die Welt offenbart ihr zweites Gesicht nur dem Auge, das sich dafür öffnet" (1966, 113). The existence of this "second world" was then the basis for deriving Musil's theory of feeling (117–18), which was in turn tied to the hope of realizing an alternative to the problem of living in the world: "Das ungefähr ist wohl die utopische

Hoffnung der Geschwister: ihr Erlebnis als Paradigma am Anfang einer Epoche, in der mindestens eine 'Ekstatische Sozietät' von Gleichgesinnten diesem Beispiel folgen und damit die Welt als ganze verändern könnte" (140). That this utopia was, in von Heydebrand's view, mystical in outlook, was again thoroughly in keeping with the spirit of existential critique.

Elisabeth Albertsen's Tübingen dissertation of 1966 was published under the title *Zur Dialektik von "Ratio" und Mystik im Werk Robert Musils* in 1968. Albertsen's study revealed the influence of philosophical positions taken up by Theodor Adorno in postwar German letters, in particular his condemnation of totalizing systems of thought in the German tradition of ideas since Hegel. In following Adorno, Albertsen echoed the skepticism about the Enlightenment project of reason that was evident in emerging social criticism, without abandoning existentialist positions that were dominant in Musil scholarship throughout the 1960s. The starting point of her analysis — building on Berghahn's insight that "Denken und Erzählen beinah zu Synonymen werden können" (1956, 5) — was the relationship of philosophy to poetry in Musil's work. In Albertsen's view, the discussion of ideas on the reflective level of the novel amounted to a type of attenuated literary philosophy that used the capacity of philosophy to generate theoretical positions while avoiding the logic of closure that philosophical systems imply. In setting out her analysis in this manner, Albertsen was one of the first critics in Musil scholarship to attach significance to the question of the interconnectedness of art and philosophy in Musil's novel. This question was pursued by a number of later critics, most prominently Gilbert Reis (1983), and remains a central issue when evaluating Musil's literary project as a whole.

In Albertsen's analysis, Musil's novel became a litmus test for Adorno's critique of totalizing philosophies as well as for art's capacity to accommodate non-rational aspects of life. Albertsen's idea that the vision of artists could be understood as "unsystematic philosophy" affirmed Adorno's position about modernist fiction in general: "Musil will kein 'System,' weil es doch nie vollkommen sein kann, sondern er will Gestalt, die imstande ist, auch Irrationales zu integrieren" (1968, 16). In considering the question of such integration, Albertsen found that the dialectical tension between rational and irrational levels of meaning in Musil's novel was not sublated in the manner, say, of Hegel, on a higher plane of consciousness. On the contrary: "Die Synthese Seele-Ratio [. . .] ist mißlungen. Dies führt in direkter Linie zum Krieg" (122). Such a conclusion left ground either for a stoical acceptance of the imponderable nature of life or for a celebration of life's more mystical aspects. Albertsen struck out in both directions by conferring on the mystical union of the sibling lovers a religious aspect, as Karthaus had done before her (cf. "Works Consulted," 1965). The Other Condition, whose mystical aspects in Albertsen's view revealed the influence of Buber's *Ekstatische Konfessionen*, did not, however, lead to Christian belief. Ulrich's non-dogmatic commitment to a dimension above the concerns of material life retained existentialist aspects through the category of possibility: "[Ulrich] setzt alles daran, [diesen Glauben] nicht durch Dogmen zu materialisieren, weil er Angst hat vor der Umwandlung des erlebbaren Ahnens in den nicht erlebten Glauben [. . .]" (1968, 41). Albertsen's analysis concluded by affirming Adorno's view of art as an "open dialectic system." In taking over the language of Adorno's reply to Lukács on the question of realism in the modernist novel, Albertsen remained skeptical of overdetermined rationality and the "erpreßte Versöhnung" that would accompany any attempt to deliver finality to the world in the name of an "ultima ratio" (126–27).[3]

Bernd-Rüdiger Hüppauf's study of 1971 has proved to be one of the most influential as well as most frequently quoted studies in Musil scholarship. Turning attention away from the question of Musil's use of direct quotation from mystical thinkers, Hüppauf advanced the view that Musil's novel was a work of mystical inspiration for an altogether different reason — its very structural organization placed Musil's novel in a direct line of descent with the literature of mysticism. Although a catalog of direct and indirect sources was still valuable — Hüppauf indicated that Musil's use of mystical sources was largely unconscious or at times even accidental — it was of secondary importance. More valuable was the *structure* of Musil's "mystical thought." Here Hüppauf revealed correspondences between Musil's novel and the triadic structural pattern of mystical writing. He noted that it was particularly the second stage of the triadic movement, the movement from thesis to antithesis, which betrayed Musil's affinity with mystical literature, "denn [die Antithese] bildet die grundlegende Kategorie von Ulrichs und Musils Zeiterfahrung und Weltverständnis" (1971, 15). The movement to transcend the intermediary phase of antithesis in an overarching synthesis was then the task of the final section in Musil's novel, the Other Condition. Even though this third stage remained incomplete, Hüppauf was still able to detect a concern for staying within the immanent realm of process — a characteristic feature of mystical literature. Connecting this final section of Musil's novel to Enlightenment discourses, Hüppauf made a marriage of unusual bedfellows, namely, mysticism (or, perhaps, inner enlightenment) on one side and rationality (as outer Enlightenment) on the other — a partnership which would be consummated in the upper reaches of consciousness, where spirituality meets intellectuality. Such a partnership was made possible because Musil had already emptied reality of worldly concerns over the middle stretches of the novel and opened up ground for untrammeled reflective thought. For Hüppauf, then, the philosophical side of thought emerged out of the artistic substructure of Musil's novel more or less naturally. Accordingly, there was no sense in faulting Musil, as Schramm had done in 1967, for mixing "fiction" and "reflexion" in synthetic ways (1971, 170). Even so, Hüppauf's approach betrayed a synthesizing intention of its own, since it sought to rescue reflective intellectuality from the attacks of its detractors and collapse art into philosophy on the grounds that they were essentially related undertakings.

Dagmar Herwig's study of 1972, which was submitted as a dissertation at the University of Munich in 1971, may be considered a classic example of existential critique. The existentialist signposts of boredom and a sense of futility toward life were established early in the analysis in relation to autobiographical aspects and Musil's first novel *Die Verwirrungen des Zöglings Törleß*. Reference to the English psychotherapist R. D. Laing illustrated a dilemma Herwig considered central to Musil's outlook in the novel.[4] This was the desire to reach objective understanding of individual human beings, on the one hand, while resisting the depersonalizing of individuals through the application of scientific principles of inquiry, on the other. Between this Charybdis of rational science and the Scylla of emotional empathy, Musil appeared as a type of frustrated positivist, longing to apply the exactness of science to understanding the individual, but exactly fearing to do so. At the same time, Herwig contended, Musil did not wish to throw out the baby with the bathwater, that is, he did not wish to sacrifice the emotional and religious dimension of life, as might result from the introduction of science to the study of the inner self. In *Der Mann ohne Eigenschaften,* this occasioned a disjuncture of "Gefühl" and "Verstand" that Herwig interpreted in terms of an underlying "schizophrene Struktur [des] Denkens" (96). Herwig's study uncovered a political aspect of the "Utopie des motivierten Lebens" in Ulrich's ethical disposition. Nothing concrete resulted, however, from this aspect of Musil's novel, in part because human experience — as Herwig skeptically held — did not widen the capacity of human beings to formulate models for rational action in the world (144). In the final analysis, the man without qualities shared features in common not with the political reformer, but with the revolutionary, whose hopes for a better social order could only be realized in some far off imagined future.

Marie-Louise Roth took Herwig's reference to Ulrich's ethical disposition to greater depth in a major study that also appeared in 1972. Approaching the question of ethics from the vantage point of Musil's essays, Roth formulated the central question of the novel, and indeed of Musil's oeuvre generally, as the relationship between art and ethical understanding — realms long held to represent distinct levels of response to the world (cf. *TB I,* 941). Roth's study became important for the new interest in Musil's ethics that has dominated approaches to the novel since the early 1990s.

In Roth's analysis, Musil opposed the disparity between ethics and art, attempting to reconcile the theoretical and critical dimensions of the ethical approach to life with the technical and aesthetic demands of poetry. Roth's approach implied a response to Benjamin's question about the status of art in an age of technology, and Brecht's desire to break with Aristotelian conceptions of theater in the new scientific age. At the same time, it also engaged with the question of the role of criticism in the hermeneutic tradition at a time when hermeneutics was being assailed both by new scientific discourses and the new aesthetics of structuralism. Musil's idiosyncratic conception of art, which was conservative of humanistic impulses and yet progressive in aesthetic terms, could thus be enlisted in the broader defense of hermeneutics at a time of great change in literary criticism: "Schreiben ist bei Musil Selbstfindung, Suche nach dem 'rechten Leben,' ein Akt aggressiver Verteidigung gegen die Einreihung in die gesellschaftliche Mechanisierung und das kulturelle System" (12). This defense of art — and, by implication, scholarship in the hermeneutic tradition — against new forms of cultural expression was an ethical struggle that Musil launched as a conscious undertaking in the essays. In considering Musil's early study of biology and mathematics, and, later, his thorough acquaintance with Gestalt theory, Roth made the new discovery that Musil's attempt to reconfigure the relationship of art and ethics had been undertaken not from the standpoint of art in the first instance, but had arisen out of a spirit of scientific understanding. Since Musil had been a scientist before he became an artist, it was now possible to suggest of the struggle between scientific and artistic impulses that science had taken too little notice of art, that science had been too "unaesthetic." This turned the traditional attack against art on its head, for art had always been held to be too unscientific. For this reason, Roth's detailed study of scientific influences on Musil[5] drew attention to the feeling dimension of artistic understanding ("die Fruchtbarkeit eines Gefühls") as a rational proposition, that is, a fruitful "Idee" possessing "verborgene geistige Energie und [. . .] Anwendbarkeit" (41). This suggested new goals for rationally based scientific understanding. In Musil's scientific vitalism, for example, thought became an "adventure of the spirit" directed at uncovering the unique quality of life; it did not subsist in "thought-systems" that stayed below the facts of life (77). This vitalistic quality in Musil's — still preeminently scientific — thinking became essential to the project of harmonizing aesthetics and ethics: "Das Streben nach Bewußtsein und Objektivierung liegt in dem Menschen. Hier identifizieren sich Ethik und Ästhetik. Der gleiche Drang sich zu übersteigen, sei es im Kunstwerk oder im sittlichen Verhalten, kennzeichnet den Menschen" (109).

That art and ethics, and, by extension, artistic and scientific understanding, could be reconciled through the moral outlook of literature, as Roth contended, again revealed a strategic choice of existential critique. However, as ethics began to assume importance in its own right in approaches to literature by the late eighties, its need to seek resolution with artistic activity seemed increasingly less pressing. Indeed, equating aesthetics with ethics today implies a mutual dependence that does not appear essential for either activity. Musil's project, as Bonacchi has recently argued, is now more typically seen as "eine Art Methoden- und Terminologietransfer von der Wissenschaft zur Kunst und von der Kunst zur Wissenschaft," where points of convergence are identified between the two different areas (1998, 173). Nevertheless, Roth's study was a significant point of departure for ethical criticism, and has remained a work of importance for Musil scholarship in general.

Judith Burckhardt's study of 1973 was pervaded above all by the insight that modern life was founded on an absence of authenticity. This lack of authenticity, already announced in the title of *Der Mann ohne Eigenschaften,* had been proclaimed by Ernst Mach, whose functionalist philosophy had contributed to a sense of existential uncertainty in the late nineteenth century. Indeed, notions of the "unsaveable self" ("das unrettbare Ich") in the early twentieth century had originated in Mach's philosophy and now recurred in programmatic form in the title of Musil's novel. Since Burckhardt criticized Mach for bypassing the moral problem of the right way to live, her study can be considered, along with that of Stephan Reinhardt (1969), one of the most prominent polemics against Mach's functionalist philosophy. The "lack of qualities" in the novel's title, therefore, did not in Burckhardt's reading imply that the subject lacked a purpose in life. It rather set out a point from which the insistent shaping of finished forms conditioning behavior in the Austrian state could be critiqued, if not resisted altogether. "Eigenschaftslosig-keit" thus established a positive attitude of opposition to conditioning influences. Burckhardt then described a program of self-realization fol-lowing Sartre's idea that human beings are not finished forms, but ideas, or remnants of ideas. In Burckhardt's conservative approach to the problem of value, however, neither the attempt to find new moral cate-gories, nor the ideal of brotherly and sisterly love (a variation on the search for qualities) could be sustained (1972, 68). Instead, she pointed to the need to uphold a rational value scheme, even as it remained unclear what these values might actually consist of: "Ulrich selbst sieht sich wieder vor die gleiche Aufgabe wie zu Beginn der Roman-handlung gestellt: er muß versuchen, zu sich und seiner Zeit in ein 'ver-nünftiges' Verhältnis zu kommen." (123) That the likely failure of this endeavor suggested a return to religious thinking, was underscored at the end of her study in the observation: "Musil streift denn auch immer wieder die religiöse Frage, ohne aber auf sie eine endgültige Antwort zu geben" (128).

The main undertaking of Jochen Schmidt's important study of 1975 — a study that overshadowed Dietmar Goltschnigg's approach to a similar topic of the same period (1974) — was to demonstrate a basic correspondence between Ulrich's attitude of "Eigenschaftslosigkeit" and mystical writing. Whereas Hüppauf's earlier study of 1971 had sought to demonstrate structural correspondences between mystical writing and *Der Mann ohne Eigenschaften*, Schmidt uncovered Musil's appropriation of mystical ideas from actual sources, in particular the writings of Meister Eckhart. According to Meister Eckhart's teachings, human qualities connected social selves with worldly values and experiences and thus represented obstacles to accessing higher mystical truths. The goal of communion with the divine was only possible where the human being weakened such insistent ego attachments and put her- or himself in a direct line with God. Schmidt's investigation of the mystical thought of Meister Eckhart established that "Gelassenheit" and "Abgeschieden-heit" — characteristic aspects of Ulrich's denial of qualities — had the aim of breaking down the attachment to human qualities. According to Schmidt, they also accrued positive value, since they promoted the pro-tagonist's search for mystical union with God.

Martin Menges's study of 1982 approached the state of absence of qualities from a similar point of view, but reached different conclusions. His study approached "Eigenschaftslosigkeit" as a modular category that described various attempts undertaken in the narrative to abstract from the concrete facts of life. This approach led naturally to a consideration of the Other Condition, insofar as the siblings' idyll sought to realize a new level of abstraction on a higher plane of ecstatic experience through an experiment of the mind. That this experiment also entailed a "destruction" of concrete experience was a typical observation of existential critique. Menges concluded that "in jedem Abstraktionsprozeß findet etwas von jener Entgegenständlichungs- und Vernichtungsarbeit statt, die in der Geschwisterliebe ihren Höhepunkt erreicht" (249). Menges's study therefore ascribed no final value to transcendent impulses in Musil's novel, even where they sought to remain — albeit abstractly — within the purview of immanent experience. To existential critique of the eighties, therefore, the insistent utopian thrust of the major novel had become a pointless abstraction, if not to say, distraction, from the real concerns of life. If, as Menges suggested, "form" indeed needed a new accommodation with "matter" (250), this would have to be assayed in an entirely new set of critical assumptions about Musil's oeuvre.

Philip Payne's 1988 study of Musil — an extended meditation on the nature of free will — in many ways brought the tradition of existential critique in Musil scholarship to an end. In constructing a drama of choice for the main character, where Ulrich would be given precisely as many reasons to reach a decision as not to reach one, Musil's novel could be read as a literary experiment that discussed how much true choice was left in the world. Part of this experiment involved considering Ulrich in juxtaposition with Moosbrugger, the prostitute murderer, who, from the point of view of free will, seemed at the greatest remove from the "man without qualities." Accordingly, Payne says: "Through him [Moosbrugger], Musil seeks an answer to the question 'Can human beings determine actions themselves, or is freedom an illusion?' The answer from the narrative is 'Yes, human beings *are* free agents'" (147). According to Payne, Musil discovered that free will contained "both mystery and fact" in more or less equal measure. This finding constituted grounds for basing a sense of life on the mystical activity of really existing human subjects. To this extent, Payne's study was able to rehabilitate the subject, whose sense of certainty about the world had been eroded by "the march of a militant objectivity" as well as the pre-eminence of scientific thinking, under whose terms the observer had become alarmingly absent from the field of observation. Payne's existential focus sought to return this observer-subject to the world, and, in so doing, reacquaint the existentially ailing, morally alienated human being with "his intellectual, emotional and moral centre" (211).

Notes

[1] Jean-Paul Sartre, *Being and Nothingness. An Essay on Phenomenological Ontology,* trans. by Hazel E. Barnes (London: Methuen, 1958), 19.

[2] Karl Menges was one of the first scholars to discuss the influence of Husserl on Musil in an essay that appeared in 1976, "Robert Musil und Edmund Husserl. Über phänomenologische Strukturen im *Mann ohne Eigenschaften,*" *Modern Austrian Literature* 9 (3/4): 131–54.

[3] "Nur so [. . .] kann Musils Roman enden, denn jedes Ende, jede gewaltsame Versöhnung, die sich als ultima ratio gebärdet, wäre nur erpreßt, eine bequeme Patentlösung, die Musils Forderung nach Genauigkeit widerspräche." Elisabeth Albertsen, *"Ratio" und Mystik im Werk Robert Musils* (Munich: Nymphenburger, 1968), 126–27.

[4] R. D. Laing, *The Divided Self: An Existential Study in Sanity and Madness* (London: Pelican, 1965), 24.

[5] Roth set out a list of these influences in an appendix: Marie-Louise Roth, *Robert Musil: Ethik und Ästhetik* (Munich: Paul List Verlag, 1972), 538–48.

2: From Social Criticism to Cultural Critique

*Selbst der Sternenhimmel ist eine soziale
Erfahrung, ein Gebilde der gemeinsamen
Fantasie unsrer Gattung Menschen, und
ändert sich, wenn man aus ihrem Kreis
austritt.* (*MoE,* 1720)

*Aber dieses groteske Österreich ist nichts
anderes als ein besonderer deutlicher Fall
der modernen Welt.* (*TB I,* 354)

SOCIAL QUESTIONS HAVE never been far from scholarship on Musil's
novel, even where other approaches have held sway. Identifying the
moment when social criticism became a popular, and for some time even
a dominant, point of departure in approaches to the novel is therefore a
matter of some conjecture. Nevertheless, such a moment could be said
to have occurred with the appearance of Helmut Arntzen's doctoral
dissertation in book form in 1960. Arntzen's book, which announced a
new approach to understanding Musil's novel under the title of *Satirischer Stil,* has been of general significance for Musil scholarship, but it
was especially important for social criticism of the novel. Although the
presence of satirical elements in Musil's portrait of the Austrian state,
which Musil gave the name "Kakania," had struck many earlier commentators, Arntzen was the first to see in Musil's use of satire a major —
if not *the* major — stylistic category at work in the novel. Arntzen's
analysis, however, was not restricted to an enumeration of stylistic features. Crucial was his analysis of the historical emergence of satire, which
he linked to the underlying moral intention of the novel since its beginnings in the eighteenth century.

The historical context in which Arntzen placed Musil's treatment of
satire offered an early response to the question of Musil's modernism,
since scholarship was beginning to ask whether the fragmentary novel
connected with the nineteenth-century tradition of the novel, or rather
whether it was to be reckoned among the works of the literary avant-
garde of the early twentieth century, which broke with this older tradition at several points. The Hungarian literary scholar Georg Lukács,
writing in the late 1950s, was one of the leaders of this debate. He rejected the view that the freely associative techniques of the avant-garde,

such as inner monologue, laid bare the human individual. Instead he made the claim that these doggedly individualistic creations of the avant-garde were tied to actual historical and social circumstances. He further held — with an eye on the inwardness of Musil's Ulrich as much as Joyce's Dedalus — that: "Nur in einer lebendigen und konkreten Wechselwirkung von Menschen und Umwelt kann die konkrete Möglichkeit eines Menschen aus der schlechten Unendlichkeit seiner abstrakten Möglichkeiten heraustreten [. . .]" (1958, 17). Neither Ulrich's longing to dispense with reality, nor his desire to live for the abstract sense of possibilities he found within himself, therefore, drew much sympathy from Lukács. Rather, it was Musil's observation that modernist art implied a level of neurosis that struck Lukács as proof of a pathological quality in the literary avant-garde — a quality that Musil's fiction in general upheld. While Lukács stopped short of condemning Musil's novel outright, his serious charge against Musil was not Ulrich's denial of reality alone, but Musil's failure to offer any alternatives to this "Verweigerungshaltung." Ulrich's stance was thus an empty gesture — as bankrupt as the reality he sought to protest against. From this perspective, Musil's novel appeared not only pathologically inward-looking like much of modernist fiction; it was now also regressive in a political sense. Moreover, as long as Musil's protagonist remained within the confines of existential critique, which had conditioned the approaches to the novel in the 1950s and held firm well into the 1960s and even beyond, Ulrich's "lack of qualities" could, with a shift of perspective, indeed appear as the self-indulgence of a morose antihero unable to withstand the sweet lure of bourgeois decay. That these existentialist views had been ethically compromised — as Heidegger's collusion with the fascists as "Rektor" of Freiburg University in 1933 had shown — was a key element in the emergence of social criticism, and one reason for the indignant tone that it adopted, particularly in the immediate aftermath of the student movement of the late 1960s and early 1970s. For this reason, Musil's novel provided a litmus test of early social critique, which was beginning to reassess the moral trajectory of modernist fiction in the postwar period in general.

Against this background, Arntzen's study of Musil represented an important contribution to the moral dimensions of the debate about modernist fiction. Arntzen suggested that Musil's outlook was not shaped by nihilistic elements present within Austrian modernism in the manner of Hofmannsthal or Schnitzler, but took root in the deeper and less morally compromised soil of the German Enlightenment. Musil's literary cousins were therefore not his direct compatriots and coevals in turn-of-the-century Austria, but Schiller, Kant, and German idealism in the eighteenth century. Although Musil's adherence to this arguably still bourgeois intellectual tradition did not disqualify the objections raised by Lukács's Marxist critique, it did suggest the need for a more complex understanding of Musil's historical position. For this reason, Arntzen's approach influenced not just the aesthetic response to the novel of later years, but was also to exercise a decisive influence over socially critical approaches, which set out to appraise the historical conditions in which Musil was writing and the wider social dimensions of his portrait of Kakania. Arntzen's category of "satirical style" allowed these social aspects of the novel to come into view, without losing focus on the novel as a work of literature. His analysis was built on the substructure of existential critique, which had been sympathetic to the protagonist's attempts to gain distance from a flawed social order. At the same time Arntzen questioned the nature of that distance, seeing in it as much socially critical as nobly ironical intent, and thus adding important qualifications to Allemann's study of 1956, which had affirmed the inviolability of authorial perspective through Musil's use of irony.

Whereas the alienating effects of society were felt within the individual in existential critique, social criticism increasingly opened up the social effects of individualism to analysis. For this reason, the focus on satirical style in Musil's novel led directly to the question of whether not just Kakania, but also Musil's characters and indeed the main character himself might be considered an object of Musil's satirical gaze. This question surfaced as an issue at several points in Arntzen's analysis. Although Arnheim and Diotima, the chief ideologues of the Kakanian state, still occupied center stage, the character of Ulrich in Arntzen's analysis was also drawn with pointed satirical intent. As Arntzen put it: "Gerade er [Ulrich], der von der Gesellschaft sich lossagte, als er für ein Jahr vom Leben Urlaub nahm, sehnt sich nach ihr zurück. [. . .] noch in der Distanz will er sich mit der Wirklichkeit arrangieren" (1960, 166). Such a judgment suggested that Musil's protagonist conspired in some way with the general social decline of the Austrian state. Ulrich, accordingly, could not escape the moral censure that had hitherto been reserved for other characters in the novel. While this view was resisted, notably by Ulf Schramm,[1] whose study of 1967 was devoted to formal genre categories in the first instance, it was echoed by a number of socially minded critics such as Laermann (1970) and Böhme (1974) and was the basis on which the social opposition to Musil's novel in the early seventies was mounted.

Such opposition was strengthened by the climate of skepticism about the goals of the modernist project in the early postwar period. Of the many charges leveled against modernist writers by Georg Lukács, the charge that the apparently self-obsessed and inward-facing literature of modernism was profoundly indifferent to concrete historical circumstances was perhaps the most serious. Since these historical circumstances had largely brought about the social malaise that now confronted postwar European societies, the failure to address history, even in the rarefied air of imaginative writing, was open to scrutiny and indeed condemnation. In East Germany and other countries of the Eastern Bloc, including Lukács's native Hungary, the cultivation of inner states in literary writing ran counter to the egalitarian outlook of the Communist social experiment and was considered perverse, if not diseased. Understanding the ways in which social bondage had come to be visited upon the laboring classes through historical processes, moreover, had been part of the theoretical underpinnings of Marxism since Marx and Engels's foundational study of 1848, *Das Manifest der kommunistischen Partei*.

Ulrich Schelling was one of the first scholars to undertake a study in broad sympathy with Lukács (1968). For Schelling, Musil was an ironist for whom the collapse of the Austrian monarchy also signaled the breakdown of any single, reliable perspective on the past. Schelling made the failure to locate stable points of reference for subjective identity part of a broader failure of tradition to stabilize society and its cultural formations. Musil's portrait of Kakania, accordingly, was marked by the abandonment of one of the classic narrative means to stabilize the perspective on the past — the device of epic narration. What emerged instead in Schelling's judgment was an all-pervasive narrative irony that encompassed the main character and his critically distant attitude toward Kakania. Even the epithet "man without qualities" could not be affirmed, Schelling held (following Arntzen), but had an ironic intention.

The focus of Schelling's essay was Ulrich, whom Schelling compared with Hofmannsthal's Claudio in *Der Thor und der Tod* (1893). This comparison was instructive, for Schelling viewed Ulrich very much through Hofmannsthal's eyes as a type of wandering aesthete disconnected from reality, for whom the play of possibilities had few redeeming features and little positive value: "Allseitig beweglich im Geist, aber ohne Mitte, schwankend in sich und ohne eine Welt, die er als die seine, gültige anzuerkennen vermöchte, negativ frei, allem Endlichen überlegen, aber ohne Gegenwart, ohne wirkliches Glück und ohne wirklichen Schmerz" (33). Ulrich's experiment of the mind could therefore bring no joy, but was instead a "dangerous" game with a nihilistic purpose, for it induced a "Schwindel erregende[n] gottähnliche[n] Machtvollkommenheit der Subjektivität" (45). Even Ulrich's utopia fell short of delivering any advantage to the sibling lovers, since it removed them further from Kakania into the vainglory of private emotions. The one concession Schelling made, at least by implication, concerned the fate of the sibling lovers. In invoking history in partial explanation of their experiment of the emotions, Schelling undertook an interpretative maneuver that has become familiar to social criticism on Musil in general: Schelling viewed the excesses of Ulrich and Agathe as a "Symptom der Zeit [. . .], ein Zeichen für das Mißverhältnis zwischen dem Einzelnen, der sich um eine Ordnung des Lebensganzen bemüht, und dem Zustand des öffentlichen Lebens" (82).

Schelling's approach, which demonstrated the influence of the Marxist account of modernist literature, was notable for its condemnation of inner states, its characterization of Ulrich's lack of qualities as "negative freedom," and its failure to endorse the private idyll of the sibling lovers. Such an idyll, indeed, held little appeal for early social criticism, and drew even less sympathy from critics at the beginning of the seventies whose outlook had been sharpened by the student protest movements of 1968–69. For these critics, Adorno's response to Lukács's condemnation of modernist fiction — that Lukács's attack on modernist formalism rested on a dogmatic and non-dialectical understanding of nineteenth-century literature and failed to appraise the underlying historical nature of all literary writing[2] — could itself be interpreted as a rearguard action of the literary establishment. Even so, as Karl Corino has reported, Musil was able to draw support from left-wing circles in Italy in the late 1960s, where his satirical portrait of Kakania and his belief in the inevitability of the First World War revealed a keener, if covert, Marxism than that of many avowed Marxists of the day (1990, 98).

The less tendentious response of the Italian Left notwithstanding, social criticism in Germany widened the attack on bourgeois literature of the modernist period and Musil in particular by embracing the critique of reason put forward by the Frankfurt School philosophers. Stephan Reinhardt's study of 1969 was one of the first works of Musil scholarship to strike out in this vein, viewing modern society as a thoroughly artificial and unnecessary construct fashioned around increasing refinements to knowledge and the emerging specialist fields that apply knowledge. The outward success in promoting the technical quality of modern life, Reinhardt argued, had not been matched by a keener sense of the value of the individual. Musil's novel therefore gave evidence of an underlying conflict between the rational side of life embodied in the intellect, and the intuitive side issuing from human emotions. Bringing both these aspects of the human being back into alignment was the task Musil had set himself in *Der Mann ohne Eigenschaften*.

At the heart of Reinhardt's study was not merely the age-old problem of the individual's relationship to society; more particularly, Reinhardt considered how and to what extent collective modes of behavior promote or militate against authentic expressions of individual life. This issue was one of the central concerns of the generation of 1968, and, in Reinhardt's analysis, again revealed the influence of the wider conflict in the late 1950s between Theodor Adorno and Georg Lukács on the question of realism in the novel. Reinhardt enlisted Musil's reflections on the pitfalls of the collective endeavor, especially in the essays, to underscore not the triumph of individualism, but rather its failure, and specifically the failure of individualism to sustain unambiguous ethical values in the Other Condition. Here Reinhardt expressed strong agreement with Lukács's sentiment about the alluringly naive aspect of all utopian fancies. As Lukács had argued, such utopias, in establishing merely surface harmony, debase life more than they elevate it. Unlike Lukács, however, Reinhardt stopped short of condemning Musil merely on the grounds of his bourgeois appearance. Instead of condemning the bourgeois values in the novel, as Lukács did, Reinhardt looked to the positive aspects in Musil's notion of spiritual life, which aimed at overcoming the underlying "antinomy" between the intellect and the emotions. In Reinhardt's analysis, however, the attempt to envision a reorganization of the spiritual inventory of human beings would ultimately lead up a blind alley. This was suggested in his conclusion, which linked the programmatic absence of qualities in Ulrich's ethical outlook and the Other Condition to the functionalist view of life — a view of life Reinhardt found wanting. Both the Other Condition and the failure to endorse qualities, he argued, could neither establish enduring values for individual human beings nor redirect the human being to more satisfactory forms of collective endeavor. In Reinhardt's analysis, the dream of collectivism remained perpetually distant.

Lothar Georg Seeger was another scholar clearly influenced by Arntzen's pioneering study of 1960. In 1969, viewing *Der Mann ohne Eigenschaften* as a socially critical historical novel, Seeger focused attention on Musil's portrait of Kakania. His study was paralleled in the same year by Günter Graf's assessment that "Unwahrheitstypik" represented a "condition" in the novel — and by implication in the Austrian state — in its own right. In Seeger's view, Kakania was stable and ordered only on the outside. Inwardly, it was corrupt and disordered and could only be sustained by an underlying "Lebenslüge" — the energy-sapping lie perpetuated in the form of the Parallel Campaign that sought to deny the forces of chaos that inhabited the substructure of the Austrian state. Seeger highlighted the specifically Austrian elements in this portrayal of Kakania. Adapting a reference from Albrecht Schöne's 1961 essay on Musil, he characterized Kakania as "das eigentliche Land des Konjunktivs" (82). Moreover, this lie about society was not peculiar to the social fabric of the Austrian state, but could be seen as part of a crisis of culture affecting European society as a whole. Kakania was therefore not merely an Austrian phenomenon, but also betrayed the wider affliction of European society on the brink of world war. The Other Condition provided the only relief to what was otherwise a bleak portrait of a society caught in the grip of an "Irr- und Wahnglaube[ns]" (8). As Kakania succumbed to the wider paralysis and decay of European society, not even Musil's idyll — the attempt to create a synthesis of moral and spiritual values through an experiment with "other possibilities" — could in Seeger's analysis avert the collapse of "helpless Europe" (146). In a conclusion that raised the question of a wider generational conflict lying behind not just Musil's novel, but the postwar world of Seeger's present, Seeger upbraided the older generation in the novel — Ulrich's father and Graf Leindorf, for example — for their corrupt values and moral failure. This generation of fathers, he concluded, anticipating other studies that were to take up the question of a generational conflict in Musil's novel more directly, had been "ungenügend im Moralischen" (141).

Klaus Laermann's study of 1970 provides one of the clearest examples of how criticism in the late 1960s and early 1970s was heavily indebted to the Marxist critique of Western culture. Already in Laermann's introduction a challenge was issued to what he polemically labeled "bourgeois scholarship." Laermann revealed no uncertainty about the meaning of "Eigenschaftslosigkeit," the state of being without qualities embraced by Musil's protagonist, viewing it in thoroughly negative terms as a capitulation to resignation, indifference, and melancholy, and as congenitally self-destructive. Laermann rejected this pusillanimity out of hand. He urged the enterprise of criticism to display the sense of character he found absent from Musil's writing as a whole. Criticism, for Laermann, was not the business of interpreting texts so much as the business of taking issue with them: "Denn die Widerstände der Eigenschaftslosigkeit sind zugleich die Symptome, an denen deutlich wird, daß ihre selbstzerstörerische Konsequenz reale Entsprechungen in objektiver Zerstörung hat [. . .]" (x). Laermann's study was committed to uncovering elements that could exemplify such "objective destruction." While drawing on philosophy and Freudian psychology to explain the mental disposition of the main character, his study was ultimately less psychological than political in outlook. Forging links with aspects of existential critique, especially Heidegger's theoretical account of the loss of authenticity from the world, Laermann's approach also radicalized those links, and Heidegger's existentialist lament inflamed the running sore of Laermann's deeply oppositional study throughout.

Laermann's analysis pulsated with polemical formulations, and sometimes rhetoric, at every level. Ulrich's openness to the world was read as a lack of moral commitment. Its analog was "the morality of money," which was indifferent to good and bad outcomes and failed to generate morally desirable social behavior. Money, power, and rationality in the novel, in turn, were the instruments of a social system that exercised profoundly alienating effects on the individual. This individual, as a result, was called upon to oppose such a system. The core issue in *Der Mann ohne Eigenschaften* was therefore "decisionistic" in nature — the question of how to commit to (political) action and so help promote the conditions under which authenticity could return to the world.[3] In this way Laermann's study — more directly than any other work of criticism on Musil at the time — could be read as a thinly disguised, Marxist inspired political tract dedicated to the overthrow of bourgeois institutions in general and bourgeois writing in particular. That Ulrich failed to commit to action was partly attributable in Laermann's judgment to his "narcissism without ego ideal" — libidinal energy that found no proper outlet (31) — and partly to the nature of reality itself, which, following Heidegger, impressed itself upon the subject in thoroughly inauthentic ways. Ulrich's refusal to be bound by social roles represented a type of bourgeois disease — a cultivation of superficiality, a love of harmonious appearances. Laermann made this clear in his final chapter, which dealt with the mystical union of Ulrich and Agathe. The love discussed here was unable to shed its own solipsism, its own focus on self. Agathe, viewed from this perspective, represented Ulrich's "ego ideal," not a fully fleshed out character in her own right. The Other Condition accordingly became a flight from the world and an ecstatically self-interested, if ultimately self-denying, glorification of the loss of authenticity. In the end, Laermann deemed the virtues of reflection and inwardness exaggerated, for they issued no call to action in the sphere of reality. Laermann could thus consign both the ideal that Ulrich and Agathe had aspired to, and indeed the two lovers themselves, to the finality of death: "Die Geschwister selbst werden zur 'nature morte.' Das sich rein in sich zurücknehmende Leben, das mit allen qualitativen Veränderungen deren letzte, den Tod, bannen will, muß sich ihm angleichen" (163).

Götz Müller's study of 1972, eschewing the polemical focus of La-ermann's discussion, argued for a more complex understanding of Musil's politics. At the same time, his study was remarkable for the note of resistance it struck to the critical assumptions of the immediate postwar era. These readings had sprung in Müller's judgment from a type of "'false' reception" — they overlooked the parodistic intention of *Der Mann ohne Eigenschaften* by uncritically accepting as their own the ideals Musil seemed to put forward rather than throwing them open to question. Müller, moreover, could provide evidence of a methodological flaw in these critical approaches, arguing that they had failed to appraise Musil's method of "montage," that is, the extent to which Musil's characters are cobbled together from quotations derived other literary sources (one example among many is Musil's use of quotes from Nietzsche to stitch together the character of Clarisse). These quotations were not smoothed out and "integrated" into the narration, as Heydebrand's harmonizing account of the intellectual influences on Musil had suggested in 1966, but indicated a deliberate patterning of the author. In Müller's view, Musil did not deploy ideas uncritically, but incorporated them into the narration in ways that both revealed and rendered intact their ideological substructure. Müller, in reaching such conclusions, ascribed importance to Horkheimer's notion of "Ideologiekritik," a form of which, he argued, Musil had effectively engaged in by using ideas without embracing the historical consciousness (or "Geist") that had inspired those ideas into being. In this way, Müller suggested, Musil was able to establish both a dialogue with the dominant ideas of his time and a distance from them. This distance, which Müller held to evince satirical intent, revealed the formal, historically determined quality of those ideas without implying any endorsement of them by the author. Müller's approach therefore suggested that Musil's novel and his characters could not be taken at face value, but required of critics and readers alike a deep familiarity with the intellectual sub-traditions from which the ideas in his novel had been taken.

The efficacy of Müller's method was demonstrated in the discussion of the Other Condition, where a type of "false consciousness" (Lukács) was seen to arise from the aesthetic ideal of the lovers. Although rendered problematic by the unfinished nature of the novel, Müller found that the aesthetic ideal of the Other Condition was not affirmed. As he noted: "[d]er ästhetische Lösungsversuch wurde von Musil als ungenügend angesehen" (66). The fragmentary quality of Musil's novel, the failure of its — historically posited — "internal" ideals ("die Utopie des ästhetischen Lebens," "die Utopie der induktiven Gesinnung," etc.), even Ulrich's lack of qualities, all resulted from the more generic failure of mythic thinking to resist the alienation flowing from totalizing thought. This was a conclusion reached in sympathy with Horkheimer and Adorno, who had shown in their major work *Dialektik der Aufklärung* (1944) how reason took on the totalizing aspects of the mythic thinking it aimed to resist. The result was that the claim of the work of art to represent the world became problematic: "Die Legitimation von Kunst in ihrem Verhältnis zur Wissenschaft wird damit vollends zum zentralen Problem des Romans" (89). At the root of the problem of art's "legitimacy," as Müller argued at the end of his study, was a fundamental problem of language akin to Nietzsche's perspectivism: "Musils Sprachkritik relativiert jede bestimmte Sprache durch den Aufweis der Bedingungen, die ihr zugrundeliegen, und der Grenzen, die ihr durch diese bestimmte Perspektive gesetzt werden" (141).

Janik and Toulmin's *Wittgenstein's Vienna* (1973), although only peripherally concerned with Musil's novel, represented a significant early contribution to cultural critique, a line of inquiry that has strong links with social criticism and cannot satisfactorily be separated from it. In building on Claudio Magris's pioneering account of Habsburg Vienna (1966), which had made prominent reference to Musil and his novel, Janik and Toulmin's study illustrated the value of approaches that attribute importance to the immediate socio-cultural environment in which writing of all descriptions — philosophical no less than literary — emerges. Their cultural focus had both a more narrow and, simultaneously, a wider remit than social criticism. While cultural critique is not directly concerned with the broader discussion about civilization and society that has been a part of social criticism since the early sociology of Durkheim and Max Weber, it adds the full array of cultural forms of expression to the restricted field of aesthetic analysis in literary studies, allowing any form of social, political, and religious behavior to meet the criterion of cultural expression, provided these can be seen to take root in a particular cultural environment. As a result, cultural critique has come to engage with wider forms of collective identity, such as nationalism and political involvement, and has added significantly to a general understanding of local influences on human behavior and identity. Recent studies by Bringazi, in 1998, and Jonsson, 2000, illustrate the extent to which cultural critique, with points of focus on nationalism and global identity, has had significant impact on Musil scholarship.

The argument that a diverse range of poets, painters, philosophers, musicians, and even physicians was enriched by a cultural environment that they in turn enriched, seems particularly apposite in the case of turn-of-the-century Habsburg Vienna. Janik and Toulmin's study presented not only an analysis of Viennese society and citizens, it also highlighted new connections that linked Mahler to Freud, Bruckner to Boltzmann, and, less directly, the architecture of Loos and the philosophy of the young Wittgenstein to Karl Kraus. Although not discussed at length, Musil appeared in the study for two reasons. On the one hand, Musil's picture of Kakania put succinctly the "constitutional and social paradoxes embodied in the Habsburg monarchy and its capital" (36). On the other hand, literature gave Musil an opportunity to pursue fundamental problems of philosophy that could not be addressed in the academic philosophy of his own day (118–19). In this latter observation, Janik and Toulmin's pointed to the importance of a proper understanding of Musil's philosophical position — a methodological consideration that has become an important part of ethical approaches to Musil.

After this brief flowering of cultural critique, Hartmut Böhme's study of 1974, one of the best works of criticism to have been written on Musil, signaled a resumption of the dominance of the social critically approach to the novel.[4] The importance of Böhme's study lies above all in its understanding of the critical enterprise. Musil scholarship had hitherto, with few exceptions, seen itself as a "secondary" undertaking seeking to elucidate a "primary" work of literature. Its authority had been drawn not from the critical enterprise itself, but from the authority of literature and the author. Böhme departed from this approach. He not only put forward a new type of analysis — a synthesis of socially critical Marxism and sociology in the tradition of Weber and Durkheim — but he also saw this analysis as a rejection of most of the scholarship on the author that had preceded it. Moreover, Böhme's study — along with that of Laermann (1970) and Götz Müller (1972) — was one of the first works of the younger generation of postwar German scholars to have internalized the ideological conflict raging in Germany in the late sixties and early seventies. This conflict indicated a rift between the so-called perpetrators, who had lived through the Third Reich and in some cases actively conspired with it, and the new generation, born mostly in the 1940s. This new generation was deeply suspicious of those who had fought in Hitler's armies or otherwise shared Hitler's ambitions and were now living — and frequently prospering — in postwar German society. Böhme's disdain for most of the Musil criticism from the 1950s and 1960s reflected this wider rejection of the generation that had preceded his own. It is significant that Böhme, together with his brother Gernot Böhme, was subsequently to write *Das Andere der Vernunft*, a work that outlined an uncompromisingly critical approach to the idea of reason in the Enlightenment (1983). This important study, which was built on the bedrock of Horkheimer and Adorno's critique of Enlightenment rationalism, opposed the systematic devaluation of non-rational ways of understanding evident in the works of rationalist thinkers of the late eighteenth century. It also helped to give an ideological foundation to the first postwar generation's disagreement with the values of its predecessors. Hartmut Böhme's study of Musil, which had a similar orientation to that of the later study with his brother Gernot, represented the culmination of the first phase of social criticism in Musil studies. This phase aggressively disavowed earlier, allegedly ahistorical, existentialist scholarship, and underscored the importance of connecting literature both with the social context of the historical period in which it arose and, by implication, the social imperatives obtaining in the present.

Böhme's study appeared under the title of *Anomie und Entfremdung*. "Entfremdung" was a term that had been used extensively in Marx's early writings, particularly the *Deutsche Ideologie* (1845–46) and *Das Manifest der kommunistischen Partei* (1848), to register the sense of alienation afflicting the industrial laboring class under the conditions of early nineteenth-century capitalism. In the manner of the early Marx, Böhme applied a similar "materialist" approach to Musil's intellectual position, centering his analysis on the claim that knowledge is determined historically and cannot exist at a remove from history in a realm of pure ideas. For Böhme, as for Marx, consciousness was determined above all by material conditions, and not vice versa. It was the historical figure of Galileo, Böhme argued (quoting Musil), who had installed rationality as the highest authority in human life and thereby ushered in the modern secular state. This Marxist account of the progress of civilization substituted the question inherited from older criticism, namely "Wer ist Musil?" — a question that had been approached in terms presupposing the pre-eminence of the writer and of the writer's outlook — with the new question "wer ist Musil und wo steht er?" (1974, 56). Böhme was therefore driven by the need to make the author socially "relevant" and not simply admirable in intellectual ways.

Böhme's approach brought a new Musil into view — the Musil of the "cultural crisis" of the early twentieth century. This cultural crisis was at the same time a crisis of modernity, and allowed Böhme to broaden the scope of his analysis to include the sociological critiques of Durkheim and Weber, who, like Böhme, were driven by a deep suspicion of bourgeois values ("bourgeois," unsurprisingly, is used frequently in Böhme's analysis, in the main to express reproach). Böhme viewed Musil as one of the prominent voices of the transition from a premodern, early industrial society to the modern technologized secular state. In living through such transition, Böhme argued, Musil had inherited a dilemma peculiar to the historical circumstances of his time: how could modern society, which was constructed around technical advances and the prestige of technological rationalism, make use of the innovative potential of technology without sidelining values that derive from the much older era of European humanism? For Musil, a trained engineer who had turned away from the rationalistic sciences after reading Nietzsche in early adulthood, this dilemma became an abiding concern. *Der Mann ohne Eigenschaften*, accordingly, had two parts: a socially critical, but at the same time deeply conservative part, which revealed Musil's trenchant criticism of the new rationalistic, bourgeois society of Kakania; and an emotively subjective, "Nietzschean" part, which sought to advance an alternative vision in order to redeem society. Böhme, however, showed little interest in the socially progressive aspects of Musil's utopia. Instead he portrayed the choice facing the hero of the novel as a thoroughly invidious one: "Zwischen die Refugien der Innerlichkeit und den Sozial-prozeß legt Musil eine so 'unüberbrückbare Kluft,' daß im Verhältnis von Individuum und Gesellschaft nur noch die gegenseitige Negation möglich erscheint: entweder vereinnahmt die Gesellschaft das Individu-um, oder verfällt das Individuum in einen Zustand der Nur-Distanziertheit, durch den es zu einer nicht lebensfähigen Monade wird" (3).

It is hard not to see in this social entrapment and subjective isola-tion — "Nur-Distanziertheit," as Böhme called it — the circumstances of the alienation of the 1968 generation. This generation had itself been caught between politically compromised parliamentary processes (the grand coalition government of right- and left-wing parties in the Federal Republic between 1966 and 1969, which had ostensibly ended opposi-tion within the Parliament), and attempts to generate political opposition outside the federal parliament in West Germany (the so-called "außer-parliamentarische Opposition" erected by student groups in 1968) which had spiraled into violence by the early 1970s. Böhme's doctoral disserta-tion had been written in the aftermath of these events — events that provided the pessimistic backdrop for the "objektiv gewordene Krise der europäischen Gesellschaften" (1974, 56) perceived in Musil's novel. Böhme's interest in psychoanalysis, which came to the fore in the later work *Das Andere der Vernunft*, was subsumed here in a less advanced stage of evolution under the technical term of "Anomie" (self-alienation), and allowed Böhme to draw a link between social processes and the effects they engender in individuals. Later chapters took this interest further, connecting the self-alienation of the hero to oppressive family circumstances in ways that again revealed the wider dominance of the older generation over the younger that informed his approach as a whole. In the end, neither the constructive aspects of Musil's discussion of technological modernism — contained, for example, in the "Utopie der Exaktheit" (cf. chapter 61 of the novel) and the "Forderung eines Generalsekretariats der Genauigkeit und Seele" (chapter 116) — nor the progressive nature of Musil's portrait of individuality, as exemplified by Ulrich and Agathe's relationship, could survive the overwhelming sense of pessimism that pervaded Böhme's work. Instead, the man without qualities was transformed into the "man without identity" (261–62); the imminence of war provided the note of resignation into which — in Böhme's reading of the novel's conclusion — all lines in the novel descended.

If Böhme's Marxist-inspired pessimism represented the culmination of the left-wing response to the novel, David S. Luft's historically based approach of 1980 broke new ground by considering Musil in the light of his membership in the Austrian mandarinate. This mandarinate was a liberal elite with a commitment to Enlightenment and positivism caught "in the transition from traditional-status to industrial-class society" (10). In Luft's analysis, it was not bourgeois values or an emerging nationalism from below that helped Austrian liberals negotiate the transition to modern industrial, technological society. This liberal elite instead sought direction from "an aristocratic culture that was more aesthetic than moral, more psychological than political, more inclined to respond to the inroads of mass society with an ironic smile." In this general cultural outlook, the figure of the artist appeared central and supplied the model for the reflective inwardness of Musil's protagonist. Musil was animated as a representative of this liberal elite above all by the question of "the right way to live" ("die [Frage] des rechten Lebens": cf. *MoE*, 255), which Luft understood as the problem of how to live in a pluralistic, industrializing, mass society at a moment of great social upheaval. The medium Musil used in posing this question was the philosophical essay. Although not used in the service of any grand vision, the essay helped, according to Luft, to express "the smallest step" in conceptual thought, "the insight, the broken form" (19). Musil's extensive use of the essay form in the novel led Luft to consider him "the representative philosophical essayist of the generation of 1905 in Central Europe" (21).

In a key chapter entitled "Ideology and Civilization: 1911–1924," Luft analyzed the intellectual background of the period, especially the works of Mach (whose functionalist approach, Luft argued, Musil rejected), and those of Emerson and Nietzsche (who were interpreted as kindred spirits). Luft accordingly identified Musil's intellectual position as lying between the values enshrined in modern science on the one hand, and the more speculatively intellectual, emotional and moral spheres on the other. Musil attempted to forge a union of both rationality and emotion that would "apply the precision of intellect to the realm of the 'non-ratioïd,' to the realm of the 'ethical and aesthetic relations, the realm of the idea'" (87). Nevertheless, Musil never withdrew into pure intellectuality to escape the problems of his day. On the contrary, he remained vitally concerned with social issues and the need to embrace a "shared, active life" (107). Luft mixed conventional social criticism with cultural critique focused around the crisis of bourgeois culture in the early part of the twentieth century. "Bourgeois metaphysics," he found, "had failed to be empirical, to respond to the concrete individuality of lived experience" (115). He concluded that Musil, though unimpressed by many cultural manifestations of capitalism, nevertheless accepted as inevitable the capitalist-democratic version of mass society and the imminent collapse of bourgeois culture. In view of such resignation to inevitability, the essay assumed an even larger importance: "In the absence of philosophical totality and narrative coherence, essayism provided the thread of continuity for Ulrich and the novel, as the form of spirit appropriate to the dissolution of bourgeois culture" (227).

Josef Strutz's study of 1981 continued the interest of earlier studies in the special position of Musil's generation with respect to the past. In his broad opposition to older generations of all descriptions, Strutz expressed perhaps even more uncompromisingly than Böhme had in 1974 the hostility of the first postwar generation in German society toward those who had failed to oppose and prevent the rise of fascism. Basing his study of Musil's novel on Böhme's Marxist analysis and Dieter Heyd's psychoanalytical approach of 1980, Strutz postulated a broad generational conflict in the period before the First World War, and cited Freud's concept of the superego and Kafka's *Brief an den Vater* as literary examples of such a conflict. In Strutz's analysis, it was not the main character Ulrich so much as the more marginal figure Feuermaul who typified this generational conflict, in particular because Feuermaul could be seen to suffer from an unconscious repression of the figure of the father. In Strutz's view, Feuermaul was a representative of a lost world with an archaic understanding of culture and no sense of political activism. Tellingly, it was his extreme passivism that disrupted the deliberations of the Parallel Campaign. In a passage striking a note of protest typical of the first postwar generation of Musil scholars, Strutz turned Feuermaul into a figure of wider importance in the novel: "Feuermaul kann als Sinnbild, als Symbol jener Bewegung genommen werden, die alle Krisen der Gesellschaft im Medium der 'Kultur' zu überwinden sucht" (1981, 47). Elsewhere Strutz detailed how the established classes in the novel achieved their dominance of other social groups through manipulation and control. Outlining the special role attaching to socially activistic literature, Strutz argued that literature represented a means to combat the sense of social and political alienation felt outside the ruling establishment. Using extracts from the essays and thinkers who influenced Musil, Strutz drew an overtly political conclusion that indicated disagreement with postwar social and economic conditions in the Federal Republic. Property-based capitalism, he argued, could never successfully reconcile socially progressive individual identity with collective forms of identity (69–75).

While Strutz's view did not establish any final position about the political Musil, his approach suggested that Musil's novel was anything but quietistic. Clearly, Musil's ironic picture of Kakania and the true nature of his utopian visions still needed detailed examination. Friedbert Aspetsberger's essay of 1982 represented one such attempt to interrogate Musil's utopian conceptions more directly, adding contextual information about the Other Condition that threw light on Musil's social and political intentions. Aspetsberger found that the Other Condition was a topic "appropriate to [Musil's] times." "In the 1930s," he argued, "it met with a very specific political reaction in the real world, resulting in something which many adopted in blind faith" (63). Aspetsberger also shed light on confessional questions, revealing that Musil was not the atheistic-minded thinker he was frequently taken to be. Aspetsberger emphasized Musil's concern about a fundamental confusion between two types of belief: the belief in living *for* God (the example of the character of Lindner in the novel) and living *in* God, which had more positive associations for Musil (66). In the same collection of essays, the noted Nietzsche scholar J. P. Stern made clear where historical reality and Musil's presentation of fictional reality intersected:

> The narrator (and through him the author) sees the Empire and the Vienna of the higher civil service, of the patritiate and the middle classes which constitute the imperial centre, not as finite historical "reality" [. . .] but on the contrary as a very special possibility of being in the world, as a social existence that is intent on preserving its aspects as a provisory world. Here, then, is a society engaged on the experiment of living in the *coniunctivus irrealis* [. . .]. (79)

In this new spirit of non-polemical engagement with social and political questions, an essay by Lucas Cejpek, published in 1984, addressed the topic of conflictual relations. Quoting Cassirer's distinction between the cultural sciences and the natural sciences in building a focus on social relations in the novel, Cejpek indicated the existence of a profound antagonism underpinning bourgeois social and sexual relations. This sense of antagonism meant that the states of war and peace were not sharply opposed in the novel; any distinction drawn for the purposes of appraising Musil's picture of society (and, by implication, whether peace would be displaced by war as the final outcome of the novel) ultimately had to be seen as quantitative rather than a qualitative in nature. The novel described a society in a state of civil war, where this society stood for the entire world (205).

Cornelia Blasberg's attempt, also published in 1984, to link the general crisis of culture at the turn of the century to the position of the intellectual during this period, and to see both cultural crisis and the position of the intellectual as compelling themes in Musil's novel, while indebted to David Luft's earlier study of 1980, opened up fresh perspectives on *Der Mann ohne Eigenschaften*. The psychological discontinuity Blasberg analyzed assigned importance to a feeling of disconnectedness from history experienced by Musil's intellectual generation. Blasberg identified Berlin and Vienna as the dominant localities, and the period immediately before, during, and after the First World War as the temporal focus for the sense of loss and decay that overtook this generation. Musil's novel could therefore be read as a particularly vivid portrayal of the mental disposition of the European intellectual in the early twentieth century, or, as Blasberg put it, as a "document of the experience of crisis" (6). In doing so, her analysis broadened the understanding of Musil's novel at a time when opposition to "bourgeois literature" was still a popular topic in Musil studies.

In Blasberg's study, the philosophy of Nietzsche was of crucial importance to the generation that entered adulthood in the years immediately before the First World War. Blasberg characterized Musil's connection with the thought of Nietzsche, which Musil's diaries had indicated was life-long, as of significance. Nietzsche's aphoristic style, for example, was important for the development of the essay form in the novel. Even more than this, however, Nietzsche's thought addressed an intellectual elite that at the end of the nineteenth century had suddenly become aware of its own loss of status. Nietzsche, in Blasberg's judgment, found a ready audience in the new generation of intellectuals in the early twentieth century who were beginning to grasp the full extent of their estrangement from society. Nietzsche's thought — a blend of cultural critique and radical utopianism — offered a compelling diagnosis of the age as well as an alternative to the preoccupations of the age. Blasberg used the word "Ungleichzeitigkeit" (discontinuity) in a variety of contexts to characterize the sense of intellectual displacement and estrangement felt by this generation of intellectuals.

The central aspect of Musil's reaction to this wider cultural crisis was his critique of rationality. In breaking with aspects of rational civilization, he set his protagonist on a course of openness and autonomy typical of the general intellectual response of his time. Blasberg analyzed how the critique of rational civilization became not just a catch-cry; it was a moment of "identity formation" that led many intellectuals to cultivate and glorify non-rational and even irrational positions in a "conservative revolution" against the dominant culture of the time (109–12). For Musil, however, opposition to the culture of his time took the form not of irrationalism, but of what Blasberg called a "de-ontologizing of reality," a view according to which life and history lost its sense of underlying necessity (147). In the utopian outlook of the final section of the novel, Musil's interest was shaped by methodological considerations and the problem of making the Other Condition a genuinely sensed and lived alternative to the dominant forms of rationality of the day. To this extent, Blasberg argued, Musil's fashioning of a viable alternative to rationality in the realm of art led even beyond the exhortatory philosophy of Friedrich Nietzsche.

In an introductory study that situated Musil within the intellectual climate of turn-of-the-century Vienna, Hannah Hickman (1984) echoed Blasberg's analysis of the significance of Nietzsche for Musil's generation. Interweaving an evolving account of Musil's biography with a close study of the text and a broad intellectual discussion about influences, Hickman viewed Musil as a type of broker of different intellectual traditions, wedged firmly between the "two cultures" of art and science, and uniquely placed by dint of his education and intellectual disposition to bridge the gulf between them. While rejecting Kaiser and Wilkins's overly harmonizing account of the novel's conclusion (1962), Hickman nevertheless identified moments of genuine transcendence in the lovers' attempt to marry the scientific ideal of exactness with the needs of the emotions (181–82).

In 1993, Jacques Bouveresse advanced one of the first attempts to see in Musil's use of history a postmodern aspect — an aspect that, in historiographical terms, moved beyond Leopold Ranke's notion of the "great man" as the agency bringing forth the great deeds and events of history. In Bouveresse's analysis, the dominance of great men and their discourses converged — and were ended by — the First World War (227). This eclipse of the great men of history revoked all views about the ends of history. Bouveresse's important finding was that the First World War was the moment from which the decline of history as a reliably narrated, teleologically understood unfolding of events in time could be dated.

In Wolfgang Schraml's 1994 study, the important years 1914 and 1918 became reference points for a wide-ranging consideration of anthropological influences on Musil's novel. Schraml asked the historian's question of how the conflagration of world war had occurred, but broadened the scope of this question by estimating the role that emotional and intellectual confusion had played in the period immediately preceding the First World War. This climate of confusion had spawned in Schraml's opinion a type of general cultural "relativism" inhibiting both collective and individual action. Schraml noted that the confusion of the prewar period that the novel narrates also dominated the postwar period in which the novel was actually drafted and written. When the German and Austrian monarchies metamorphosed into democracies in 1918–19, a new pluralism emerged that was confronted and resisted across vast sections of the community. The result was even greater cultural disorientation. Schraml therefore endorsed Vogt's earlier finding of 1984 in adjudging Musil — like many of his contemporaries — ambivalent toward democracy: "Auch der Nietzscheaner und Demokratiegegner Musil akzeptier[te] nach 1918 die Prinzipien einer liberalen Gesellschaft nicht mit innerer Überzeugung und nur vorübergehend. [. . .] auch er [identifizierte] in den zwanziger Jahren die liberale Demokratie immer mehr mit einer nach seiner Meinung nicht tolerierbaren 'Ordnungslosigkeit'" (14).[5] One path out of this general disorientation was the totalitarian reaction that the novel in part describes. Schraml also considered two other paths. First, a flight from the present that is evident, among other things, in the tendency to make the legitimacy of political decision-making dependent on the degree to which it accorded with decision-making in the past (and thus to "historicize" political action). Second, and more importantly, a program of "geistige[n] Organisationspolitik" — Musil's abiding concern from 1918 on which gained expression in the novel in his vision of a "Erdensekretariat für Genauigkeit und Seele" (cf. *MoE*, 597).

The need for order and the ubiquity of relativism thus set the initial bearings for Schraml's study. In response to the relativism of the immediate postwar period, Musil developed by the early 1920s, particularly in his essays, an idiosyncratic cultural anthropology based on the idea of human formlessness. These ideas were influenced by the growing interest in anthropological discourses that had grown out of the revolution in the biological sciences in the nineteenth century. Schraml linked the idea of human formlessness to the central idea in the novel of being without qualities: if possession of qualities implied that human beings were susceptible to social conditioning, then the openness that lack of qualities implies could remove the alienating effects of conditioning and bring about a positive outlook on self and society. By showing how Musil's novel took root in the fertile soil of 1920s anthropology, Schraml demonstrated how profound Musil's "geistige Bewältigung der Zeit" — the conceptual dealing with his time he had promised to undertake in the novel in his interview with Fontana in 1926 — actually turned out to be. In sum, Schraml's study revealed significant new connections between literature, science, and anthropology. He even argued at the end of his study that the diplomat Tuzzi's Machiavellian qualities might be linked to ideas about cannibalism discussed in Musil's time! (470–81).

Cay Hehner's study of 1994, a published version of his 1992 dissertation submitted to the Faculty of Politics at the Free University of Berlin, took up the question of Musil's political allegiances — a topic frequently held to be highly problematic.[6] In some ways, Hehner's study promised to do for Musil scholarship what Pierre Bertaux's study of Jacobin influences had done for Hölderlin scholarship, namely, to open up an entirely new understanding of the author by appraising that author's political allegiances. The controversial idea Hehner presented was found in Musil's connections with an Austrian secret society, "Die Katakombe," immediately before the First World War.[7] This secret society, initiated by Robert Müller, was formed in response to the visible infirmity of the aging Austrian monarch, Franz-Josef II, and his increasingly debile and infirm cabinet. Müller put together a secret shadow cabinet drawn mostly from the ranks of progressively minded artists and writers with the unabashedly treasonable aim of ultimately replacing the official cabinet. This society of writers and intellectuals stood — however ineffectually — for an "antiauthoritarian revolution from below," to some extent in opposition to a more prominent later attempt, led by Egon Erwin Kisch, to launch an Austrian socialist revolution "from above." Although Hehner was unable to demonstrate any active involvement of Musil in the secret society, he nevertheless argued that Musil sympathized with Müller's aims. For one thing, Musil drafted a plan for a novel under the title of "Katakombe" that seemed to set out an antiauthoritarian political agenda. In other ways, Musil revealed in his essays and to a lesser extent in other works a broadly similar social and political outlook ("[a]uch bei Musil finden wir unzweideutig anarchistische genauer antietatistische Elemente" [445]). In the major novel, Hehner interpreted references to the utopian ideal of an "ekstatische Sozietät" as evidence of a political program of ebullient anarchism. Musil's 1921 play *Die Schwärmer*, Hehner pointed out, had appeared under the title of *Die Anarchisten* in Musil's early notes. In his 1913 essay *Politische Bekenntnisse eines jungen Mannes* Musil even declared himself to be a "conservative anarchist." Stitching these political themes, statements, and asides together, Hehner concluded:

> daß die Programmatik des Mann ohne Eigenschaften oder des eigenschaftsfreien Menschen schwerlich anders zu begreifen ist, als als Überhöhung und Paradigmatisierung des Anarchisten, des Geistherrschers oder des libertären Menschen, eine literarische Sublimierung des Geistohne-Geist-Aktivismus von Müller, Hiller, u.a., einem Ideal, dem Musil, trotz der erheblichen Schwächen in der praktischen Realisierung, zeitlebens verpflichtet blieb. (590)

Hehner's attempt to uncover a political agenda in Musil's writings remained at best speculative. The strength of his approach — that attention was drawn to Musil's notes and fragments from 1911 to the early 1920s that had otherwise escaped notice in Musil scholarship — also turned out to be a weakness. The one-sided treatment of this material skewed the analysis toward Musil's person and away from the novel. The unitalicized subtitle of Hehner's study, "Der Mann ohne Eigenschaften als 'Übergangswesen,'" indeed, can be taken to refer more to the person of Robert Musil than to the novel itself. Furthermore, there was no contextual discussion about the multiplicity of voices encountered in the novel, whose function is to relativize most of the aspirational statements made by the characters, including those characters expressing sympathy for the idea of an Austrian republic of soviets. Clarisse's blindly ecstatic vitalism, for example, can easily be taken as evidence against the worth of anarchical causes. Despite this, Hehner's study delivered important new insights about Musil's reception of Nietzsche (Musil is "kein richtiger Nietzscheaner [. . .], mit dem man auf reaktionäre und genozidäre Raub- und Vernichtungszüge gehen kann" [168]), his understanding of positivism ("es [ist] nicht zulässig [. . .], Musil schlicht und gänzlich unter die Positivisten zu subsumieren" [200]), and his portrait of the Other Condition, which he considered a trenchant critique of millenarianism and of emerging totalitarianism.

In an essay in the *Musil-Forum* for 1993–94, Alexander Honold examined apocalyptic dimensions in the major novel. Following the cue given by Musil himself— "Grundidee Krieg: Alle Linien münden in den Krieg" (*MoE,* 1851) — Honold engaged with the question of the inevitability of war and the unconscious role the Parallel Campaign played in promoting it. "Die Wahrheit," he found, "wird in dieser unabsichtlichen Vorhersage als ein Textereignis inszeniert, als Entgleisung der Rede, die genau dadurch ihr wahres Ziel findet" (146). Uncovering a naive belief in untrammeled progress, Honold asked, with Musil, why no one had foreseen the catastrophe of 1914: "Man wohnte also auf einem Vulkan. Trotzdem stellten es die Seelen und Geister nicht in Rechung" (*TB I,* 1005).

In a longer study published in 1995, Honold connected history with the medium of literature in important new ways. Narrative became the means to preserve essential aspects of historical experience in memory, in particular in order to forestall the "Auslöschung der Spuren" that war otherwise effects. Honold's aim was not to retell history through the novel in any conventional way. Rather, he sought to demonstrate how history is memorialized and reconstructed at the level of individual experience. In comparing the separate claims of historical analysis and "poetological" experience, Honold offered two different perspectives on the use of history in the novel. The first approach aligned the novel with the events of history. The second approach showed how history is absorbed, transformed and "re-invented" in the novel to serve aesthetic purposes. Honold juxtaposed these two perspectives on history in order to return to one of the most intractable problems to have vexed Musil scholarship — the question of Musil's realism.[8] Honold asked whether Musil could be considered a historical realist who places himself "below" the facts of history in drawing a portrait of the collapsing Austro-Hungarian empire, or whether he was rather to be imagined as a different type of realist, who reconstructs reality with a view not to its outward veracity, but more to its authenticity as directly lived experience. The former perspective engaged with Georg Lukács's understanding of the novel. Lukács had viewed the novel as a failed bourgeois attempt to command temporal reality. In the end, Lukács argued, Musil was unable to extricate himself from the satirical picture he drew of a bankrupt bourgeois social order. His novel therefore represented a document of failed bourgeois sensibility. The latter perspective on the question of realism was aligned more with Adorno's reply to Lukács, who viewed the failure to sustain a comprehensive sense of reality in Musil's novel as part of Musil's "Realismus der geschlossenen Augen" (99). Honold's view about the realism of Musil's novel endorsed Adorno's perspective and has delivered the most authoritative account of Musil's realism thus far: "Musils Roman ist 'realistisch' im Sinne einer Intentionalität [. . .]: Er ist auf Wirklichkeit aus, behandelt diese jedoch nicht als schlichtweg abbild-bare oder gar 'widerspiegelnde,' sondern als noch ausstehende, zu kon-struierende — 'als Aufgabe und Erfindung' (*MoE*, 16) und knüpft damit an das aristotelische Konzept der energeia an, der Wirklichkeit, die als Komplementärbegriff zur dynamis (Möglichkeit) fungiert [. . .]" (16).

As announced in the title, Honold's study linked this notion of real-ism to the entities of "war and the city." Both entities were then ana-lyzed as typical aspects of modernity, bound to a particular place (Vienna) and time (the First World War) and yet representing general phenomena that brought about a fundamental sense of alienation and social dislocation. Honold treated both aspects at length and from differ-ent conceptual standpoints. Crucial was the fact that both war and the city could appear as the central points of focus of the novel precisely because the novel failed to address either in overt ways. Instead, as Ho-nold observed: "Wien und der Weltkrieg fehlen in diesem Roman, blei-ben der Fiktion unerreichbar von Beginn an" (23). The incapacity of fiction to circumscribe and name actual historical experience thus became the underlying "problem situation" of the novel. Reality resisted narra-tive closure on all fronts and indeed from the very first lines of the novel: "Musils Romananfang [. . .] zeigt, daß er etwas voraussetzt, was er nicht zeigen und erst recht nicht erzeugen kann" (43). This failure to effect narrative closure, while broadly characteristic of modernist literature, was attributable in Musil's case, as Honold argued, to a double disruption of textual construction and historical experience. In historical terms, the novel described the collapse of the Austrian-Hungarian monarchy; at the same time, the novel was constructed against the backdrop of a second collapse, the decline of the Weimar Republic and the emergence of German fascism: "Die Darstellung des altösterreichischen Panoramas trägt in sich den Zeitindex eines Zerfalls, den die Zeitumstände der Werkgeschichte negativ bekräftigen" (98). Honold's conclusion about Musil's novel therefore formulated a problem at the heart of all modern-ist literature: the description of dissolution (of the Austrian state) was connected not with the issue of what the text described, but with what it programmatically and openly failed to describe.

Klaus Mackowiak's 1995 study, outwardly directed at uncovering Musil's "concept of art," was in fact drawn to considering the historical conditions that Musil faced in the 1920s. Musil's problem, in Macko-wiak's eyes, was to explain the sense of social dislocation and "anomie" apparent even before the war. In Mackowiak's view, following Horkheimer and Adorno, the social dissolution Musil's generation faced had resulted above all from the historical development of reason. By the early twentieth century reason had taken on overdetermined and "instrumental" aspects that Musil rendered under the neologism "ratioïd." This dominance of reason in all aspects of life had made even moral concepts empty and unusable. Musil therefore constructed an alternative value scheme based around a new approach to rationality. In this value scheme the term "nichtratioïd" indicated a new type of thought based not on abstract concepts, but on holistically applied concrete ideas (24–33). Mackowiak demonstrated how Musil's critique of rationality was indebted to Nietzsche, Heidegger, and the critical approach of the Frankfurt School. The final section of Mackowiak's analysis considered the extent to which the "pre-logical" and mythical dimensions of Musil's utopia, the Other Condition, could be said to accord with Durkheim's understanding of the elemental features of religious life.

Harald Haslmayr's published version of his dissertation (1997), which had been presented for examination in the history department of the University of Graz in 1994, revealed how the postmodern understanding of "text" had served to break down the boundaries separating traditional discipline areas. In the 1990s, Musil's novel had attracted the interest of disciplines outside literary studies such as history and politics. At the same time, Haslmayr's study took further the earlier work of Jean-Pierre Cometti (1987) and Jacques Bouveresse (1993), who had witnessed an entropic movement in Musil's account of history. From this postmodern perspective, Haslmayr's study reflected on how the emergence of cultural studies had changed the way history itself was viewed. The central problem Haslmayr identified was the new difficulty for historians in legitimating universalist positions (such as human rights, etc.) when the study of the past indicated that these positions had emerged historically and could not be considered to have general or unchanging application to human affairs. Haslmayr's study represented a response to the so-called "historians' debate" ("Historikerstreit") of the mid to late 1980s in Germany.[9] In that debate, attempts by the German historian Ernst Nolte to set Hitler's concentration camps in a historical context and thus diminish the singularity of the Holocaust drew sharp responses from philosophers and historians in Germany, notably Jürgen Habermas. That debate itself seems to have marked the arrival of "posthistoire" within the mainstream of the German academy. Haslmayr, reflecting on the implications of "posthistoire" in *Der Mann ohne Eigenschaften*, put Musil in a line with the cultural critics Nietzsche, Freud, and Horkheimer and Adorno, all of whom pointed out aspects of the decline of what Lyotard had called the "grand narratives" — in particular, the incapacity of such conceptually based narratives to find validation beyond the logic of their own totalizing constructs.[10]

As Haslmayr implied, Musil had foreseen such difficulties long before Lyotard. Musil's rejection of causality in history and his discovery of functionalism through his reading of Ernst Mach was the conceptual breakthrough that revealed how the Austrian state remained entrapped within its own systemic logic (the problem alluded to in the second part of the novel under the heading "Seinesgleichen geschieht"). In describing the breakup of the Habsburg empire, Musil was not concerned to undertake a historical case study in the manner of Joseph Roth or Hermann Broch, but rather to account for the decline and fall of a totalizing historical meta-narrative centered around the artificial construct of Kakania. For Haslmayr, accordingly, the dissolution of Kakania was not just a peculiarity of Austrian history, but was a more general phenomenon. It could be seen as part of a movement that had witnessed the breakdown of universalizing discourses and grand narratives and their replacement with particularizing new ones. Indeed, Haslmayr's study can be read as a call for the same displacement of traditional arts curricula ("Geisteswissenschaften") by new particularizing discipline areas such as cultural studies ("Kulturwissenschaften"). In the first part of his book, Haslmayr examined instances in the novel where history was problematized. The second part of the analysis then revealed how the study of history can be usefully informed by the study of culture, or, even more than this, that the study of the past and the study of culture amounted to the same thing. Haslmayr concluded by challenging the edifice of history. The events of history, he argued, did not throw light on Musil's historical position; there was no unraveling, as Bouveresse had already shown in 1993, to any final end of history. Instead history was by its very nature fragmentary and open, and could be unlocked only by the limited means of establishing cultural reference points for historical understanding (254, 267).

If, as Stephen D. Dowden suggested, "cultural critique is understood to mean an analytical exploration of the ways in which imaginative writing is positioned with regard to history, politics, and religion,"[11] then Friedrich Bringazi's 1998 study of the idea of nation and nationalism in Musil may be taken as a good example of this critical tradition. Bringazi used Musil's work to consider what lies behind an individual's sense of belonging, and, by way of extension, why individuals develop a sense of the importance of the nation. This "inside perspective," however, assumed a negative view of nationalistic consciousness, since nationalism was held to arise from maladjusted personal identity formations. Bringazi's aim was to investigate how such maladjusted identity results from social, political and economic circumstances in a given historical period. To this extent, Bringazi's study may be read as a political response to the rising tide of reactionary nationalist movements sweeping across Europe in the 1990s in general and Bringazi's native Austria in particular.

Bringazi's contribution to the under-researched[12] area of nationalism in Musil scholarship opposed an earlier study by Hüppauf (1983). Hüppauf had not able to establish any real interest on the part of Musil in the question of nationalism. Bringazi, by contrast, showed that nationalism emerged as a significant topic in Musil's essays, particularly the essay *Die Nation als Ideal und Wirklichkeit*. Musil had given expression to nationalistic sentiment, for example, in speaking out in favor of the *Anschluß* with Germany. In the middle chapters of his study, Bringazi showed that Musil approached nationalism from the viewpoint of the individual. Here he referred to Musil's "Theorem der menschlichen Gestaltlosigkeit" in support of the view that the human being was predisposed to manipulation through suggestion and violence — a concern of Musil's since his first novel, *Die Verwirrungen des Zöglings Törleß*. In *Der Mann ohne Eigenschaften*, the demonstration before the palace of Graf Leinsdorf (cf. *MoE*, 625ff.) shed light on the individual's psychological response to living in mass society. Elsewhere, the tension between individual and collective levels of identity formation was at issue. The last two chapters treated the issue of nation and anti-Semitism, and the problem of jingoistic fervor. In Bringazi's view, Musil was deeply suspicious of collectivism, and especially critical of those forms of collectivism that manipulated the individual in the name of a particular ideology. Musil favored, instead, an "open society" such as that later advocated by Karl Popper. In such a society, the "other" would be welcomed into the collective rather than excluded from it — an idea of which the "ecstatic society" ("ekstatische Sozietät": *MoE*, 1307) of the sibling lovers represented an early prototype.

If, as some have argued, postmodernism is contained within the discourse of modernism rather than emerging *post hoc, ergo propter hoc* in reaction to it, then the same argument might hold in relation to postcolonialism and colonialism. The Swedish-born Germanist Stefan Jonsson, who undertook the first attempt at a postcolonial reading of Musil, followed such an assumption by arguing that Musil's Austria was "the first postimperial culture in modern Europe" (2000: x) and that *Der Mann ohne Eigenschaften*, accordingly, could be read as a "postimperial novel" (14). In setting out this view, Jonsson suggested that Musil's interest in the question of Austrian politics remained paramount throughout the novel. He thus opposed the popular view that Musil had progressively lost interest in depictions of Kakania as the novel unraveled and was increasingly drawn to the utopian story of sibling love in the Other Condition. Throughout his analysis, therefore, Jonsson aligned himself with history and the primacy of Musil's historical situation. His aim was to show how individuals are conditioned by historical forces acting from outside; they are not shaped by any innate "subjectivity."

In Jonsson's view, Austria's postimperialism did not merely enact the conflict between a receding feudal system and an emerging capitalist society, but was dominated by "the struggle between a crumbling imperial regime and various movements of what we today would call identity politics: Zionism and anti-Semitism; women's movements and antifeminism; nationalism, racism and fascism" (x). Moving then to the level of the individual, Jonsson argued that Musil's historical position forced him to "conceptualize the possibility of a human subject who would not be captivated by homogenizing ideologies" such as imperialism or fascism (9). Endorsing a finding of Honold's earlier study of 1995, Jonsson held that Musil's ideal of subjectivity was posited within a "historically specific experience of urban space" as part of a "specific experience of modernity" (93–94). Human subjects were therefore to be understood more from their "singularity" in time (what Jonsson called their "ipseity") than from any view of their inward natures, that is, less as subjects and more as part of an overriding historical process (164–70). This contentious position on Musil's portrayal of his characters in the novel opposed notions of subjectivity that implied an inherent unity of the subject. Instead, Musil set out a counter view in the tradition of Adorno, Kristeva, and Lacan. According to these critics, the subject entirely lacked positive identity from the beginning, and was impelled, through action in the world, to overcome this lack. Extending this account of postrational subjectivity to posit a "subject without nation," Jonsson added, by implication, a reply to Bringazi's study of 1998. Bringazi had maintained that Musil was vitally concerned with the problem of nationalism. Jonsson contended that while the nation had imposed models of collective identity on individuals in Musil's time, Musil himself rejected such models in formulating a prototypical version of global supranationality.

The "subject without nation" in Jonsson's analysis was the underlying "project" of Musil's novel. In some ways, this understanding of the novel brought the protest tradition of 1968 in Musil scholarship to an end, since it engaged with the socially critical philosophy that had inspired such a tradition while pointing beyond its incipient pessimism about identity and social and political action in the world. Jonsson found, instead, that the ideal of the "nationless subject" that inspired Musil's outlook could not be evinced through philosophical argument, nor could it be accessed via the "expressivist paradigm," that is, following Ferdinand Tönnies, through the externalization of an underlying essentialist "natural will" (cf. 25–26). Jonsson ascribed no importance to art as expressive activity. Instead, he held that history naturalizes the subject and gives credence to the collectivist endeavor. Where, in the Other Condition, Musil's notion of the subject broke both with conventional sense and, in the vision of incestuous love, good taste, Jonsson followed the lead of Ulrich Schelling's 1968 study in placing what he called these "figures of monstrosity" (205–16) into a historical context. The idiosyncratic behavior of the siblings could therefore be explained with reference to an "historical trauma" that had an observable etiology, since it was typical of cases where "ideological appellations malfunction and the normative point of identification on which the citizens normally rely recedes" (11). Thus purged of its antinormative features, the utopian conclusion of Musil's novel could be upheld in the name of a positive and more open conception of global nationlessness. Jonsson concluded by linking the lovers' ecstatic vision to other ciphers of behavioral "multiplicity" that had direct appeal to posterity.

Notes

[1] Ulf Schramm, pointing out that no overall satiric intent is apparent in the drawing of the character of Ulrich, opposed Arntzen's assumptions about the use of satire in the novel — cf. Schramm, *Fiktion und Reflexion. Überlegungen zu Musil und Beckett.* (Frankfurt am Main: Suhrkamp, 1967), 54.

[2] Stephen D. Dowden, *Kafka's Castle and the Critical Imagination* (Columbia, SC: Camden House, 1995), 55. Cf. Georg Lukács, "Die Gegenwartsbedeutung des kritischen Realismus," in *Probleme des Realismus I: Essays über Realismus* (Neuwied/Berlin: Luchterhand, 1971), 457–603 (1957); Theodor W. Adorno, "Erpreßte Versöhnung. Zu Georg Lukács: 'Wider den mißverstandenen Realismus,'" in *Noten zur Literatur* (Frankfurt am Main: Suhrkamp, 1981), 251–80 (1958). Note an earlier essay by Georg Lukács, first published in 1933, "Totentanz der Weltanschauungen," in *Literatur und Literaturgeschichte in Österreich,* edited by Ilona T. Erdélyi (Budapest/Vienna: Akadémiai Kiadó, 1979. Sondernummer der Zeitschrift Helikon), 297–307, here 302: "[Musil] ironisiert schart das Österreich der Vorkriegszeit und seine Satire dehnt sich darum auch auf alle aktuellen Fragen der deutschen Intelligenz in der Faschisierungsperiode aus. Aber diese Ironie ist der Witz eines

mitten in der Sache drin Stehenden, dessen Horizont ebenfalls nicht weiter reicht, als der von ihm Verspotteten."

[3] Cf. a passage in *MoE* on reaching decisions: "'Alles das muß entschieden werden!' Er wollte es nicht mehr im einzelnen wissen, was 'alles das' sei; [. . .] alles das führte auf Unmöglichkeiten [. . .]" (*MoE* 653).

[4] A similar socially critical orientation can be perceived in Hartmut Böhme's 1976 essay, "Theoretische Probleme der Interpretation Robert Musils Roman *Der Mann ohne Eigenschaften*," *Musil-Forum* 2 (1): 35–70.

[5] Musil's feeling of uncertainty about democracy was also underscored by Guntram Vogt in his article, "Robert Musils ambivalentes Verhältnis zur Demokratie," *Exilforschung* 2 (1984): 310–38.

[6] Several commentators, including Maier-Solgk ("Musil und die problematische Politik: Zum Verhältnis von Literatur und Politik bei Robert Musil, insbesondere zu einer Auseinandersetzung mit Carl Schmitt," *Orbis Literarum* 46 (1991): 340–63, have expressed this opinion.

[7] This reference to the "Katakombe" was, admittedly, not completely new. Wilkins and Kaiser had referred to Achilles' plan to found a new secret order of "extra rationalists," the "Katakombe," in connection with the early fragments *Der Spion* and *Der Erlöser* (1962: 137).

[8] Cf. Freese, "Robert Musil als Realist. Ein Beitrag zur Realismus-Diskussion, *Literatur und Kritik* 9 (1974): 514–44; Karthaus, "War Musil Realist?" *Musil-Forum* 6/1 (1980): 155–227; Zeller, "Musils Auseinandersetzung mit der realistischen Schreibweise," *Musil-Forum* 6/1 (1980): 128–44; Fourie, "Musil als Realist?" *Musil-Forum* 19/20 (1993/94): 132–43.

[9] Halsmayr admittedly does not make explicit reference to this debate, but instead refers to the debate about positivism in Germany in the 1970s (*Die Zeit ohne Eigenschaften: Geschichtsphilosophie und Modernebegriff im Werk Robert Musils* [Vienna: Böhlau, 1997], 122).

[10] This was a point already alluded to by Jean-Pierre Cometti in his article "Es gibt Geschichte und Geschichten," *Musil-Studien* 13, 175.

[11] Stephen D. Dowden, *Kafka's Castle and the Critical Imagination* (Columbia, SC: Camden House, 1995), 95.

[12] Only Bernd-Rüdiger Hüppauf and Peter Pfeiffer have undertaken studies in this area: Hüppauf, "Von Wien durch den Krieg nach nirgendwo," *Text und Kritik* 21/22 (1983): 55–69; Pfeiffer, "Nicht Fisch und nicht Fleisch. Robert Musil's Reaktion auf den Nationalsozialismus," in Josef Strutz, ed., *Robert Musils "Kakanien" — Subjekt und Geschichte: Festschrift für Karl Dinklage zum 80. Geburtstag* (Munich: Fink, 1987), 145–63.

3: Psychological and Psychoanalytical Readings

> *Soviel Agathe sehen konnte, hatte er die*
> *Psychoanalyse dabei außer Betracht gelassen*
> *[. . .]; aber Ulrich sagte, er ließe sie nicht*
> *deshalb beiseite, weil er die Verdienste dieser*
> *bedeutenden Theorie nicht anerkenne [. . .],*
> *sondern es hänge damit zusammen, daß bei*
> *dem, was er vorhabe, ihre Eigenart nicht so*
> *zur Geltung komme, wie es ihres immerhin*
> *auch sehr anspruchsvollen Selbstbewußtseins*
> *würdig wäre.* (*MoE*, 1138–39)

T HE PSYCHOLOGICAL NATURE OF Musil's fiction struck Musil's literary public from the beginning. His first novel *Die Verwirrungen des Zöglings Törleß*, for example, deals with the anxieties of a young schoolboy. Young Törleß finds himself unable to become master of his troubled inner state, and therefore unable to commit to action to end a campaign of brutality of two schoolboys against a fellow pupil. That these "confusions" were not confined to adolescence, but referred to wider confusions in the social world of turn-of-the-century Austria, was one reason for the immediate success of the novel. Since Musil's later works did not end this exploration of states of inner confusion, but extended them into all areas of mature life, his concern with psychological states was quickly held to be programmatic. Moreover, the fact that Musil's career as a writer was exactly contemporaneous with early psychoanalysis — *Törleß* was published in 1906, only six years after Freud's pioneering work *Die Traumdeutung* — and that Musil, like Freud, lived and worked in Vienna, added to the impression that his works were preeminently psychological in outlook. For this reason, analyzing the conflicts of subjectivity at all levels of conscious and unconscious awareness has become a popular point of departure in approaches to Musil's work in general and the major novel in particular.

In 1970 Erhard von Büren undertook the first comprehensive study of Musil's works from a psychological perspective. Von Büren identified psychopathological aspects, particularly in Musil's early fiction. He noted how Musil's portrayal of unusual or even extreme mental states in his characters was duplicitous, in that it served an underlying literary purpose. The two stories of *Vereinigungen*, for example, were not "about" perverted behavior. The perversions that Musil portrayed in treating the theme of adultery were instead "der konstruktive Entwurf einer neuartigen Möglichkeit des Erlebens und Seins" (50). In the case of *Der Mann ohne Eigenschaften*, Musil had not intended to throw light on the condition of schizophrenia in drawing the character, say, of Moosbrugger. Instead, his intention was to treat the general theme of subject-object relations at a time when these relations were profoundly disturbed. As von Büren put it: "Der Lustmörder ist das krasse Symptom einer Generation, deren 'letzte Zuflucht Sexualität und Krieg' ist" (115).

Other early psychological approaches appraised the extent of Musil's debt to psychoanalysis — a movement that had begun in Austria at the end of the nineteenth century with the work of Freud and Breuer on hysteria. In a 1973 essay, Karl Corino found many points of contact between early psychoanalysis and Musil's fiction. Indeed, Corino published a full-length study on Musil in 1974, applying the main principles of psychoanalysis to the two early novellas of the *Vereinigungen* (1911). For Corino, the case for the influence of psychoanalysis on Musil was self-evident. From 1913 at the latest, he found, Musil had taken note of Freud's major publications; by the early 1920s he had already acquired a high degree of familiarity with the key ideas of psychoanalysis. Despite later attempts to throw off this influence, or at least to qualify it, Musil remained under the sway of psychoanalytical theories throughout his life. Corino concluded: "Er begrüßt den kollektiven Impuls, die psychoanalytische Theorie in der Praxis zu verifizieren und aus der Praxis neue theoretische Erkenntnisse zu ziehen. Den Grundansatz der Psychoanalyse hält er für richtig, nur die spekulativen Auswüchse müßten beschnitten werden" (1973, 191).

Corino's account of influence revised an earlier opinion of Ulrich Karthaus (cf. "Musil Bibliographies," 1965, 459) that had maintained that Musil did not draw any inspiration from psychoanalysis. Frederick Peters, accordingly, felt some "trepidation" when he approached this same question in a study that appeared in 1978. The subtitle of Peters's study announced an interest in Musil's "major fiction" as a whole, yet this was somewhat misleading, since the primary focus of Peters's study was not Musil's major work of fiction *Der Mann ohne Eigenschaften;* rather, as with Corino's longer study of 1974, it was the comparatively minor early work *Vereinigungen*. The discrepancy between the real and stated ambition of Peters's study immediately suggested a difficulty that has come to characterize psychological approaches to Musil's work as a whole. This difficulty arises from differences between the psychosexual orientation of the early works up to and including *Drei Frauen* (1924), and the complex conceptual outlook of the later major novel. Whereas Musil's early work has frequently been read in sympathy with the psychoanalytical approach, the complicated and more diffuse outlook of the major novel allows no simple reduction to psychoanalytical categories of understanding. While attempts to apply such categories to Musil's novel have nevertheless been undertaken, they have in the main only had limited success. For this reason, new "psychopathological" categories were adduced in psychological approaches in later years, starting in the early 1980s, in an attempt to comprehend Musil's complex picture of subjectivity. These later approaches explored links between psychological understanding and the process of writing, and took inspiration from new forms of literary analysis, such as semiotics and structuralism, that were emerging in other areas of literary criticism at this time.

As if sensitive to the difficulties presented by the psychoanalytical approach, Peters's 1978 study abandoned the Freudian psychosexual methodology operative in the first and longer part of his study of Musil's early works, turning to the psycho-mysticism of Jung in his reading of *Der Mann ohne Eigenschaften*. The "master of the hovering life" named in the title of Peters's book was Ulrich, the great essayist, whose aim was to achieve a union of "the exact and the nonexact," of "precision and passion." The essay form was the vehicle that enabled Musil-Ulrich to pursue such a synthesis, and, through its consistent deployment in the novel, brought about in Peters's judgment "the most directly philosophical work in the history of the novel" (19). Peters treated the first part of *Der Mann ohne Eigenschaften* as a "scientific experiment" that attempted to base an approach to life around reason. Upon the failure of this experiment to realize any tangible results in the wakeful world of reason, a new approach was undertaken in "a kind of second reality," a mystical experiment at less conscious levels of understanding designed to realize Ulrich's wish that everyday reality be totally abolished (224). Yet this second experiment of linking "science and love, precision and soul" also foundered, bringing about a decidedly pessimistic conclusion. In an ending marked by a lack of final resolution, Ulrich's life became, like the novel itself, "fragmented and paralyzed" and therefore ultimately "sterile" (239).

The beginnings of a shift away from a direct application of psychoanalytical method to a more general account of psychological categories of understanding was already evident in an essay of Johannes Cremerius which appeared in 1979. In this essay, both real and imagined psychopathological disturbances in Musil's character — among them, Musil's extreme reserve and his incapacity to make decisions — were adduced in an attempt to throw light on Musil's literary concerns. At the same time, Cremerius did not abandon the question of Freudian influence. Instead, he found that Musil had repressed Freudian psychology in his novel. This repression had led to a displacement of Freudian principles onto more covert levels of the text. Cremerius took such displacement as proof not of attenuated influence. Instead, he found, to the contrary, that Musil had effectively written a "psychoanalytical novel par excellence" (767–68).

The argument that the repression of psychoanalytical categories of understanding highlighted Musil's debt to Freud, rather than diminished it, was in some ways an attempt to deal with the change in the type of psychology practiced by Musil in the major novel. In a study *Der Buchstabe und der Geist*, which appeared in 1980, Peter Henninger viewed the question of the influence of Freud from the reverse perspective, asking why Musil did not arouse Freud's interest. The answer, he contended — maintaining Cremerius's view about the value of psychoanalysis when approaching Musil — lay with the fact that Freud did not concern himself with recent literature or the avant-garde (to which Henninger reckoned the early Musil in particular). Despite this apparent lack of interest on Freud's part, Musil was in Henninger's judgment nevertheless of singular importance to psychoanalysis; a contention he based on an analysis of *Vereinigungen*. Henninger's book, which drew on positions established by Lacan as well as Freud, took as its premise the idea that a single fragment of text could illustrate an "invariable" and unconscious feature of an entire work of art (16). Devising a new method of "textual psychoanalysis," Henninger's investigation of unconscious typologies in Musil's work assumed a broad sympathy between psychoanalytical and structuralist positions when approaching works of literature. In effecting a return of the author to the center of literary analysis, "textual psychoanalysis" also betrayed a conservative intention. This attempt to reinstate the author can be considered a response to the wider dethronement of the author emerging in aesthetic criticism of the same period.

In Henninger's analysis, the author was not recoverable in any direct way. Instead, he attempted to locate the author in the interstices where the text betrayed signs of repressed desire or "unconscious determination," that is, in areas of "disturbance" in the "syntagmatic" flow of the narration (23). Although such disturbances were not obvious to conventional critical analysis, they could be rendered intelligible on a conscious level through the literary-psychological approach Henninger advocated.

Introducing the author as "self" into the analysis, Henninger accorded basic importance to Musil's decision to become a writer. In this decision, Henninger saw a complex of ideas and emotional issues arising from the infantile childhood imagination — issues that were later embedded in the desire to write, as well as in inhibitions about writing. Corino had already pointed out the importance of these inhibitions in considering *Vereinigungen* (1973, 206ff.). Since these stories had proved difficult for Musil to finish at the time, they could be used as an indirect commentary about the nature of literary production. Henninger now linked the question of literary production to expressions of sexual desire — quite literally. The letter "V" of the title of *Vereinigungen*, for example, was accorded particular significance, representing both a pictogram of the open-legged woman (and therefore of erotic desire) as well as the Roman numeral "5." The significance of these aspects, taken together, was then traced to the fifth hour of the afternoon on which the child witnessed the coitus of his parents in the fragment *Grauauges nebligster Herbst* (92–96).[1] From this connection between the "letter" and the "spirit" of literature announced in the title of his book, Henninger formulated a general position about the literary process. This was the controversial proposition that the process of writing — the flow of ink through a tube onto a white sheet of paper — was a cipher for coition. The unfinished nature of *Der Mann ohne Eigenschaften*, accordingly, could be read in psychosexual terms as a denial of orgasm, and so represented another attempt to explain the problem of the unfinished novel: "Insofern stehen also auch die den Abschluß des Romans verhindernden Retardierungsmanöver letztlich im Dienste der Triebbefriedigung. *Der Mann ohne Eigenschaften* ist das Werk eines Autors, der seine 'Geschichte' nicht beenden wollte" (139).

For Dieter Heyd (1980), Musil's novel was a springboard to advance not merely a psychoanalytical reading, but also to embark upon a complex meditation on literature, criticism, and the nature of literary process. His aim was to link textual "commentary" with the more active pursuit of textual "criticism" — a term implying no necessary agreement between reflection on literature and the work of literature. In fact "criticism" could even suggest an attitude of profound disagreement with the writer, as Laermann's deeply oppositional study of 1970 had demonstrated. Following Derrida as much as Freud and Lacan, Heyd held that meaning in the work of art was not unlocked through a process of textual exegesis — a compliant attitude towards the author that in any case stayed "below" the author's intention and at a distance from the work of art — but was in fact "disseminated" into the world in the process of literary reception. Accordingly, an active strategy of interpretative engagement was required to locate the "traces" of the disseminated text and forge connections with other texts and discourses — sometimes in ways that were in variance with the author's declared intentions. Here Heyd affirmed Derrida's strategic move against "logo-centric" tendencies in the text that imply a self-justificatory idea of authorship. Interpretation in Heyd's analysis thus became an open-ended task, an endless endeavor that followed the conscious and unconscious traces the work of art left behind in the world.

Heyd's understanding of textual criticism connected with psychoanalysis at the level of the unconscious. Since the text wrote itself as much as it was written, a psychoanalytical reading could bring to the surface what the rational and literal level of consciousness otherwise repressed. Heyd, following Lacan, referred to such rational oppressive consciousness as the "Zwangsalphabet" of wakeful life (109). The "psychodynamic power" of writing that was embedded in such concepts as "Essay," "Möglichkeitsdenken," and "Leben-als-Experiment" could be released by addressing the nonrational aspects of the text (296). Criticism, conceived in this way, functioned as a type of "dream-work" in Freud's sense, that is, as a type of therapy. Since the therapeutic dimension implied a restitution of rational perspective — that is, the ordering of the repressed or displaced components of the dream, in order to relieve the psychic burdens endured by the unconscious — Heyd also found on meta-narrative levels of the text elements of "positivistic" activity. This positivistic aspect connected with what the text conveyed about itself on a preconscious or subconscious level. Heyd was thus able to postulate a theory of literary production as "subcutaneous" activity (66). In such deeply inward regions where the self entered into a dialog with the self, Heyd identified elements of neurosis and even madness that showed that literature was steeped in prerational primitivism as much as ethereally rational intellectualism. Heyd referred to literature as "vernünftig-unvernünftige und real-phantastische Produktivität" (22).

Heyd's expansive reflections on the literary process and textual criticism were in many ways more engaging than his reading of the novel. In approaching it, he followed the model of wish fulfillment and repressed desire outlined in Freud's *Die Traumdeutung*. The repression and displacement of desire Freud analyzed in this work helped account for the stance Musil's protagonist adopted toward reality over vast stretches of the novel. Ulrich's negative strategy of "Eigenschaftslosigkeit" also stood for the dissemination of textual traces into the world — what Heyd elsewhere termed a "Desanthropomorphisierung der Welt" (39). "Eigenschaftslosigkeit" therefore entailed a double response to the world. In one sense, Ulrich's lack of qualities signaled a basic uncertainty about life. In another sense, "disanthropomorphizing" conveyed a positive account of the way in which texts insert themselves into the world in connection with other texts. In Heyd's analysis, the textual strategy of disanthropomorphization thus expressed the subject's need to overcome desiring consciousness — somewhat in the manner of Schopenhauer. Desire was thereby rendered both impossible and counterproductive ("[die Geschichten des *MoE*] enthüllen immer aufs neue die Unmöglichkeit des Begehrens"), and, in the idyll of the siblings, also strangely possible and therefore productive: "[d]er Roman arbeitet der pessimistischen Geschichte des Begehrens dort entgegen, wo er in einem utopischen Akt (Gegen-)Geschichte erfindet" (166–67). Heyd's best insights related to what he saw as the shortcomings of Musil scholarship. In linking Musil terms like "Gefühl," "Erregung," "Ergriffensein," and "Ekstase" to a writing strategy of "intensity" ("eine Schrift der Intensität" [173]), Heyd was able to show how Musil scholarship had become preoccupied with secondary aspects of the novel: "Der Dualismus zwischen Verstand und Gefühl, Ratio und Mystik, der bei Musil im Vordergrund zu stehen scheint, und der in besonderem Maß die Aufmerksamkeit in der Rezeption auf sich zog, entpuppt sich als ein sekundärer, abgeleiteter Effekt der Intensität" (174).

Musil scholarship in the 1980s developed a number of new insights by applying psychoanalysis to Musil's works. In 1981, for example, Peter Dettmering took up a lead given by Hartmut Böhme in 1974 in analyzing forms of narcissistic behavior in *Der Mann ohne Eigenschaften*. In 1984, Marianne Charriere-Jaquin revised Christiane Zehl-Romero's judgment, in an article of 1978, about the "last love-story" narrated in the final section of the novel. Whereas Zehl-Romero had found the non-idealized aspects of love in the utopian concluding sections of the novel to be preponderant, dismissing any notion of a redemptive conception of love, Charriere-Jaquin attributed positive dimensions to Musil's notion of hermaphroditic love in these sections. Among other approaches to the novel, Josef Strutz connected what he viewed as a conception of "still-life" in the major novel with Freud's notion of the death drive (1987b). In a 1985 article, Jean-Pierre Cometti postulated broad links between the expressivist quality of narrative and the activity of psychoanalysis. In her 1991 book *The Vanishing Subject,* Judith Ryan analyzed the influence of early experimental psychology on literary modernists, including Musil. And in the same year, Hildegard Lahme-Gronostaj, in a study focused mostly on Musil's story *Tonka,* linked Freud's allusively plural "psychic reality" to Musil's notion of "Möglichkeitssinn." Following ideas explored in Dieter Farda's study of 1988, Lahme-Gronostaj reconceived the role of literature as the introduction of the multiple, overlapping possible realities of the unconscious into the wakeful world of rational consciousness. The aim of this connection between inner psychic states and literature was the expression a new form of knowledge about the world. Literature, accordingly, made accessible "ein Modus des In-der-Welt-Seins [. . .], dem noch das Modell von Neurose und Verdrängung als Vorbild dienen konnte: Der Modus der Perversion, in dem [. . .] die 'Urszene' als Ursprung sowohl erkannt als auch verleugnet wird, was durch eine Spaltung im Ich ermöglicht wird und diese wiederum fixiert" (195).

Hans-Georg Pott's 1984 general introduction to Musil's life and works, subtitled "the endless text," took the question of science's relationship with everyday reality as its starting point. In his preface, Pott struck a decidedly pessimistic note about the prospects of knowledge in the world: reason, a notion issuing from Europe's glorious heritage of the Enlightenment, had been handed down to posterity as a poisoned chalice. Accordingly, Pott was moved to ask why in the age of rationality human beings now appeared *impelled* to fall back into barbarism. Proceeding to a consideration of Musil's novel, Pott painted a picture of profoundly alienated human subjects: mind-directed subjects who lived not in harmony with, but at odds with their physical bodies, especially so those "men with character"; psychotically ill subjects who, like Clarisse, were ruled not by their passions, but by symbols and signs (91–96). Using positions established by Freud and Lacan, Pott highlighted the prevalence of "repetitive force" (or "Wiederholungszwang") in the unconscious lives of Musil's secondary characters.

By contrast, Pott approached the character of Ulrich with a different methodology in mind. Quoting from Musil's notes on the novel underscoring the influence of Mach, Pott demonstrated the importance of functional categories in seeking to comprehend the "Eigenschaftslosigkeit des Ich" (110–11). Viewing the "man without qualities" from this functional perspective, his conclusion about identity was, as before, pronouncedly culturally pessimistic: possibilities in life diminished with advancing age, and identity was rather much of an illusion — perhaps no more than the sum of what we have been in the past, as Sartre had suggested. Despite this, Musil, in establishing the idyll of the final section of the novel, attempted to reacquaint body and mind on a higher plane of sensibility. Pott showed how the mystical elements of this section were sustained through image and allegory, that is to say, more by dint of artistic categories than from any independent position in logic. For this reason, Pott concluded by considering the novel's aesthetic dimensions, and specifically the question of art's relationship to the everyday. In following poststructuralist notions opposing the closure of the text, Pott discovered a liberating dimension to the endless work of art: "Man kann daraus folgern, daß es Kunst gibt, solange es kein vollkommenes Leben gibt (und daß das vollkommene Leben das Ende der Kunst wäre) [. . .]" (169).

Two studies of the late eighties returned to the question of literature's capacity to broker the expression of preconscious states in the rational world of understanding. Ralf Bohn's study of strategies of inversion and Hartmut Cellbrot's assessment of the influence of Edmund Husserl on Musil, both appeared in 1988 and presupposed a phenomenological understanding of reality. Phenomenology had arisen out of the paradigm shift in the natural sciences in the early part of the twentieth century, according to which the invariable and fixed time-space continuum had been broken down by an awareness of the operation of perspective and of the quantum forces of complementarity and relativity in the universe. Phenomenology was in some ways an attempt to shore up the position of the material sciences, since it suggested that phenomena, although not directly observable, still appeared to the subject, but in ways that indicated a split between actual physical observation and "ideal" awareness. The question of ideal awareness, in turn, connected with the idealist tradition of German thinking at the end of the eighteenth and the beginning of the nineteenth century. Recording this dual aspect of phenomena, therefore, required a comprehensive understanding of the nature and limitations of perception, as well as a high degree of precision in assessing the impact of objects on subjective states of both conscious and unconscious awareness. Musil's ideal of exactness with respect to emotional understanding appeared to parallel this interest in phenomena and the way they impinged upon subjective awareness.

Bohn's complicated study saw in the later Schelling's understanding of subjectivity — at least by implication — an early statement of the phenomenological position. "Alle Subjektivität," Bohn held, "wird, um sich zu begründen, von einer Tötungsabsicht ausgehen müssen, von einer Gewalt, die den Leidensdruck der Krankheit der Verdinglichung verschiebt" (284). Subjectivity, accordingly, was caught between the desire to posit itself in absolute terms — a prospect Schelling had held to be fatal to the self — and an equally insistent desire to defer the moment of this self-positing. Bohn discussed two important considerations arising from this view of subjectivity. On the one hand, subjectivity was inseparable from pathological aspects. (This consideration made Musil's notion of subjectivity appear particularly open to psychoanalytic interpretation.) On the other hand, the deferral of the moment of posited identity was linked to the notion of possibility explored by Musil in *Der Mann ohne Eigenschaften*. In fact, the idea of possibility was actually a way of achieving such a deferral of identity formation, by direct and indirect means: "Menschsein gleichsam als Gedicht (miß)verstehen, heißt, die Krankheit als Fall einer offenen Möglichkeit zu lesen" (286). Bohn, accordingly, saw the central drama of subjective awareness in Musil's novel in such openness to possibility, but also in resistance to an absolute self-positing of subjective identity. If Schelling's thinking provided a model for Musil's conceptual understanding, it also provided for a way of overcoming its insistent paradoxes. This was entailed in the idea of "inversion." According to this idea, the beginning of subjective awareness could be reclaimed at its end through the medium of imaginative language: "Die mimesistheoretische Divination durch die 'Einbildungskraft' erschafft die Idealität aus der prinzipiellen Möglichkeit der Realität. Der zweite Anfang ist in Wahrheit der erste." Inversion provided a way to address — and ultimately overcome — the problem of consciousness. This same problem had been implicit in quantum theory, since physics in the early twentieth century had already demonstrated that the phenomena were subject to disturbances by the very subjective attention that wished to render them sensible to perception. Inversion could now appear as a solution to the problem of subjective awareness that had tendentiously postponed the moment of grounding subjective identity. A moment of inversion was thus to be found in Musil's ideal of otherness in the Other Condition. Bohn concluded: "Der erste Anfang ist erst in einen zweiten begriffen, in dem er sich in einem Anderen begreift" (334–35).

Thomas Pekar's study of 1989 focused on the discourse of love in Musil's novel. This was a topic that suggested parallels with Roland Barthes's *Fragments d'un discours amoureux* (1977)[2] and Niklas Luhmann's codification of love in systems theory.[3] Moving beyond Luhmann, Pekar's basic assumption was that love was not just a codified semiotic system linked to social change, but a highly individual affirmation of life and personal identity. Pekar, accordingly, sought to plot a path between these social and personal markers in defining the status of love in *Der Mann ohne Eigenschaften*. For Ulrich and Agathe, love was a unifying experience and could be classified into three variant scenarios: a narcissistic scenario providing for an endless mirroring of self;[4] a hermaphroditic scenario, involving a coming together in order to create something new; and a Dionysian perspective, according to which a union, expressed in terms of "die Sprache der Tiere," "die Sprache der Affekte," ultimately meant a dissolution. Musil's difficulties in completing his novel arose, Pekar further argued, from problems in effecting a resolution between these three — in part contradictory — models of love.

In Ralf Bohn's 1988 study, discussed above, the question of subjective identity had psychopathological aspects, precisely because it bore on the essentially indissoluble problem of how the subject posits (and therefore grounds) itself in existence. In 1990, Ruth Hassler-Rütti, pursuing related questions of identity, probed the connection between the madness of Clarisse and Moosbrugger, and the mental disposition of Ulrich and Agathe.[5] In her analysis, good health and disease are not sharply opposed, but continuous states, connecting with each other in the same way that reality and madness are connected: "Niemand kann eine Krankheit beschreiben, ohne sich nicht gleichzeitig oder vorgängig bestimmte Vorstellungen und Begriffe von Gesundheit zu bilden" (10). Considering both published and unpublished materials from the novel, Hassler-Rütti's study focused on the "Clarisse-Komplex" as well as the character of Moosbrugger, the prostitute-murderer. Moosbrugger was important because he took over completely what Ulrich, the protagonist, only represented in part, namely "die Eigenschaftslosigkeit schlechthin." The character of Moosbrugger, accordingly, represented those pathological aspects attaching to the expression of individuality in Bohn's sense:

> [an Moosbrugger] [. . .] stoßen alle Denk- und Begriffssysteme, alle wissenschaftlichen Theorien, alle Wirklichkeitskonstruktionen an ihre Grenzen und darüber hinaus ins Leere, Phantastische oder Eigene, wodurch sich jede Realität selbst als eine bloß fiktive, vorläufige, gewähnte im infiniten Produktionsprozess hergestellte und unvollständige zu erkennen gibt [. . .]. Wirklichkeit und Wahn bleiben wie "Gewalt" und "Liebe" getrennt *und* aufeinander bezogen, miteinander verbunden, *sind* eigenschaftslos. (254)

The starting assumption of Hans-Rudolf Schärer's 1990 analysis was Musil's ambivalent and highly problematic relationship with psychoanalysis. Rejecting Musil's avowedly low opinion of psychoanalysis, Schärer subscribed to Cremerius's 1979 assessment that Musil — against his own declared intention — had employed Freudian psychology in his novel. Schärer set out to probe the psychology not of the author Musil, but of individual characters in Musil's novel, especially Ulrich, Clarisse, and Moosbrugger. Whereas Clarisse and Moosbrugger represented clear examples of psychotic disturbance, Ulrich suffered in Schärer's analysis from a personality disorder rooted in narcissism. While noting the early work of Freud on narcissism, Schärer used the more recent work of Heinz Kohut to show that narcissism derived principally from disturbances in the child's relationship to its parents, in particular to its mother. On a reading of the chapter "Heimweg" (chapter 122), Schärer identified a "narcissistic trauma" in the young Ulrich not balanced by Ulrich's relationship with his father (18–20). This disturbance brought about a desire for recognition of individual aspects of self in later life, as well as occasioning an imbalance between mind and body and ambivalent sexual feelings. Using Kohut's notion of "mirror transference in an extended sense" ("Spiegelübertragung im weiteren Sinn"), Schärer interpreted Ulrich's encounter with his "twin" sister in the second part of the novel as a therapeutic reinvigoration of the monumental self (73). In a strong condemnation of the utopian section of the novel, Schärer considered the Other Condition regressive for its failure to confront the moral dilemmas of reality, and narcissistic for its failure to abide the grounded aspects of mundane life (134).

Ulrich's relationship with his sister Agathe has been a favorite topic of psychological approaches. Among several approaches to have focused on sexual psychology in Musil's work was Ortrud Gutjahr's comparative study of Musil and Ingeborg Bachmann (1990), Anja Elisabeth Schoene's study of the theme of incest from Ibsen to Musil (1997), and Ina Hartwig's discussion of sexual themes in literature of the twentieth century (1998). Schoene regarded the sheer frequency of incestuous relationships in the literature of Musil's era as a sign of a new, more progressive, understanding of subjectivity. Hartwig's comparative study of 1998 also highlighted the importance of the progressive potential in new ideas of the subject and intersubjectivity.

The question about incest, Hartwig argued, had been read in two ways by Musil scholars: either as the (spiritual or physical) fulfillment of what Musil called "die letzte Liebesgeschichte" (*MoE*, 1094),[6] or, as a confirmation of the asocial position taken up by Ulrich and Agathe.[7] As Musil remained undecided about incorporating the incest motif into his story, and it never became part of the published version of the novel, the issue was rather "warum Musil an dem Motiv des physisch vollzogenen Inzests, nachdem er einmal erzählt war, *nicht* festgehalten hat" (140). Crucial was a new element of discursive communication in the erotic and intellectual relationship of Ulrich and his sister Agathe: "Es sind Gesprächssituationen, keine Bettsituationen, in denen Musil sein Geschwisterpaar diese Form ekstatischer Übereinstimmung erleben läßt" (154). Because this coming together of the siblings took place principally in and through language, it grounded, in Hartwig's view, a "Liebessemiotik" and a new "Poetik der Liebe" (168).

In presenting a view of the importance of the communicative dimension of Musil's ideal of love, Hartwig's approach suggested Musil's interest in sexual psychology was primarily philosophical in nature. The idea that Musil's psychology had been conceived from a philosophical point of view had already been maintained by Margaret Kaiser-El-Safti in 1993. In endorsing a view of the importance of philosophy in his study of 1999, Uwe M. Maier suggested that Musil's interest in psychopathological states — such as those that afflicted Moosbrugger and had also been read into Ulrich's failure to embrace fixed qualities — had not been significant. Certainly Musil's psychological approach to writing and Freudian psychoanalysis were related undertakings. Both announced a primary interest in the mental disposition of human subjects. Yet here — in Maier's view — the parallels ended:

> Musil war weniger an dem psychopathologischen Aspekt der Depersonalisation interessiert. Ihn machten die Befunde neugierig, weil sie Parallelen zur Bewußtseinslage des modernen Menschen aufwiesen. Die Sinnkrisen und Verlusterfahrungen seiner Zeit bringen moderne Subjekte in ähnliche Gegenlagen zur Welt, wie die (häufig organisch bedingten) krankhaften Gefühlsdefizite des am Depersonalisationssyndrom erkrankten. (169)

While psychoanalysis is economical in outlook, reducing the complexity of human mental states to a structural typology, Musil's psychology scales up to ever-increasing levels of mental and emotional complexity. Musil's subjects, accordingly, are never reducible to a single or basic psychopathology, just as their actions are never reducible to a single or dominant motivation. Their outlook is rather more akin to the situation of the writer, who attempts to distill a sense of the ineffable quality of life — even as that life, in all its manifold complexity, continues to elude him. This special dimension to the artist's outlook on the world has been explored further in aesthetic readings of Musil's novel.

Notes

[1] That psychological disturbances could result from the child's witnessing of the coitus of the parents was alluded to in Freud's case study of the "Wolf Man."

[2] Translated as *A Lover's Discourse: Fragments* (New York: Hill and Wang, 1978).

[3] Niklas Luhmann, *Liebe als Passion: Zur Codifizierung von Intimität* (Frankfurt am Main: Suhrkamp, 1982).

[4] Cf. earlier view of Hartmut Böhme that maintained that Ulrich's narcissism prevented him from establishing unity within himself and with others.

[5] Ruth Hassler-Rütti, *Wirklichkeit und Wahn in Robert Musils Roman "Der Mann ohne Eigenschaften"* (Bern: Peter Lang, 1990), diss. Zürich, 1989/90.

[6] Cf. Ernst Kaiser and Eithne Wilkins, *Robert Musil: Eine Einführung in das Werk* (Stuttgart: Kohlhammer, 1962, 89); Werner Fuld, "Die Quellen zur Konzeption des 'anderen Zustands' in Robert Musil's Roman *Der Mann ohne Eigenschaften*," *Deutsche Vierteljahrsschrift für Literaturwissenschaft und Geistesgeschichte* 50 (1976): 677.

[7] Cf. Wolfdietrich Rasch, *Über Robert Musils Roman "Der Mann ohne Eigenschaften"* (Göttingen: Vandenhoeck & Ruprecht, 1967), 127.

4: Aesthetic Readings

*Das Problem: wie komme ich zum Er-
zählen, ist sowohl mein stilistisches wie
das Lebensproblem der Hauptfigur,
und die Lösung ist natürlich nicht
einfach.* (B I, 498)

WHEREAS EXISTENTIALIST VIEWS in Musil criticism in the postwar
period cultivated an understanding of the position of the individual, social criticism adopted history as "first philosophy" in assaying
conceptions of social truth. Neither view, however, could be said to have
addressed adequately the question of the function of art in society. Nor
did these views throw light on the special circumstances in which art is
produced. These questions were taken up in aesthetic approaches, which
now constitute one of the most popular pathways to understanding
Musil's novel. In the early postwar period, aesthetically based inquiry
found common ground with existential critique, since the artist's struggle to respond to the world was understood to relate to the more general
problem of how the individual might meet the demands of increasingly
problematic social life. Gerhart Baumann's two essays of 1953 and 1960
and his full-length study of 1960, all of which investigated stylistic features and the shifts in perspective that lie behind the narration of Musil's
novel, were based on the conviction that art could illuminate the problems of life in this way. By the late fifties and early sixties, however, the
question of the artist's exemplary individual existence had become secondary, as aesthetic criticism was increasingly drawn to formal questions
of style and text type. Joseph Strelka's comparative study of Kafka, Musil,
and Broch, published in 1959, was one of many early studies to register
this new interest in the formal quality of Musil's prose. Ulf Eisele later
gave clear expression to this view in an important essay that first appeared
in 1979 and was reprinted in Renate von Heydebrand's collection of
Musil essays in 1982.[1] Eisele turned around notions of the priority of
existential questions by highlighting the issue of literature and literary
production: "Nicht 'das Existenzproblem Ulrichs wird zum Formproblem des Romans,' es verhält sich genau umgekehrt: Die dem *Mann
ohne Eigenschaften* zugrunde liegende literarische Problematik ist verant-

wortlich zu machen für die prekäre Situation Ulrichs als Romanhauptfigur" (1982, 167).

The movement away from existential questions in Musil scholarship, therefore, was not just a shift in emphasis, but marked a significant departure. It drew inspiration from the Adorno-Lukács border dispute over realism, while implicitly endorsing Adorno's argument that questions of realism were not only a function of the social or historical reality of the artist. In defending a more writerly conception of the artist, aesthetic approaches progressively weakened the writer's historical position in favor of the claim that art constituted a realm apart from ordinary life, and, by extension, that artists could not be comprehended in any final way by assessing the social or historical circumstances into which they were born. In this way, notions of artistic truth were advanced in opposition to the underlying assumptions of existential critique and social criticism, even as it remained unclear in this early period precisely what type of artistic truth Musil actually defended.

A major signpost of this early period appeared in an essay by Maurice Blanchot, first published in French in 1958 and in German translation in 1962. Blanchot was one of the first critics to anticipate the new Musil of the aesthetic approach, while still upholding links to existential critique. He showed how the question of the protagonist's individual identity connected with the self-constitution of the novel as narrative. In his interpretation of Musil's novel, the categories of fiction and historical reality ran together in a new understanding of the term autobiography: "Das Buch ist an der Oberfläche und im tiefsten autobiographisch. Ulrich verweist uns auf Musil, zugleich aber klammert sich Musil angstvoll an Ulrich, findet nur in ihm seine Wahrheit [. . .]" (191). For Blanchot, writing did not represent the world under any theory of correspondence; rather, it *was* that world. Similarly, autobiography was in fact "auto-Biography," a narrative of self-constituting individual life that borrowed from the structures of fiction in decisive ways. For Blanchot, the inseparability of fiction and life brought about what he elsewhere called "automatic writing," since it "put the hand that writes in contact with something original; it made of this active hand a sovereign passivity, [. . .] an independent power, over which no one had authority any more, which belonged to no one and which could not, which knew not how to do anything — but write [. . .]."[2] In one sense, the "dead hand" of the narrator was also Musil's ideal, since it opened out onto the idea of self-constituting, self-narrated personal identity Musil had discussed in chapter 122 of *Der Mann ohne Eigenschaften*.[3] These views of the intertwining of narrative and individual identity have been taken further outside Musil studies in the new sociology of Ulrich Beck, where biography unfolds as a creative form of risk management in a world of singular dangers, but also opportunities.

Blanchot's understanding of writing profoundly opposed postwar hermeneutics, which betrayed a far more rigid understanding of the author and the critical enterprise. Hermeneutics, for its part, had emerged out of a concern with subordinating textual sense to a fixed conception of historical reality, leading back to early nineteenth-century notions of teleological history and possibly even further.[4] In rejecting speculative metaphysics in favor of a more concrete understanding of language, hermeneutics had attempted to establish a "scientific" notion of the critical enterprise. By contrast, the broadening of the categories of narrative and fiction that underpinned Blanchot's understanding of autobiography were more aligned with Nietzsche's sensitivity to the coexistence of different conceptions of history and his utter rejection of the fixed categories of scientific truth. Of later Musil critics, Marike Finlay, taking Blanchot's essay as one of her starting points in a 1990 study, advanced one of the clearest assessments of the way Musil's novel overturns the "classical episteme" of hermeneutics in its adherence both to plural perspectivism and Nietzsche's understanding of creatively evolving, heroic self-identity. Finlay identified three key components in Musil's conception of reality, "a constituting discourse, an object-reality, and a knowing subject" (29), all of which deserved equal treatment in scholarly approaches.

The flowering of hermeneutics in criticism of the fifties and sixties — of which most of the existential and social criticism of this period may be cited as examples — was therefore matched by a new interest in the self-constitution of narrative. Wolfgang Iser's notion of the "play of the text,"[5] which developed out of a broader interest in the reader's response to literary texts in the early 1970s,[6] suggested that meaning in the narrative could be found in the complex patterning of different rhetorical features and "strategies." Interpretation was not a matter of locating texts along a fixed historical continuum, but was subject to rhetorical patterns the text set up within itself. These patterns, in turn, could be approached as self-enclosed games with their own rules and regulations, where sense issued from the way in which the text marked off its limits and free areas of play. The meaning of a text, accordingly, arose from the way each rhetorical pattern upheld or deposed its own game-rules. Iser's idea of "the play of the text" was indebted to French structuralism of the early postwar period and shared many features in common with it. At the same time, it upheld links to the older philosophical tradition of phenomenology, widening phenomenology's distinction between real and ideal objects to incorporate the intentional structures of the work of art.[7] Most importantly of all, the idea of "the play of the text" was part of the emerging movement of poststructuralism, which, in Derrida's idea of deconstruction, followed the same understanding of the independence of the text from a world to which it had hitherto been held to refer. Derrida's famous dictum, "il n'y a pas de hors-texte" ("there is nothing outside the text; there is no outside-text"), stood for every new notion of the self-reflexivity of literature and the self-enclosed nature of writing and writers.

Werner Hoffmeister's 1965 study of inner monologue in Musil was an early work of criticism that demonstrated a similar awareness of literature's self-reflexivity. While yet to acquire the more radical aspects of later aesthetic criticism, which downgraded literature to "text" and saw writing exclusively in terms of the self-generation of discourses, rather than the communication of any inherently referential sense, Hoffmeister already divined in the novel a retreat of the author from outside reality. Writing, accordingly, expressed not the contours of a liberated self at the center of the world, but the shifts of perspective of individual consciousness taking flight from it: "Dem Autor, der die erlebte Rede verwendet, ist es darum zu tun, ein direktes Schlaglicht auf die geistig-seelische Situation seiner Figur zu werfen. Er muß daher unvermittelt seine objektive, übergeordnete Erzählerposition aufgeben und in das Innenleben seiner Gestalt tauchen" (22). To some extent, Hoffmeister's study of the melting of the narrator into the narration and the loss of the epic distance of the conventional narrator was inseparable from the concerns of existential critique, which also saw a withdrawal of God from the world: "[. . .] so könnte man sagen, daß geschichtlich gesehen der persönliche Erzähler im Roman ebenso wie der persönliche Gott in der Religion verschwunden sei." While traditional epic perspective had realized omniscient control over narrative perspective, the appearance of inner monologue as a literary device betokened a loss of control and a new level of ambivalence toward the world. For Hoffmeister, however, inner monologue also signaled a gain, since it conveyed an urgency about inner states, enriched these still more with intense feeling, and so brought about a whole new dimension of authentically sensed, poetic inwardness (166–68).

Dieter Kühn, in a 1965 study that exhibited a new focus on allegory and parable (Gleichnis) in Musil's novel, was one of the first critics to suggest where this retreat into "poetic inwardness" might lead. Although indebted to previous studies focusing on the ironic and satiric content of the novel, notably those of Beda Allemann (1956) and Helmut Arntzen (1960), Kühn also broke with them in viewing allegory not just as a formal poetic device, but also as a content aspect of Musil's prose. For Kühn, allegory in fact marked out the ambiguous nature of the narration. For this reason, he warned against interpreting any single statement of a character or the narrator in an unambiguously affirmatory way. Kühn's approach instead showed how Musil set one utterance in the novel against other utterances, often putting several different viewpoints together in a single passage. Accordingly, no single utterance could be endorsed on an absolute level of meaning. At most, Musil's statements yielded "Annäherungswerte" (12) — rough approximations of relative truth-value only.

Kühn's study ushered in a new understanding of the formal quality of Musil's prose, suggesting that meaning could not be gleaned from "straight" readings of textual passages taken in isolation, but merged fully with the complex formal structures of Musil's narration taken as a whole. Later works, such as those of Ulf Schramm (1967) and Jörg Kühne (1968), were to take these insights further. Kühn, for his part, reached limited conclusions about how meaning is communicated in Musil's novel, focusing his discussion on individual characters rather than teasing out broader lines of ambiguity in the novel.[8] Moreover, Kühn's approach, while upholding ambiguity in the narration, also smoothed out the contrasts of Musil's highly allusive style. This had the effect — the title of Kühn's book *Analogie und Variation* notwithstanding — of reducing variation rather than evincing it at greater levels of complexity. Nevertheless, his study, which examined all the major figures in the novel, shed useful light on the multidimensional thought-world of individual characters in *Der Mann ohne Eigenschaften,* drawing out lines of connection with Ernst Mach in the case of Ulrich, Nietzsche in the case of Walter and Clarisse, and the Swedish educationalist and early feminist Ellen Key in the case of Diotima.

Ulf Schramm's 1967 comparative study of Musil and Samuel Beckett was the most important among early aesthetic approaches to Musil's novel. In moving the drama of formal language to center stage, Schramm followed early structuralism as well as the discussion about the pitfalls of rationalist thinking that had emerged out of early social criticism. The underlying problem of Musil's novel, in Schramm's view, related to the question of whether and how science and technology — new features of modern life in Musil's day — could be reconciled with the needs of individual human beings. In terms of narrative content, this was the question of whether the novel could establish a dialogue between individuals and their rapidly technologizing world. In formal terms, the issue was how far theory (as technology-affirming) and art (as culture-conserving) could work together to make accessible a new type of truth. In responding to this question, Schramm put both art and theory below an ideal conception of narrative truth in a way that connected with existential critique: "die Konvergenz von Vermitteltem und Mittel, die dann entsteht, wenn Wahrheit erst ermittelt werden muß, drängt Kunst und Theorie dazu, selbst Wirklichkeit zu werden: diese ist als solche weder Fiktion noch Zweck, sondern Dasein" (40). This framing of the issue of technology and art in Schramm's analysis was taken further in this period, notably by Gerd Müller, who in 1971 analyzed how far the literary tradition of German Romanticism, to which Musil arguably belonged, mediated between literature and science in establishing a synthesis based on humanistic values.

Whether and to what extent humanistic values could be affirmed was also a question that animated Schramm's study. A key point of focus was his discussion of "Möglichkeitssinn," a category which also informed Peter Nusser's approach (1967) of the same period. Whereas Nusser had developed his understanding of "Möglichkeitssinn" through a consideration of Musil's diary entries and essays, Schramm linked "Möglichkeitssinn" to the issue of satire with the explicit aim of revising Arntzen's findings of 1960 on the same topic. Since everything in Musil's novel — even its form — was satirical, Schramm contended, no ideal reference point could be said to stabilize Musil's satire from without. This became obvious when "Wirklichkeitsdenken" was considered in contrast with "Möglichkeitsdenken." Under the terms of Musil's polyvalent perspective, Schramm demonstrated that neither reality on its own, nor possibility on its own, could be completely affirmed:

> Mit diesen Gedanken kann grundsätzlich alles (und grundsätzlich nach zwei entgegengesetzten Richtungen) kritisiert werden: das Konkrete, weil es normiert sei (oder noch nicht konkret genug); das Ideelle, weil es nicht real sei (oder noch nicht rein geistig genug); das Ineinander beider, weil jedes Moment das andere verdecke (oder das Ideelle nicht vollkommene Realität, das Reale nicht reiner Geist geworden sei). (57)

The conclusion Schramm reached about Musil's literary intentions — "Musil gibt allerorts Satire — und dennoch fehlt dem Roman die Entschiedenheit von Satire" (57) — was of great importance for Musil scholarship, since it indicated the limits of socially critical studies that had been chiefly concerned with Musil's portrait of Kakania. Schramm, by contrast, now directed attention toward formal and aesthetic categories, indicating that Musil's fictional style described a less concrete and more general, "modular" reality. Schramm showed how this modular reality incorporated speculative and reflective aspects that could not be ascribed with any confidence to the standpoint of the author or his narrator. Instead, they had to be understood as the process by which the narration constituted itself as text. In this way, Schramm highlighted how Musil's narration makes overt its own structures of communication: "Vermittlung ist das Grundprinzip des Sinnzusammenhangs, daß es keine Grenze zwischen Kunst und Wirklichkeit gibt, und daß es doch entscheidend um diese geht: sie ist je neu durch Ineinanderarbeiten von subjektiven Intentionen und objektiven Gegebenheiten, durch deren Vermittlung also, zu ermitteln" (140–41). In comparing Musil to the absurdist Samuel Beckett, Schramm revealed how the narrative ultimately conveyed no more than the "truth" of the communicative strategy of the main character Ulrich and his congenital attachment to scenarios of possibility.

Jörg Kühne's 1968 study was enlivened by the same sensitivity to plural perspectives in the novel. His starting assumption was that Musil's novel — never completed despite Martha Musil's attempt to publish a "finished" version in 1943 after Musil's death — admitted of such kaleidoscopic variety that the thought of a single reading of the text was precluded from the beginning. The absence of a definitive version of Musil's novel in fact formed the unspoken "problem situation" of Kühne's book, indicating how much Musil scholarship at least until 1970 remained preoccupied with the need to find a final answer to the problem of the fragmentary nature of Musil's text. Kühne's response to this problem was imaginatively deft: he highlighted the operation of a rhetorical figure in Musil's novel, the *Gleichnis* (allegory or parable), which allowed the "inner form" of the novel to reveal itself. (Musil refers to the *Gleichnis* as evincing the "gleitende Logik der Seele" [cf. *MoE*, 593]). That such inner form was manifest on the allegorical level of the novel allowed conclusions to be drawn about the novel's trajectory, while avoiding the technical aspects of the debate about the novel's conclusion that was showing no sign of abating in the late sixties. Applying a combination of close textual reading and stylistic analysis, Kühne widened the application of this admirably useful rhetorical figure to include metaphor, simile, and symbol. He concluded that the *Gleichnis* encompassed both formal and content levels of the narrative without being reducible to either. To this extent — endorsing the findings of existential critique still influential at this time — the open-endedness of allegory could also stand for the ambiguity of human existence, for the very indecipherability of that existence at the threshold of immanence and transcendence.[9] Appraising this poetic use of allegory, Kühne situated Musil at the end of a line of continuity that reached back in the German literary tradition to the late eighteenth and early nineteenth centuries.

Kühne's imaginative reading of the inner form of Musil's novel sought justification in the absence of any palpable action — the sort of action that would have permitted the author to develop a plot line in the normal manner. The term that characterized this paucity of "outward" action was "Seinesgleichen geschieht," the title of the second part of the novel, in which the Austrian state Kakania is described. In Kühne's analysis, this term stood for the duplication of forms and the reduction of action to stasis, but a stasis that obscured a deeper movement on the plane of ideas. Kühne therefore focused on the subtle unfolding of ideas that lay below the surface of human action — an inner logic of the shape of things he called, following a formulation from Musil's interview with Fontana in 1926, "das Gleichnishafte und das Gespenstige dieses Daseins" (61). This "Gleichnishafte," Kühne argued, was expressive of a type of indicative possibility about life. Allegory dominated the first part of the novel, and ultimately connoted a passive attitude, whereas "Möglichkeitssinn," which shaped the second part of the novel and the posthumous notes to the *Mann ohne Eigenschaften,* took its cue from the need to leave the province of reflection and make a final commitment to action in the world (85).

These influential approaches to allegory by Kühn and Kühne drew attention to the subtle shifts in perspective of the writerly Musil.[10] Jürgen Thöming's study of 1974 demonstrated that these perspectival shifts were not merely a question for writers, but also impacted on the reception of writing. Following Iser's notions of reader response and the implied reader, Thöming focused attention on the way Musil's writing drew upon, and also relativized, the expectations of readers:

> In der Tendenz läuft alle Metaphorik Musils darauf hinaus, nicht eine in sich und in einer poetischen Scheinwelt kreisende Symbolik zu konstruieren, sondern die Bildersprache aus den Alltagserfahrungen des Lesers heraus zu entwickeln, sie in der Bedeutung nicht zu stark zu determinieren, sondern variable Bildprozesse im Leser freizusetzen. (173–74)

For David Dawlianidse (1978), Thöming's approach invited a reappraisal of the first chapter of Musil's novel in a similar spirit of open readerly engagement. At the same time, his essay demonstrated the general importance of philosophy in approaching Musil's novel — a finding subsequently confirmed by Friedrich Wallner in 1984. In a later study in 1989, Wagner-Egelhaaf widened the readerly experience to accommodate the mystical levels on which Musil's novel operates. For Wagner-Egelhaaf, the close connection between writer and reader suggested in reader response theory had a divine emanation; reading itself could therefore be conceived of as a second order mystical activity. Later critics like Peter Nadermann (1990), however, opposed such readerly mysticism, which appeared scarcely different from the veneration of the author dominant in the existentialist tradition of Musil scholarship — a tradition that by the end of the eighties had largely run its course. Instead, Nadermann set about dismantling this ideal of writerly mediation of readerly reception, arguing that writing represents perhaps no more than an "exzessiver Versuch der Selbstbestimmung im Medium der Literatur" (3). Nadermann, analyzing biographical aspects, instead emphasized in a far more modest way the value writing had come to hold for the author.[11]

Dietrich Hochstätter's study of 1972 was part of the groundswell of interest at the end of the 1960s and at the beginning of the 1970s in the formal quality of Musil's language, particularly the way the category of radical possibility seems to bend language toward dissonance and perspectivism and against any single view of reality. Hochstätter's study was important for later approaches, like that of Dieter Fuder (1979), who argued that the open structure of *Der Mann ohne Eigenschaften* aimed at stimulating a potentially limitless engagement with ideas and concepts. Hochstätter's study provided a critical underpinning for such later approaches, since he viewed Musil as a perspectivist and pluralist whose ideal of artistic practice was inclusive of, as well as open to, other conceptual positions.

In Hochstätter's view, reality in Musil's novel was not fixed or given; rather, it appeared as the shifting sands of quotation, formula, and the rhetorical gestures of a narrator who relativized and made dynamic the very quality of things. Informing this new view of the quality of things was "variable function," a stylistic device of Musil's that Hochstätter linked to an entry in his diaries (but which as a conceptual approach can also be traced to his encounter with the philosophy of Ernst Mach during his doctoral years at Berlin University). Reaching conclusions similar to those of Schramm's 1967 study, Hochstätter showed how the functionalist way of understanding reality is essentially linguistic in nature: it is — like material language itself— non-ontological, highly modular in nature (since it can be shaken out like the kaleidoscope into an endless series of combinations) and descriptive of notional possibilities about life rather than of a single fixed reality (which also meant that it was antimimetic). In viewing language from such a dynamic perspective, Musil rejected the highly artificial, moralistic, and positivistic language he had encountered, for example, in the work of Maeterlinck and Ellen Key. Since this literature had initially left a strong impression on him, Musil had come to think of his own early adherence to positivism, somewhat self-critically, as similar to a "gekränkte Kinderliebe zu Gott" (74). Applying a structuralist analysis to the novel, Hochstätter then divined a basic dichotomy in Musil's work. This dichotomy, for which Hochstätter used the Musilian terms "Spekulation à la baisse" and "Spekulation à la hausse" as conceptual markers, was roughly consonant with the division between Books One and Two of the novel. Accordingly, Musil's project represented the attempt to combine "low" and "high," earth-bound and transcendental concerns in a speculative utopia that nevertheless sought to remain within the realm of concrete experience.

The desire to see an underlying harmony in opposed aspects of life seemed particularly linked to Hochstätter's historical position. Writing in the immediate aftermath of the political upheaval in Germany that began with the student demonstrations in Berlin in 1968, Hochstätter's approach appeared as a conservative reaction to the conflict and change of this period. It is remarkable, for example, that Hochstätter, while ultimately sympathetic to the sense of possibilities that attach to "Möglichkeitssinn," began his analysis with a focus on the protracted disputation and negativity that arises when language is used to shore up ideological positions. The destruction of "formulaic reality" brought about by functional language, therefore, initially only had negative aspects, since it stood for the agonistic quality of the narration and the world opposed to it. The ledger, however, was squared in the second half of the book, where Hochstätter investigated the Other Condition and its positive account of alterity. Here it was notable that Musil renounced the use of irony in this section in favor of a more inward language of the emotions that drew on mystical writings such as Buber's *Ekstatische Konfessionen* (122–24). Yet even here, Musil's language remained more concrete than any high-flown mysticism, and his utopia was ultimately more sensually suggestive. In an interesting passage, Hochstätter returned to the theme of the child, comparing the idyll Musil constructed to the promise of childhood. Musil's protagonist, accordingly, was a "backward facing prophet" who longed for a childhood that might nevertheless include those "corrective moments" of conceptual understanding that modern consciousness is able to call upon (143). This conclusion about Ulrich's double focus in life also seemed to apply to

Hochstätter's scholarly generation, since it contained the same mix of nostalgia and escapism that characterized the 1968 tradition of critical engagement with literature, particularly in Germany.

Annie Reniers-Servranckz was one scholar of this period for whom Musil's attention to the future, rather than the past, was the primary point of focus. Her 1972 analysis of Musil's development as a writer revealed an artistic intention that could be read into Musil's earlier works and literary writing with as much conviction as the later major novel. Reniers-Servranckz found those approaches wanting that excluded the earlier works of Musil from view or measured Musil by the sole criterion of *Der Mann ohne Eigenschaften*. In her view, Musil's career was informed from the very beginning by an ambition to inspire a new spiritual concept of humanity. Such a concept would expose the shortcomings of existing reality and offer alternatives to it. Presupposing not merely a new conception of being, but a new way of seeing, as the miniature piece "Triëdere" from the *Nachlaß zu Lebzeiten* showed, Reniers-Servranckz's study forged connections with ethical approaches to Musil's novel that were emerging at this time: "Die Aufgabe des Künstlers ist eine ethische: sie ist ein Herstellen der 'richtigen optischen' Beziehungen zur Welt, ein Entdecken und Enthüllen der 'wirklichen' Zusammenhänge, ein Deuten des geheimnisvollen Lebens" (46).

Alan Holmes's 1978 study announced a new emphasis on the question of narrative perspective, approaching *Der Mann ohne Eigenschaften* from the viewpoint of the changes affecting the German novel in the period from realism to relativism and perspectivism, that is, "from nineteenth-century traditionalism to Modernist twentieth-century experimentation" (206). Such a point of departure paid homage to Wolfgang Kayser's groundbreaking work on perspective and narration in *Das sprachliche Kunstwerk* (1948) — a debt Holmes acknowledged, with some qualification, in his introduction: "Kayser's theory on the position and role of the narrator in fiction may apply to the norm but does not apply to Musil's exceptional experimental novel except in considerably modified form. It does, however, serve to define and clarify the relationship between Musil and the narrator in *Der Mann ohne Eigenschaften*" (5–6). Holmes's aim was to establish the level of identification obtaining between the author and his protagonist. He proceeded from the view that literature represented "a constructive alternative to the real world, more fluid, less fixed, because it is a possibility and not a reality" (47). Rejecting the epic narrative that held sway in the nineteenth century, Musil's narration incorporated rationality and theoretical reflection in an attempt to access the rich complexity of life in the twentieth century. The key to elucidating this "complex contemporary life" in Holmes's analysis was the "new Narrator," who moved effortlessly between close identification with particular characters, and great distance from them. Turning his attention to the deployment of the essay form in the novel, Holmes argued that Musil's essayism did not aid philosophical expression, as Luft's study from the same period also suggested (1980), but was deployed mainly as a framing device, a technique: "Essayism is fundamental to Ulrich's quest for self-fulfilment, the right life for him. As an attitude and technique it saves him from distortion and allows his true development" (140). The result of the partnership between the "new Narrator," the protagonist Ulrich, and the essayist Musil was an experimental novel that aims to supply "constructive alternatives" (236) to contemporary life.

Siegfried Rinderknecht unfolded in his 1979 study a conventional view of the crisis of bourgeois culture in the late nineteenth and early twentieth century and the loss of moral and ethical certainty as the backdrop to a more urgent undertaking — the need to reacquaint the disparate areas of ethics and aesthetics, an issue that had earlier been pursued by Marie-Louise Roth in 1972. This, then, was the "form problem" at the center of Musil's novel and at the same time the crisis at the heart of the bourgeois novel. Musil's "aesthetic essayism" was seen as its solution, a grand attempt to overcome the "Zusammenbruch aller verbindlichen Wertorientierungen" (17) by erecting in its place a new hierarchy of values. In so doing, the modality of possibility acquired significance, particularly for Ulrich and Agathe, who embark on a series of experiments to realize the lost harmony of ethics and aesthetics. The final section of Rinderknecht's book sought to deliver on the promise to foreground the problem of form, but did not provide much more than surface statements about the operation of narration and irony in Musil's novel.

Two studies at the start of the eighties revealed the influence of French structuralism, particularly the work of Michel Foucault. The first of these, Walter Moser's 1980 study of reason and madness in European civilization,[12] advanced a detailed investigation of scientific, political, philosophical, jurisprudential, and psychiatric discourses. In such allusive manner, Moser's study forged connections with other discipline areas at a time when traditional notions of genre and stylistic classification, such as irony and satire, still provided the main line of approach to *Der Mann ohne Eigenschaften*. Moser showed that aesthetic approaches needed to take account of Musil's novel as a historical document and the way it constructed, at times unconsciously, an evolving engagement with quite separate, extra-literary modes of thought. Ulf Eisele (1982) was another critic who pursued the implications of Foucault's "archaeological" approach to human understanding laid down in discourse analysis. Unlike Moser, who indicated that Musil's novel is embedded in a wider discussion of reason and madness, Eisele ascribed importance, as Blanchot (1958/62) had done before him, to the way fictional categories shape the conduct of life. For Eisele, therefore, literature itself was the main topic of Musil's novel. Engaging with the question of Musil's realism, which was hotly debated in Musil scholarship at this time,[13] Eisele showed not only that realistic description had come upon its limit in Musil's novel, but also that the complex social and historical circumstances of Musil's time suggested the failure of writing to encompass life at the level of poetic understanding (193). Eisele's study was therefore notable for proclaiming the failure of early aesthetic approaches to reach a broad understanding of Musil's novel based on aesthetic and literary categories alone.

Against this background, Gilbert Reis's 1983 attempt to defend the work of art against the encroachment of the neighboring disciplines of philosophy, sociology, and psychology appeared as a conservative reaction to the emerging crisis of literature and of the literary criticism that, in aesthetic approaches, had accompanied it. Reis's "question about reality" from the title of his study (*Musils Frage nach der Wirklichkeit*) was therefore made urgent by the entry of scientific discourses into literary criticism in the postwar period and the increasing separation of science from art (disseminated since the fifties in anglophone countries through C. P. Snow's important reference to the "two cultures"[14]): "Es gibt keinen Bereich des Wirklichen," Reis held, "der nicht für den Wissenschaftler so gut zugänglich wäre wie für den Dichter: aber eben in anderer Weise" (9).

Reis's aim was to define the specific quality evident in the literary approach to reality — "dichterisches Erkennen" as he called it. This type of literary understanding proceeded not from isolated fragments of reality, which science analyzed, but from the work as a whole. This led to the further question of how the cognitive aspects of highly contemplative art, such as Musil's, invest the art form. Are they "intuited" a posteriori from the whole, or do they actually precede the creation of the work of art? The answer to this question turned up surprising similarities in the approaches of philosophy (as a discourse of science) and of art to the problem of reflective understanding. For Reis's comprehensive treatment of Musil's works from *Die Verwirrungen des Zöglings Törleß* to *Der Mann ohne Eigenschaften* indicated a central difficulty for a work of the imagination in making plain the idea that underlies it: "Die Reflexion der

Dichtung auf sich selbst führt somit, und zwar unausweichlich, in eine geistige Krise hinein. Der Geist verselbständigt sich der Wirklichkeit gegenüber, vermag aber das letztlich Bestimmende nicht in sich zu finden" (438).

This notion of literature's inability to conceptualize its own underlying "idea" is a restatement of a philosophical problem investigated by Martin Heidegger.[15] Reis's study therefore bore on the question of literature's relationship to philosophy, and specifically whether, as Ulrich Karthaus[16] had earlier suggested, literature is to be imagined as a realm fundamentally apart from philosophy. Karthaus's assumption about the separateness of aesthetic and philosophical understanding appeared in reference to a 1960 essay by Erich Heintel, who had used Hegel to inform his understanding of Musil. Karthaus had concluded:

> Die auf hohem Niveau geführte Diskussion Heintels mit Musil wirft eine methodische Frage auf: ist es möglich, eine Dichtung von einer philosophischen Position aus angemessen zu kritisieren? Dichtung unterscheidet sich grundsätzlich von begrifflicher Reflexion, und so anregend ein Unternehmen wie das Heintels ist, so wenig ist es erschöpfend — es übersieht die in der Struktur des Werkes und nur in ihr sichtbaren Aspekte. (471)

Reis's study now showed that Karthaus's view of art's separateness from more conceptually focused disciplines such as philosophy was overstated. Moreover, he was able to demonstrate without recourse to turgid philosophical argument[17] that the ground of art is not any idea of art, but "ein Anderes," "ein Fremdes." Musil called this idea, which had progressively found its way into his literary project, "der andere Zustand." However, as Reis went on to suggest, this meditation on the reflective basis of art led to a greater and ultimately intractable problem: "wie seine Figuren, so ist der Erzähler zuletzt immer wieder genötigt, in die Wirklichkeit, die er ablehnt, zurückzufallen. Der 'unendliche Sinn' des Gefühles läßt sich in keiner Weise — weder dichterisch noch begrifflich — realisieren" (493).

As a result of such insights, a turning point in the aesthetic discussion of Musil's novel was reached by the mid 1980s. At this time, French structuralism was reverberating across Musil scholarship, and the term "postmodernism" had already been invoked to characterize the new self-consciousness of literature in its engagement with competing disciplines and nonliterary discourses. Eisele's study of 1982 demonstrated the limits of the promise of literary understanding to contain the world, while Reis, in a conservative reaction to the crisis of literature, proved — somewhat against the hope that had animated his study — that the idea of literature is "groundless" in Heidegger's sense. The crisis that these studies exposed was paralleled in the mid eighties by a prolonged dispute[18] between an elder statesman of Musil studies, Helmut Arntzen, and one of the intelligent new critics, Roger Willemsen, who had burst onto the scene with two book-length studies of Musil appearing under the titles, respectively, of *Das Existenzrecht der Dichtung* (1984) and *Robert Musil: Vom Intellectuellen Eros* (1985). Arntzen, for his part, had added to his earlier groundbreaking study of satire (1960) with a two-volume study on Musil's works that appeared in 1980 and 1982 and set out to provide a comprehensive treatment of Musil as well as a genealogy of individual works. Willemsen's unfavorable review of this two-volume study, which started the controversy, was — it can now be said with the benefit of hindsight — part of an emerging discussion throughout the scholarly world. In this discussion the scientific impulse in traditional literary criticism was pitted against the literary impulse in new aesthetic approaches, which were beginning to draw inspiration from French poststructuralism. The conflict between Willemsen and Arntzen also gave evidence of a dispute between what Uwe Japp has called, more generally, a "Hermeneutik der Reduktion" and a "Hermeneutik der Entfaltung," where the former sought to reduce the polyvocality of the text and the latter to expand it.[19] Arntzen and Willemsen, to this extent, were representatives of opposing factions within the broader defense of literature. Where Arntzen put artistic truth below an ideal conception of socially meaningful language, Willemsen subordinated language to artistic truth. In Willemsen's view, social experience conveyed only the "Formelhaftigkeit des Daseins" (1985, 14). Where Arntzen discovered in the novel not a cultivation of story-structure, of the "Fabel," but "eine zunehmende Befriedigung an den geistreichen Exkursen" (1982, 76), Willemsen understood the novel's language in Nietzschean terms as "eine[r] Erregung, die selbst poetisch ist" (14). And where Arntzen was scrupulous in his methodology in adherence to the conviction that literature could be unraveled by scientific principles of inquiry, Willemsen was suggestively allusive. He held that sense did not arise from the openly discursive passages of the novel, as Arntzen had assumed, but was doggedly idiosyncratic and individualistic. Willemsen, therefore, could not commend the author for offering models of social practice. Instead, he found Musil's ideal of literature utterly resistant to social practice, since it represented a "Hingabe an Fallkonstellationen, an die Augenblicksdispositionen des Ich, an situative Momentfiguren ohne stereotype Ableitungen" (73–74). For Willemsen, art did not address society in any final way. The values that Musil upheld were at most private ones that were found in the isolation of the individual from the social sphere, not in the way the individual interacted with others. The idyll of the sibling lovers, concomitantly, represented a retreat from socially conditioned behavior and a cultivation of the private region of the self.

Arntzen's project, by contrast, celebrated the individual in socially inclusive ways. For Arntzen, there was no such thing as a private language, since language was tied to society by its very nature, as Wittgenstein had suggested. As an experiment that aimed to realize a private language in an asocial setting, the Other Condition was bound to fail. The ideal the siblings pursued was the exception (to social language) that proved the rule (of social inclusiveness). Arntzen, for this reason, understood the Other Condition as a "conversation" about the limits of discourse that in fact grounded a notion of noninstrumentalized language: "Das von aller Zweckhaftigkeit freie, das insofern sinnlose Sprechen, das wie ein lyrischer Vers ist, konstituiert die Gemeinsamkeit des 'anderen Zustands' als Einanderverstehen" (126). For this reason, Arntzen's Other Condition was more utopian than real, and directly opposed the alternative reality of surging individualism that enlivened Willemsen's two studies.

Friedrich Wallner's essay of 1984 suggested an early response to this dispute over the ends of literature by focusing on the overall importance of philosophical discourses in Musil. For Wallner, rejecting Ingo Seidler's 1965 view of Musil's generally limited capacity for philosophy, Musil was a thinker of great sophistication. Wallner located Musil's intellectual position between, on the one hand, the collapse of the old European ideal of knowledge and learning (predicated since the ancient Greeks on an ideal conjunction of thought and being) and, on the other hand, a more pragmatic view that conceded no inherent truth-content to concepts. As Wallner argued, Musil adopted Nietzsche's flexible path toward truth and knowledge. He put forward a less systematic and more metaphorical philosophy by approaching philosophy not as the purveyor of objective truth (1984, 99–103) — a notion of truth Nietzsche had scornfully referred to as "truth at any cost" — but as an instrument that informed action in the world. Musil's "longing for denial" (of absolute truth) — from the title of Wallner's paper, "Sehnsucht nach Verweigerung" — thus aimed to promote understanding of the philosophical content of Musil's novel in Nietzsche's dynamically conceived sense. After considering the protagonist's stance of denial, Wallner's essay underscored Musil's turning away from objective-truth-at-any-cost. Musil's ideal, which drew on the precision of mathematics, instead set out a more incremental account of truth-through-language in pursuit of a nonprejudicial basis for human action in the world (1984, 105–8).

Gérard Wicht's study of 1984 resumed the interest in the figure of allegory or "Gleichnis" of earlier studies such as Kühn (1965) and Kühne (1968), comparing the use of allegory and metaphor in Musil with that of Hofmannsthal, Rilke, Broch, and Kafka from the same period. Wicht identified a predisposition among these authors to favor allegory as a poetic device as well as a keen awareness of the limitations of language. Hofmannsthal's *Brief des Lord Chandos* was one of several texts from the turn of the century that had set out to explore the potential of allegorical language. Of the five writers Wicht considered, it was (perhaps surprisingly) Musil who turned out to be the most radical. Musil did not use allegory to illustrate or exemplify a given reality in any realistic sense, nor did he, as with Kafka, stop at the threshold separating the real and the allegorical spheres. Instead, his use of allegory linked reality and possibility on an abstract and entirely experimental third level of communication. Musil's reader was thereby not returned to any reliably "given" sense of reality, but had to move beyond the real to a higher level — the "tertium comparationis" — in order to embrace the allegorical mode, the "Modus des Vieldeutigen und Unbekannten" (8). At this level of description, meaning was not fixed, since it emerged as a complex patterning of plot, narrative, and allegory, "wobei die dritte [Stufe] nicht sichtbar, aber im Bild intendiert ist" (110). For this same reason, the allegorical level of the story established not merely a comparison with what is depicted as real, but a wholly new aesthetic dimension of really existing possibility.

Eckhard Heftrich was another critic to investigate Musil's complex narrative structure. For Heftrich, in a study published in 1986, the problem of the major novel was bound up with stylistic and formal problems of such immensity that Musil was never able to find a satisfactory way of coming to terms with them. Accordingly, the "poetological problem" at the center of the novel, which Heftrich linked to the essayistic style of the narration as well as to the characterization of Ulrich, was the question "wie denn heute noch erzählt werden könne" (100). While this problem had to be addressed in intellectual terms, Musil did not wish to write an "intellectual" novel in the traditional manner. Instead, his aim was to write a "traditional novel with intellectual depth" ("einen traditionellen [Roman], der Intellekt hat"[20]) (149). Writing such a novel was no easy matter, since Musil found himself compelled not only to break with the convention of the omniscient narrator, but also to construct a new narrative stance that would better convey the multidimen-

sional nature of reality. (Alan Holmes had investigated this same narrative problem in 1978 under the heading of the "new Narrator.") Despite
this intention, Heftrich held, Musil had only limited success in conveying
a sense of intellectual depth to life, and, ironically, only achieved this goal
where he was able to avail himself of traditional epic means such as irony
and satire.

The resilience of older traditions of scholarship was evident in Rae-
Hyeon Kim's monograph, published in 1986. This is hardly surprising,
given that Kim's mentor in this approach was the established scholar
Beda Allemann, whose research on a "functional poetics" she frequently
referred to. Kim's monograph, accordingly, may be interpreted as an
attempt to apply an idealized model of language to Musil's work, based
on Allemann's approach: "Es handelt sich [. . .] darum, die Erfahrung
von Geschichte als Möglichkeit der Sprache aufzufassen" (12). For Kim,
Musil's understanding of "history" was open-ended, functional, and
peculiarly nonhistorical — neither Hegelian dialectic nor Spenglerian
determinism had much in common with it. This conception of "history" — a misty swirl of past and present, in which factual occurrences
lose their position on the historical continuum — also weakened the
claims of social criticism to throw light on Musil's novel, since it suggested that history was not a reliable category of teleological understanding, but could always be viewed from varying perspectives: "Diese
Austauschbarkeit der historischen Daten im 'stationären Zustand' bietet
ausdrücklich die Bedingung dafür, Geschichtsvorgänge experimentell zu
modellieren [. . .]" (36). Through a progressive historical restatement of
its own structural concerns (following Allemann's term "Rethematisie-
rung"), Kim held, literature postulated in ever-changing contexts its own
"poetological" self-containment and self-fulfillment (14, 25) and, indeed, its own original "quality" or "Gestalt" (149). This concept of
literature, which gave art a pivotal role in describing the circumstances
of life, had a mystical dimension, since art was ultimately the impenetrable artifice before which living actors stand in reverence (cf. *MoE*, 971).
Such an idealization of art was therefore an idealization of the artist's
imagination. This was further suggested in the capacity of artists to
prefigure actual human experience, of which Musil's foretelling of the
experience of war before the outbreak of the First World War provided
an example: "Das Schreiben bedeutet für Musil keine bloße Umsetzung
einer historischen Wirklichkeit oder einer ideellen Konzeption in die
Sprache, sondern einen Prozeß der *Hervorbringung aus Erinnerung*
[. . .]" (41, emphasis in the original). This work of "memory," then, was
quite other than that of a fixed history. Its goal was in every sense a

return, "die 'Rückwandlung' der Sprache als Mitteilungs- und Informationsinstrumentarium in jene ursprünglichere 'Sprachverfassung,' 'die uns plötzlich wieder erkennen läßt, daß es die Sprache ist, die uns Welt eröffnet und Dinge zeigt' [Allemann]" (41). The final part of Kim's book developed this idea of memory further, reflecting on how literary criticism discussed literature as a higher form of "memory work."

Frank Maier-Solgk's study of 1992, which also appraised Musil's conception of history, reached similar conclusions to those of Kim. Maier-Solgk emphasized Musil's desire to realize an alternative to the factual history that oppressed his own time. In his analysis, "Möglichkeitssinn" was the operative category deployed to this purpose, substituting a concept of "possible history" in a new notion of historical sense that would incorporate aesthetic sensibility and writerly concerns into history and thus connect the movement of history with language.

Daniel Joseph Brooks's study of 1989 represented another response to the intrusion of cross-disciplinary approaches into literary studies, which were fundamentally altering the critical enterprise by the late eighties and early nineties. The ideal of dialogue Socrates had defended in Greek antiquity, Brooks contended, while ending the pre-eminence of art, also promoted the vision of a harmony between science and art. Drawing on the critical picture of Socrates that Nietzsche had advocated in *Die Geburt der Tragödie aus dem Geiste der Musik,* Brooks put forward the view that "the critical, destructive force that exposes the inadequacy of the absolute, and the creative, aesthetic force that enables the construction of significance for the individual, describe precisely the thematic progression as depicted in the two books of *Der Mann ohne Eigenschaften* [. . .]" (100–101). Brooks's study envisaged a similar rebirth of rationalist society from the aesthetic spirit embodied in music. The organizing principle of this new life conception, Brooks held, would be narration ("das Gesetz der erzählerischen Ordnung" [*MoE*, 650]), and the task of narration was the cultivation of an aesthetic ideal of life — "a fundamentally Nietzschean project," as Brooks observed. That the siblings might drift into private speculation, increasingly at odds with their society at the end, merely meant in Brooks's judgment that they could claim no general validity for their ideal, however "Socratic" it turned out to be (92).

Peter Pfeiffer put forward in his study of 1990 a controversial new focus on the formal quality of the novel, linking questions of artistic development to concrete historical circumstances and the biography of the author. Pfeiffer divined a formal break in the progress of *Der Mann ohne Eigenschaften* around 1933, the date of the accession of Hitler to power in Germany. A few months after Hitler's rise to power, Pfeiffer observed, Musil and his wife left Berlin to return to Vienna. About the same time, Musil began to use the aphorism as a narrative device. Pfeiffer's analysis, therefore, attempted to connect this signal moment in German history with the literary progress of Musil's novel and a new development in Musil's poetic understanding: "Das Zusammenspiel zwischen literarisch-ästhetischen und politischen Konzeptionen erhält für Musil durch die Erfahrung des Nazismus eine neue Aktualität, die sich in seiner veränderten Einstellung zum Aphorismus ablesen läßt" (48). This new interest in the aphorism also signaled the final departure from the realistic tradition of nineteenth-century bourgeois realism: "Das lineare Erzählen destruiert Musil im *Mann ohne Eigenschaften* durch zahlreiche essayistische Einschübe und aphoristische Elemente und verweist so auf den anomischen Gesellschaftszustand, der allgemeingültiger Orientierungen entbehrt" (55). The effect of this use of the aphorism was a type of "hyper-realism" that sought to "liquidate" those earlier aspects of the novel carried by the "Fabel," particularly in part one. This liquidation of the first part of the novel, in turn, represented a new kind of novel Pfeiffer called both modern and "postrealistic" (103). Since Musil also saw in the rise of Hitler the last doomed stand of patriarchy, the "new novel" would inevitably reflect the rise of women to prominence and the arrival of a "matriarchal" approach to understanding human beings. Under such circumstances, human life would be less rationally compromised and more open to matters of the heart and the soul; its cipher was Agathe — the epitome of the new "Fragment-Mensch[en]."

Following Arntzen's influential early work on satire in 1960 and his two-volume study of language in 1980/82, Gerd-Theo Tewilt reverted in his study of 1990 to an older question in scholarship, that of the capacity of expressivist language to evince truth in the world. To this extent, Tewilt's approach implicitly engaged with the Arntzen-Willemsen dispute about the nature of literature, while ultimately falling in behind Arntzen's view about the social ends of literary activity. (It is noteworthy in this regard that Tewilt's book appeared as the seventh volume in a series edited by Arntzen entitled "Literatur als Sprache."[21]) On another front, Tewilt considered a question that had long been central to Musil scholarship — whether conceptual understanding can lead to artistic truth. Although Tewilt's conviction was that conceptual understanding was ultimately different from artistic understanding, literature was still called upon to address the aporetic conditions afflicting conceptual thought outlined in Horkheimer and Adorno's pioneering work of 1944,

Dialektik der Aufklärung. Tewilt therefore asked: "wie lassen sich Magisches und Aufklärung, Erregung des Banns und Freiheit der Distanz vereinen? Wie läßt sich zugleich eine 'Dialektik der Aufklärung' vermeiden, in der Rationalität zum Rausch, zur 'Trunksucht am Tatsächlichen' (*MoE,* 215) wird?" (132). Tewilt thereby touched upon one of the most pressing issues of modernity: the problem of imagining a viable alternative to everyday experience, given that the expressive means to do so are constrained by the very rationality that pervades every area of modern technologized life.

Tewilt's analysis considered the one-sidedness of empiricism's account of modern life, while maintaining a skeptical line about the prospects of transcending the empirical worldview through the medium of language. In particular, Tewilt asked whether Musil's notion of the Other Condition could resist being sidelined as superstition and retain its potential as an alternative vision for modern life. Tewilt saw this problem as emerging from the encroachment of science and scientizing discourses upon language. Even Clarisse, Tewilt noted, refused the invitation to use the expressivist paradigm of emotive language as a means of opposing the "Rausch [. . .] der Nüchternheit" (182) typical of the age. Musil's novel therefore enacted every aspect of the entrapment experienced by modern subjects, even as it attempted through the logic of expressivist language to find a way beyond it. Tewilt's conclusion, however, suggested that no final accommodation between language and society, or art and science, could be reached through the medium of language. At most he conceded a certain limited ethical promise for language in framing and describing models for action in the world. Ulrich's outlook, for example, was obliged to accept partial truths in its avoidance of totalizing beliefs. For this reason, Tewilt effectively endorsed earlier views, notably those of Reis (1983), which had established the groundless nature of literature and literary understanding. Musil's novel — which, under such aporetic circumstances, could not but remain a fragment — thus signaled the overall failure of language to reach a comprehensive understanding of the world.

Both Irmgard Honnef-Becker (1991) and Sibylle Deutsch (1993) focused on genre considerations in the novel. For Honnef-Becker, metalevels of signification were created "recursively," such that meaning became progressively more open and less fixed in the narration. Deutsch, for her part, was more concerned with situating this interplay of genre types in a historical context, advancing the view that the novel shared many attributes of modernist writing and, more particularly, some of the concerns that characterized Expressionism. Ultimately, however, the novel could not be satisfactorily subsumed under either label, since Musil's disposition was more naturally in accord with that of Goethe and the eighteenth century. Deutsch's main argument, indeed, flowed from the observation that Musil had resisted Expressionism's radical critique of language. In her view, Musil resolved problems of an aesthetic nature not, as Tewilt (1990) and others had suggested, through experiments with language, but through a widening of the conceptual and epistemological horizon of the novel. The result was a sort of "kaleidoscopic narration" built around the perspectivism attaching to characters and their particular situations, which, taken as a whole, still registered a desire to break with the conceptual positions that had led to the crisis of Europe on the brink of the First World War.

Deutsch's approach was also interesting for its reliance on Musil's diaries — the author's "factory of ideas" (17). In fact, Deutsch held, the diaries elucidated more about Musil's production of ideas than the novel itself. What they showed was that Musil, the philosophical poet, worked more through conceptual thought than through and with the medium of language. Even Musil's utopian visions, which opened out into religion and mysticism, did not dispense with the underlying sense of rationality that makes conceptual thought possible. To this extent, Deutsch's approach, which highlighted Musil's innate conservatism with respect to the rationalist tradition of the European West, pointed beyond the aesthetic medium toward the central importance of ethical values that have taken root in this same intellectual tradition.

David Precht's study of 1996, which revealed the strong interest of poststructuralism in expanding and dismantling the notion of the author and the work of art, was directed toward uncovering the self-reflexivity and materiality of the text. Sense, Precht held, is not given to words in any a priori way, but emerges out of the shaping of context. For this reason, Musil's text was both open and unending, and evinced a "fluctuating character." This fluctuating meditation on the "logic of the soul" — from the title of his study "Die gleitende Logik der Seele" — was conservative insofar as it constituted a meditation on the heroism of art. At the same time, it was allusively postmodern, since the text was polyvocal and could never be pinned down to any singular meaning or sense. Accordingly, Precht's long discussion of the opening chapter of the novel indicated both a "verunglückte Gegenwärtigkeit des Textes für den Leser" and the "Unmöglichkeit jedweder definitiven Festschreibung von Sinn" (69). Musil's heroic art instead spoke of an underlying skepticism about language and the possibilities of communicating meaning, and gave rise to fractured perspectives in Nietzsche's sense: "Ästhetisch selbstreflexiv zu schreiben bedeutet, Räume zu entwerfen, die nicht mimetische Wiedergaben, sondern ereignishafte Inszenierungen der eigenen Perspektivität sind" (139). Despite the many possibilities attaching to perspectivism, however, Musil's skepticism about language overwhelmed the novel and allowed it to register no more than "das Unzulängliche eines jedweden perspektivischen Zugriffs auf Wirklichkeit" (288).

Agata Schwartz, in her study of 1997, abandoned the writer's skepticism about language and meaning that had dominated approaches to Musil in the early nineties. Instead, she focused attention on reading strategies and, in particular, the question of gendered perspective in the novel. Her approach, which was constructed around an analysis of chapter variants from the posthumous notes on the novel, also mirrored the new interest of philosophy in the nineties in oriental thought — notably in the work of Peter Sloterdyk.[22] Schwartz showed how reading responses to *Der Mann ohne Eigenschaften* attached to two fundamentally dissimilar perspectives: the standard perspective, that of Ulrich, and an implied and less obvious perspective, that of Agathe and to a lesser extent Clarisse. Whereas a masculinist view, focused on the character of Ulrich, ultimately led to the centrality of dystopian elements, the femininist perspective appeared less closed off and determinate. This perspective incorporated both utopian and dystopian elements in a free mix. Entering the debate about the way Musil might have concluded his novel, Schwartz identified Taoist elements[23] that were to have shaped Ulrich's third utopian "treatise" ("dritte utopische 'Abhandlung'") (12). These elements, derived from the oriental philosophy of Yin and Yang, revealed the use of Taoist symbols and emblems held together in a relationship of "reciprocal complementarity." Schwartz concluded from the posthumously published notes to the novel that Musil wished to outline a type of utopian bisexualism that could represent a response, if not the answer, to the problem of the insistent divide between the sexes. Schwartz endorsed this account of bisexuality, arguing that bisexuality was not merely a behavioral response, but actually impacted upon human cognition. This insight allowed Schwartz to posit a utopian dimension to the Other Condition, since the Other Condition patently brought forth "Ulrich's Yin-side" (115). Schwartz concluded with a reference to Musil's statement that his utopia was addressed rather to distant posterity than to his own age. Configuring the true nature of the conclusion to *Der Mann ohne Eigenschaften,* she held, following Wolfgang Iser,[24] was ultimately a task for the "implied reader of the future."

In applying the figure of the sublime to Musil's works, Stefan Hadjuk's 2000 study set out to demonstrate the radical nature of Musil's aestheticism. The sublime, of course, had enjoyed pre-eminence in late eighteenth-century philosophy, especially in Kant's writings, as an attempt to mark off transcendent experience from the everyday material sense of being in the world. In Hadjuk's argument, this essentially historical discussion about the limits of experience, which had constituted a key moment in the emergence of modernity, was absorbed into Musil's novel, but in subversive ways. According to Hadjuk, Musil attached little importance to historical context. Instead, he was interested in a use of the sublime that registered opposition to the prevailing order of being and promoted a "break-through" to a new continuity of being (13), a new mode of experience outside history (and therefore at the origin of what has since been proclaimed as the postmodern). In Hadjuk's view, this also entailed a brokering of philosophy and literature — realms driven apart by Kant's formalization of knowledge in his three *Critiques* and since then, under modernism, held to be distinct ways of apprehending the world: "Das Ästhetisch-Erhabene ist eine aufgrund ihrer 'eigentlichen' Ortlosigkeit konfliktfähige Grenzfigur, die zwischen dem Besonderen des literarischen und dem Allgemeinen des philosophischen Diskurses vermittelt" (12).

The sublime thus became significant as a discursive figure in a "Welt des Diskursiven" (29). It implied both that modernity had hit against certain limits (which, as Nietzsche's notion of nihilism made clear, had led to the cultivation of empty values), and that it urgently needed to go beyond them. Hadjuk enlisted Musil's fiction, and specifically his idea of the Other Condition, to show how the sublime could express a new poetic attitude to life. This was the "aesthetic transgression" alluded to in the subtitle of Hadjuk's study ("Robert Musil's ästhetische Transgression der Moderne"). This aesthetic realm could be "transgressed" because it contained more than just an idea about art. It now also conveyed an idea about living, communicating by way of the poetic imagination ideas drawn from morality and ethics. Hadjuk therefore concluded:

> Die "moralische Phantasie" (MoE, 1028; 1037), die für Ulrich nahezu mit dem Begriff "Gefühl" zusammenfällt (vgl. MoE, 1037), scheint auf einer Art posttranszendentalen Freiheit zu gründen, die auf "das unendliche Ganze der Möglichkeiten zu leben" (MoE 1028) bezogen ist. (292)

Musil's aesthetics thus merged with an ethical outlook, or was that ethical outlook in action. With this new perspective on the question of aesthetics and ethics — a question that had been discussed in Musil scholarship since Marie-Louise Roth's study of 1972 — Hadjuk connected with existential critique and at the same time sought to go beyond it. What underpinned his approach was a new version of the old idea of art followed by the Romantics and reactivated by Friedrich Nietzsche in the Dionysian principle. This was the expressivist notion that art as poetic existence could overcome the limitations of mundane experience and make possible novel — and essentially "other" — ways of being in the world. Hadjuk took the conversations between Ulrich and Agathe in the final section of the novel as proof of the attempt to enliven this poetic existence and make it real. Whether, as Hadjuk's approach now implied, the discrepancy between art and life, and of culture and nature, could be annulled or somehow spirited away under the terms of a new "posttranscendent" idea of being, was to become a key issue in more directly ethical approaches to *Der Mann ohne Eigenschaften*.

Notes

[1] Renate von Heydebrand, ed., *Robert Musil* (Darmstadt: Wissenschaftliche Buchgesellschaft, 1982), 160–203.

[2] Maurice Blanchot, "Inspiration, Lack of Inspiration" (1955), in *The Space of Literature*, trans. Ann Smock (Lincoln/London: U of Nebraska P, 1982), 177–87, here 179.

[3] Cf. *MoE*, 650: "Die meisten Menschen sind im Grundverhältnis zu sich selbst Erzähler."

[4] Uwe Japp has traced the origins of hermeneutics back to the Middle Ages in his *Hermeneutik: Der theoretische Diskurs, die Literatur und die Konstruktion ihres Zusammenhangs in den philologischen Wissenschaften* (Munich: Wilhelm Fink, 1977), 9.

[5] Wolfgang Iser, "Wolfgang Iser on the Play of the Text," in *Realism*, edited and introduced by Lilian R. Furst (London/New York: Longman, 1992), 213. "*Agon* is a fight or contest, and is a common pattern of play when the text centers on conflicting norms and values. The contest involves a decision to be made by the reader in relation to these opposing values [. . .]. *Alea* is a pattern of play based on chance and the unforeseeable. Its basic thrust is defamiliarisation [. . .]. By overturning familiar semantics, it reaches out into the hitherto inconceivable and frustrates the reader's convention-governed expectations. [. . .] *Mimickry* is a play pattern designed to generate illusion. [. . .] the more perfect the illusion, the more real will seem the world it depicts; [. . .] if the illusion, however, is punctured and so revealed as what it is, the world it depicts turns into a looking glass enabling the referential world outside the text to be observed. [. . .] *Ilinx* is a play pattern in which the various positions are subverted, undercut, canceled, or even carnivalised as they are played off against one another. It aims at bringing out the rear view of the positions yoked together in the game" (212).

[6] Cf. for example Iser's important books *Der implizierte Leser: Kommunikationsformen des Romans von Bunyan bis Beckett* (1972), translated as *The Implied Reader: Patterns of Communication in Prose Fiction from Bunyan to Beckett* (Baltimore/London: The Johns Hopkins UP, 1974), and *Der Akt des Lesens: Theorie ästhetischer Wirkung* (1976), translated as *The Act of Reading: A Theory of Aesthetic Response* (London/Henley: Routledge and Kegan Paul, 1978).

[7] Iser, *The Act of Reading*, 170.

[8] A harmonizing intention, for example, can be read into the following statement by Kühn: "Nach dem Prinzip der 'konstruktiven Ironie' ist selbst im scheinbar Gegensätzlichen Verwandtes und so haben wir sogar zwischen dem Privatgelehrten Ulrich und dem Prostituiertenmörder Moosbrugger verwandte Züge gefunden — sollten nun zwischen Ulrich und Walter nur Gegensätze bestehen?" *Analogie und Variation: Zur Analyse von Robert Musils Roman "Der Mann ohne Eigenschaften* (Bonn: Bouvier, 1965), 47.

[9] Note that in Dietrich Hochstätter's later study the *Gleichnis* becomes the defining stylistic feature of the utopian section of Musil's novel. *Sprache des Möglichen: Stilistischer Perspektivismus in Robert Musils "Der Mann ohne Eigenschaften"* (Frankfurt am Main: Athenäum, 1972), 134–35.

[10] Later works influenced by Kühn and Kühne include those of Hans Wolfgang Schaffnit (1971), Gérard Wicht (1984), and Peter-Andre Alt (1988).

[11] Cf. Hans-Rudolf Schärer in *Musil-Forum* 1993/94 (19/20): 370: "Nadermann behauptet, daß die positive Wendung am Ende von Musils Leben vor allem deshalb möglich geworden sei, weil er eine neue, entspanntere Einstellung zum Schreiben gewonnen habe."

[12] Lucas Cejpek's later study of the tension between reason and madness in European civilization (1983) was indebted to positions argued by Moser. Cejpek, *Wahn und Methode: Robert Musils "Der Mann ohne Eigenschaften"* (Graz: dbv-Verlag, 1983).

[13] Wolfgang Freese argued that Musil was a realist because he "corrects illusions" (*Philologie und Kritik,* Musil Studien 7 [Munich, Salzburg: Fink, 1981]). In this way, Musil's "realism" was also consonant with Marxist views of society that had gained ground in the 1970s. Of other critics, Karthaus ("War Musil Realist?" *Musil-Forum* 6/1 [1980]: 155–227) emphasized romantic aspects in Musil's realism, and Zeller ("Musils Auseinandersetzung mit der realistischen Schreibweise," *Musil-Forum* 6/1 [1980]: 128–44) highlighted Musil's "ambivalent" relationship to realism. In a later study, Fourie ("Musil als Realist?" *Musil-Forum* 19/20 [1993–94]: 132–43) invoked the category of "anti-realism" to describe Musil's description in the novel. Following Gaede's idea (*Realismus von Brant bis Brecht* [Munich: Francke, 1972]) that realistic literature is not mimetic literature, because it expresses some form of opposition to depicted reality, Fourie concluded: "Die Vorstellung also, daß Sprache ein 'wahres' Realitätsbild zu repräsentieren hat, ist die Folie ironischer Sprach- und Wirklichkeitsskepsis, die gerade 'die Wahrheit' sprachlicher Repräsentation unterläuft [. . .]" (140).

[14] In a lecture given at Cambridge on May 7, 1959 and a subsequent book publication under the title *The Two Cultures and the Scientific Revolution* (Cambridge: Cambridge UP, 1959).

¹⁵ Cf. Manfred Frank's discussion of this same problem in his essay "Auf der Suche nach einem Grund. Über den Umschlag von Erkenntniskritik in Mythologie bei Musil," in *Mythos und Moderne: Begriff und Bild einer Rekonstruktion,* edited by Karl-Heinz Bohrer (Frankfurt am Main: Suhrkamp, 1983), 318–62.

¹⁶ Ulrich Karthaus, "Musil-Forschung und Musil-Deutung. Ein Literaturbericht," *Deutsche Vierteljahrsschrift für Literaturwissenschaft und Geistesgeschichte* 39, 3 (1965): 441–83.

¹⁷ It is particularly noteworthy that Reis was able to reach conclusions about the ground of art quite independently from Heidegger's philosophy or Heidegger's work *Der Satz vom Grund* (1957) in which the paradox of the groundless "ground" (Grund) of rational thought is expounded.

¹⁸ Cf. Werner Welzig, "Verwischte Spuren: Zu und aus Anlaß von Helmut Arntzens Musil-Kommentar (Der Mann ohne Eigenschaften)," *Germanisch-Romanische Monatsschrift* 38/3 (1988): 343–47.

¹⁹ Uwe Japp, *Hermeneutik: Der theoretische Diskurs und die Konstruktion ihres Zusammenhangs in den philologischen Wissenschaften* (Munich: Fink, 1977), 10.

²⁰ From Musil's letters (*B I,* 498).

²¹ A contrary view about the value of exclusively aesthetic approaches to Musil can be found in Friedrich Bringazi, *Robert Musil und die Mythen der Nation: Nationalismus als Ausdruck subjektiver Identitätsdefekte* (Frankfurt am Main: Peter Lang, 1998). Bringazi, whose analysis deals with the question of nation in Musil, found instructive the fact that an endless number of critical works have pursued the question of irony in Musil, although there are only thirteen references to irony in the diaries. By contrast, Musil wrote several essays on the question of nation, there are forty-seven references in the diaries to nation or nationalism, and some chapters in the novel take up the question of nation explicitly. Despite this, he noted, there is a paucity of critical engagement with this question among Musil scholars.

²² Peter Sloterdyk, *Eurotaoismus: Zur Kritik der politischen Kinetik* (Frankfurt am Main: Suhrkamp, 1989).

²³ Others to have mentioned the significance of Taoism in Musil include Helga Honold ("Die Funktion des Paradoxen bei Robert Musil dargestellt am 'Mann ohne Eigenschaften,'" diss. Tübingen, 1963, 64) and Itsuo Motooka ("'Eine Melodie ohne Töne, ein Bild ohne Form': Robert Musil und Laoste," in *"In dem alten Haus der Sprache wohnen": Beiträge zum Sprachdenken in der Literaturgeschichte,* edited by Eckehard Czucka [Münster: Aschendorff, 1991], 335–44).

²⁴ Wolfgang Iser, *Der implizite Leser: Kommunikationsformen des Romans von Bunyan bis Beckett* (Munich: Wilhelm Fink, 1972).

5: The Order of Feeling: Ethical Readings

> *Die Dinge sind anders, weil meine Ein-*
> *stellung zu ihnen eine andre ist. Es han-*
> *delt sich weniger darum, daß ich andre*
> *Seiten wahrnehme als daß ich überhaupt*
> *weniger "wahrnehme," sondern ethisch*
> *eingestellt bin.* (*TB I,* 650)
>
> *Ich will nicht begreifen, sondern fühlbar*
> *machen.* (*B I,* 24)

A ROUND THE LATE EIGHTIES a new tone could be heard in Musil scholarship. As the controversy between Helmut Arntzen and Roger Willemsen indicated, no consensus had been reached in the aesthetic discussion of the novel. In other areas of scholarship, existential critique was being displaced by social criticism, and social criticism itself had undergone transformation as a result of cultural critique, which had emerged from within it. While psychology was still an undiminished point of departure for approaches to Musil's novel, it was the question of Musil's ethics that now began to move to center stage.

The debate about modernism and its would-be successor, postmodernism, that by now was raging across literary scholarship of all persuasions, ensured that ethical questions in Musil would be conducted around a wholly new set of assumptions. Under the modernist paradigm, for example, ethics and aesthetics were anything but antithetical undertakings, as Marie-Louise Roth's study of 1972 had sought to demonstrate. The larger issue about ethics that had arisen in the seventies had been partly a matter of whether and to what extent aesthetics and ethics, and, by extension, art and science, could be connected. By the late eighties, these goals had undergone revision. Postmodernism, in collapsing the modernist obsession with comprehensive solutions to the world, felt no compulsion to realize harmony between the constituent elements of fiction (as Roth had attempted to do in her study), but a great need to see separate theoretical positions for what they were. In this context, less (comprehensive thought) meant more (clarity of thought). These insights meant that ethics — an undeniably important point of focus of Musil's novel, as Bauer and Drevermann's study had revealed as early as 1966 — could be treated on its own terms as an attempt to model forms of action under the increasingly complex conditions of "late capitalism" (Habermas). In modeling these forms of action, ethical criticism sought to understand the choices that individuals make in life and the relative value they ascribe to different types of behavior. The underlying "decisionistic" nature of Musil's novel seemed to engage with precisely such choices — all the more because there was no obvious direction in which the protagonist could strike out. Moreover, in cultivating "probabilitarian sense" ("Möglichkeitssinn") in order to imagine alternatives to established reality, Musil's lengthy meditation on possible action conferred on the novel classical aspects of the ethical disposition in Charles Alteri's sense:

> So long as we must define our categories of judgment on the basis of predicates already established as the operational vocabulary for specifying the nature of actions, our assessments will emphasize conformity or nonconformity to a norm. But suppose we can imagine actions that ask to be read as possible labels, as aligning the person with certain possible groupings of characters or of specifying qualities that warrant claiming a particular identity for oneself.[1]

That ethics was a mode of thought that invited special consideration on particular occasions, rather than a universalizing impulse conditioning all forms of behavior under the dominant sway of a "categorical imperative," was already suggested by the nature of Musil's utopia. Although Ulrich and Agathe were emissaries of a new world and an "other condition," their actions arose from the special circumstances that had brought them together at a decisive moment in their lives. Moreover, the moral reference points of their age had shifted. As war appeared not as a fleeting moment but as a new condition of the world, and as war meant — with the benefit of hindsight for an author writing in the 1920s and 1930s — world war, ethics could no longer work to reconcile its practitioners with the moral code of the prevailing civilized world. For this world was patently no longer civilized in any sense that the siblings were obliged to accept. The new discussion of ethics in the eighties and nineties, therefore, found little instruction in the Other Condition as a utopian proposition in the manner of existential critique. As scholars in the tradition of social criticism had pointed out, the fondness of existential critique for mystical thought and utopias of all kinds involved a certain escape from the world, and ostensibly "apolitical" art could still be read as highly political art. For these reasons, the new discussion of the novel centered on evaluating the Other Condition as an ethical experiment, and great significance was seen in the way Musil had set it up. Musil's intention with this experiment, it was suggested, was no longer to effect a flight from the world, but to organize a flight back into it — a return that was to allow individuals a responsible, but entirely free and flexible, accommodation with the new circumstances of life once the shattering experience of world war had been left behind. By the late eighties, the experience of a war of that magnitude was a distant memory. Scholarship now found itself drawn to considering the ethical aspects of the Other Condition in a more open and less compromised way than hitherto.

A distinguishing feature of ethical approaches was the desire to understand Musil's philosophical position. Although Karthaus had questioned the relevance of philosophy to art as a general proposition in his literature survey of 1965,[2] the view of Musil scholarship overall was that philosophy remained of importance in assessing *Der Mann ohne Eigenschaften*. That philosophy might even be the key to Musil's writing, however, because it was the key to Musil's ethics, was a notion that had slowly emerged over time. By the late eighties it had begun to appear insistent. This suggests why Musil scholarship since then has progressively taken on an impenetrable appearance to the outsider. Scholars — especially in the tradition of ethical criticism — have felt obliged to master complex philosophical arguments in framing perspectives on Musil's fiction. At the same time, their arguments have sometimes come across as arcane, if not idiosyncratic, and have occasionally aroused antipathy on the part of more traditionally minded scholars of literature. This was no more clearly the case than with Matthias Luserke's study of 1987, which applied a "Vierweltenmodell" (273) of conceptual modality to the problem of ethical behavior in *Der Mann ohne Eigenschaften*. Its complicated argument drew at least one sharp response in a book review.[3] Nevertheless, it must be borne in mind that recondite approaches such as Luserke's have arisen naturally from the nature of Musil's difficult fiction and are likely to remain a valuable guide to assessing the subtle nuances of Musil's ethical project for the foreseeable future.

Arnold Gehlen introduced the term "posthistoire" to German literary criticism in the mid 1960s.[4] Soon after, Michel Foucault published his foundational study on discourse theory, *L'Archéologie du savoir* — a study that altered the way history is understood virtually overnight.[5] At about the same time, Jean-François Lyotard revised the understanding of the term "modern" and declared the arrival of the "postmodern" in an important work subtitled "a report on knowledge."[6] This "report on knowledge" was a report on the way different forms of understanding are marked off from one another under the new terms that began to shape perception in the seventies. Lyotard found these forms of understanding worthy of a new epochal classification — the epoch of postmodernity. In developing ideas about postmodernity, Lyotard followed Nietzsche's conception of the coexistence of different forms of historical writing that had made history and the critical enterprise appear as kindred undertakings. Lyotard also went beyond Nietzsche in proclaiming the general significance of epistemology for cultural understanding, for epistemology set out the conditions under which anything at all could be known, and understanding itself, therefore, had to be seen as subject to significant perspectival changes. Thomas Kuhn's important study of the way such historical "paradigm shifts" affect scientific understanding (*The Structure of Scientific Revolutions*, 1962), gave Lyotard's new postmodernism added authority. It was now possible to see the thought of the past as the expression of "master narratives" of understanding that held sway at a particular time in history, not as any final versions of the truth. This was not just the insight that truth is in some ways relative. Lyotard's work stated that an age is defined by its adherence to particular conceptions held to be true, and that the question of the "truth" content of these conceptions, strictly speaking, was no more than a distraction.

These and other works of structuralism and emerging poststructuralism refocused the debate about Musil's novel. By degrees, the dominant paradigms of Musil studies, which had drawn inspiration from the core idea of the hermeneutic impulse — an idea of the transcendent nature of the work of art and the transcendent understanding that informed it — were increasingly displaced. Musil criticism, in overthrowing the transcendence of the author and substituting a decidedly more immanent conception of the "text," now took up the challenge that Klaus Laermann had issued as early as 1970. This was the invocation to reject those notions of the primacy of the author and the work of art that Laermann had considered manifestions of "bourgeois" consciousness. Instead of staying "under" the text, Laermann had urged, the task of Musil scholarship was to move out from beneath it. In the eighties and especially from the late eighties on, criticism began to follow Laermann's lead — with surprising results: the increasing engagement with extraliterary discourses and the desire to debunk the authority of the author in reference to epistemological shifts of understanding made Musil seem more relevant to the present age. The increasing dominance of ethical criticism among approaches to the novel has ensured that Musil remains an author of importance for the present age.

The view that knowledge in the age of the postmodern is produced under a new set of basic assumptions, which themselves might well be of a nonpermanent nature, now draws wide support. Foucault's discourse theory and Lyotard's master narratives suggested that knowledge arose from historical ways of seeing, but, equally, that history itself had to eschew any claim to represent eternally valid truth. If this were so, knowledge did not rest on supports that were tied to a concrete reality, but in some way lacked substantial reality. This was an idea Musil had confronted as early as 1908 in his dissertation on Ernst Mach. Nevertheless, it was a proposition that had not been addressed in Musil scholarship directly until the appearance of Henri Arvon's essay of 1970. Arvon was one of the first scholars to suggest the importance of functional categories in assessing Musil's approach to the question of reality. Arvon did not reject functionalism for diminishing the existentialist focus on life — as Albertsen (1968) and Reinhardt (1969) had done immediately before him. His view was rather that Musil, while reserving criticism for aspects of Mach's epistemology in his dissertation, used the functionalism he derived from Mach to outline a new type of moral and ethical project. What resulted was a productive tension between a functionalist view of reality (which could then be linked historically to the emergence of logical positivism) and a substantial view of reality (based on notions of direct causality) that informed Musil's portrait of Kakania, but also raised the question of alternatives to it, including the Other Condition. Arvon therefore held: "Das Ausspielen der Funktionalität gegen die Kausalität ist in der Tat eine der wirksamsten und meist angewandten Triebfedern des *Mann ohne Eigenschaften*. Ulrich selbst erkennt, daß eine große Anzahl von Naturvorgängen sich wegen ihrer zu großen Komplexität der kausalen Berechnung entziehen" (211) The significance of the thought of Ernst Mach for an understanding of Musil's literary project has recently been underscored by Tim Mehigan (1997a) and Hans-Joachim Pieper (2002).

This new understanding of the importance of functionalism had the immediate consequence of rendering the truth content of Musil's fiction problematic. A number of critics were drawn for this reason to considering the intellectual influences that underlay Musil's apparent abandonment of absolute truth. Among them were Yvon Desportes, who in a 1974 article followed Arvon in linking Musil with Ernst Mach's philosophy, Karl Menges (1976) and Hartmut Cellbrot (1988), who evaluated Musil's connection with the phenomenological thought of Edmund Husserl, Dagmar Barnouw (1977), who investigated Musil's relation to skepticism in the context of David Hume (whom Musil had considered in his dissertation on Mach), and Claudia Monti (1983), who analyzed Musil's critique of the rational impulse in scientific thought. These approaches attributed relatively more importance to the way truth in Musil was informed by perspectival shifts of understanding, and relatively less importance to what underlying truth-content was actually discoverable in Musil's writing. They substituted the goal of knowledge for the goal of truth in a way that made the tradition of existential critique, which had seen little difference between the pursuit of knowledge and the pursuit of truth, increasingly appear obsolete.[7] Cellbrot's analysis of phenomenological influences on Musil, which assumed the importance of functional categories of understanding, may be taken as broadly illustrative in this regard: "Die durch den Wandel der Wirklichkeit zum Wirklichkeitsphänomen sichtbar gewordenen, im sinnbildenden Leben fungierenden Bezüge [. . .] sind weder statisch noch isoliert zu denken; sie sind dynamisch und stehen in funktionalen Zusammenhängen" (1988, 21).

Sibylle Bauer and Ingrid Drevermann had indicated the importance of ethical approaches to Musil as early as 1966 in two studies published under the title *Studien zu Robert Musil*. Both Bauer and Drevermann highlighted the speculative quality of Musil's novel. In their view, the imaginary experiments Musil set up in his fiction were more compelling than the sense of reality conveyed in the narrative. For Bauer, moreover, reality was not binding or given, but merely "modular" — one of many possible expressions of reality that must be measured against the standards of ethical thought. Deciding what these standards should be, however, would imply an end to the "hypothetical existence" Ulrich had felt obliged to lead. Bauer therefore abandoned a conventional analysis of Ulrich's character in attempting to reconstruct Musil's ethics from "evidential" categories — that is, on the basis of the choices made by the main character. Drevermann, for her part, highlighted Musil's speculative search for an intellectual and spiritual response to life. Her study was principally concerned with formal questions, in particular how feeling in the Other Condition was an independent category of thought that could be modeled, modulated and ultimately made real (210–13).

One of the most distinguished contributions to understanding the ethical Musil was undertaken by Aldo Venturelli in a study initially written in Italian in 1980 and subsequently translated into German in 1988. In a wide-ranging investigation of philosophical influences that included Nietzsche, Mach, and Husserl, Venturelli focused attention on the rational content of modernism. While following the lead given in earlier socially critical approaches that had attributed importance to Musil's reception of Enlightenment thought, such as that of Böhme (1974), Venturelli moved beyond such approaches in underscoring the open-ended nature of Musil's dialogue with rationalist positions. Accordingly,

Venturelli interpreted the trajectory of Musil's ethical project as an "Ausrichtung auf ein unvollendetes Projekt der Moderne, auf das Bemühen, den Prozeß der Rationalisierung von dem Übergewicht der kognitivinstrumentellen Formen der Rationalität zu lösen und sein ganzes emanzipatorisches Potential zu enthüllen" (1988, 22). This attempt to liberate thinking from instrumental reason was indebted, of course, to Jürgen Habermas's reflections on the same topic and Horkheimer and Adorno's understanding of the pitfalls of rationalism in their *Dialektik der Aufklärung* (1944). In forging these links to the Frankfurt School, Venturelli also underscored Musil's debt to Nietzsche, in particular Nietzsche's critique of the ethical value scheme of the West and the epistemological positions that underpinned this value scheme. Indeed, Venturelli's comprehensive treatment of the influence of Nietzsche for Musil ranks as one of the most significant achievements of his study. In returning to the question posed by Roth in 1972 of the relative status of artistic and scientific understanding, Venturelli was sanguine about the prospects for reason, despite Horkheimer and Adorno's critique, and idealistic about the status of the work of art. He contended that literature, in presenting an inductive side to science, could represent "ein[em] Feld, auf dem Kunst und Wissenschaft sich gleichzeitig widerspiegeln" (250). At the same time, science's empirical dialogue with natural phenomena presented a deductive side to art in ways that constituted new gains for ethical understanding: "in der Sicht Musils wird die Wissenschaft zu einem ethisch-psychologischen Phänomen, das für die gesamte Anthropologie des modernen Menschen bestimmend ist" (263). Venturelli's study thus set out an approach to Musil that found less instruction in questions of truth than in Musil's attempts to model a new type of ethical understanding.

In constructing a similar approach to Venturelli, Josef Strutz (1984) traced the origins of Musil's ethical project as far back as the eighteenth century. For Strutz, Musil's ethical outlook, which had been worked out in opposition to objective reason, revealed several points of connection with the thought of Immanuel Kant, in particular his second *Critique*, the *Kritik der praktischen Vernunft*. Kant's formalistic approach to knowledge and morality in this work highlighted the importance of a procedural approach to ethical behavior. Musil worked out such an approach through the experimental form of essayistic narration in the novel. The combination Musil envisaged of pure and practical aspects of reason — in Strutz's analysis roughly equivalent to the Musilian terms "ratioïd" and "nichtratioïd" — also revealed the influence of Hegel and, as Venturelli (1980) had previously suggested, especially that of Nietzsche. For Musil, according to Strutz, the path toward synthesis linked analytic (or, following Nietzsche, "nihilistic") aspects with a more positive "activistic" dimension (19). Formulated as the "principle of motivated steps" ("das Prinzip der motovierten Schritte"), Musil's ethics set out a regulative principle for guiding action that sought to overcome Kakania's fatal affliction, the conditions of atrophy Musil described in the novel under the conceptual heading "Seinesgleichen geschieht."

Aldo Gargani's article on philosophy and metaphor appeared alongside Josef Strutz's essay in a collection of essays co-edited by Josef Strutz and Johann Strutz and entitled *Robert Musil — Literatur, Philosophie, Psychologie* and also addressed the problem of ethical understanding. In Gargani's analysis, it was not Kant or Hegel who were of critical importance for Musil, but Nietzsche, whom Gargani characterized above all as a metaphorical thinker. Metaphor, Gargani contended, suspends the "univocality of reason" and of "logicizing thought" (52–56) and leads to a more complex, if equivocal, understanding of the subject's position in the world. Musil's desire to embrace such Nietzsche-inspired metaphorical thinking sought to return a sense of responsibility for action to the subject at a time when the subject's capacity to influence action had been displaced by the "mechanical automatisms" of modern civilization.

In an interesting essay, originally held as a paper to a conference on Musil in Klagenfurt, Austria in 1986, Hans-Georg Pott outlined an approach to Musil's ethics from a Freudian perspective, basing his study in particular on Freud's later works, such as *Die Zukunft einer Illusion* and *Das Unbehagen in der Kultur,* which expressed an overriding cultural pessimism. The problem of an ethical response to the world, accordingly, was whether Freud's picture of the subject shaped by the process of civilization admitted of sufficient free will to make ethical responses even theoretically possible. Musil's understanding of subjectivity, in Pott's judgment, followed Freud exactly on this point: the construction of personality from which such an ethical stance would issue had been "delegated," while the master himself was "absent" (51). A possible answer appeared in the idea of an alternative "ethics of art" not unlike that formulated by Schiller in his *Briefe über die ästhetische Erziehung des Menschen.* This nonrational (but by no means antirational) ethics would reside in the emotions, eschew rule-bound behavior, and gain expression in the communicative quality of art and poetry.

The emergence of ethical criticism in Musil scholarship coincided with a recognition of the importance of Nietzsche, as the studies of Venturelli (1980), Strutz (1984) and Gargani (1984) had shown. Charlotte Dresler-Brumme confirmed this new understanding of the significance of Nietzsche in an important study that appeared in 1987. While endorsing earlier findings that Nietzsche's influence was observable across the full range of Musil's fiction,[8] Dresler-Brumme added the view that Nietzsche's importance for Musil actually increased after 1928 as his work on the major novel intensified (41). Much of this work on Nietzsche, Dresler-Brumme suggested, was directed at working out ethical positions in the novel. In taking over Nietzsche's polemic against rationalistic science, Musil could observe how scientific thought sprang from a control reflex in human beings that diminished what was intuitively valuable about individual human life. The focus on these individual aspects, accordingly, meant celebrating individual life, as well as defending a radically open, creatively inspired, and sometimes even amoral approach to living in the manner advocated by Nietzsche. Even Musil's notion of lack of qualities, Dresler-Brumme argued, was indebted to Nietzsche. The only argument Musil failed to affirm was Nietzsche's idea of the eternal return, which Musil saw as aiding and abetting European nihilism rather than working to attenuate or overcome it (150–54). Later scholars have largely endorsed Dresler-Brumme's insights. Wolfgang Rzehak, for example, agreed on the overall importance of Nietzsche for Musil in his study of 1993. His approach differed from Dresler-Brumme's primarily on matters of emphasis. One such difference concerned the relative status of the intellect and the body. Whereas Nietzsche held to the primacy of the body as the chief factor conditioning human experience, Rzehak argued, Musil accorded priority to the spirit and intellect in working out his ethical response to the world.

Just how far this recognition of Nietzsche's importance had begun to revise the older understanding of Musil can be gauged from Hartmut Böhme's essay of 1986 on the problem of the displaced modern subject. In his earlier study of 1974, Böhme had advocated a socially critical approach to Musil, viewing Musil as a member of the failed *ancien régime* of Austria-Hungary. Now, under the increasing influence of Nietzsche's condemnation of nihilism, Böhme declared reality itself to be defunct. Musil's *Mann ohne Eigenschaften*, at any rate, marked in Böhme's judgment the final departure from art's capacity to render reality through mimetic means. Moreover, the novel — a play of unrelated discourses punctuated by, rather than organized by, aesthetic considerations — had no center, nor any narrative standpoint from which reality was structured. Instead, there were only signs, discourses, and simulacra. For Böhme, a major consequence of the absence of a controlling narrative center was the ubiquity of power — the type of strategic power that Foucault saw as rushing into the gaps exposed by reason's progressive disenchantment of the world. Yet Musil, Böhme argued, drew an altogether different conclusion from the failure of subjects to remain autonomous authors of a rational world: Musil's alternative to self-authored identity consisted in submerging the subject in the Kakanian state like a "partisan of otherness," making lack of qualities a conscious alternative platform (316).[9] Musil's protagonist, therefore, did not abandon the search for happiness despite the encroachments of system, function, and inauthentic life. Instead, Böhme contended, Musil invoked the Other Condition in order to live beyond hegemonic reason and power in the midst of what reason excludes, that is, "das Andere der Vernunft" (323). The sibling lovers pursued this goal, he argued, by entering a type of fourth dimension — flattening out time and elongating it through their discussions into space. This was the "time without qualities" of the essay's title. At the same time, this utopian project of a "thousand year kingdom" of feeling had unsettling parallels with the Nazi aspirations of a similar nature (excluding the elevated discussions!), so Böhme — for all the references to Musil as a precursor of postmodernism — had to reclaim Musil at the end of his essay as a classic exponent both of literary modernism and, paradoxically, of aesthetic resistance to the logic of modernism. In doing so, Böhme also reclaimed the point of departure of his earlier study (1974), for the aporias of reason he had analyzed there were still dominant and failed to forestall the imminence of war and destruction.

By the early nineties, a number of studies — more or less simultaneously — had affirmed the need to reassess Musil's modernism. As long as Musil's novel was seen to be solely directed at questions of truth, Böhme's analysis of the aporias of reason made the case against Musil as a fatally afflicted modernist seem compelling, despite attempts to see positive aspects to subsisting in the "time without qualities." The emerging interest in functionalism and the new understanding of the importance of Nietzsche, however, brought a different Musil into view — a thinker who, as Thomas Harrison now argued in a study of 1992, was concerned "to endow feeling with the same articulatedness enjoyed by thought"; who was not concerned with reductionist systems that measure interpretation by reference to existing phenomena, but who focused on complex "anticipatory" modalities of thought admitting of many interpretations; and, finally, a thinker whose purpose was to "promote virtuality, in the Renaissance sense of virtù: dynamic preparedness, creative ability, ingenuity, resourcefulness, and abstract skill, which also means 'character' as a precondition for decisive action" (166–73). Harrison's approach took the essay as expressive of the plural sense of reality advocated by Musil. The essay functioned, he found, as a "broker" between systematic thought and the observable phenomena language sought to describe (188).

Other critics who argued for a similar brokering of reality under the dual influence of Mach's functionalism and Nietzsche's perspectivism included Marike Finlay, who likened Musil's discussion of plural realities to Werner Heisenberg's "perturbation" in experimental physics (1990, 8). That Musil's pluralism and Heisenberg's perturbation both issued from a principle of "uncertainty" indicated that truth lay less with the outcome of scientific or narrative procedure than with its process. In terms of narrative, it was now the discursive elements of Musil's fiction that took over the problem of conferring legitimacy — at precisely a moment in history when the forces of modernization, "technocratization," dehumanization, and urbanization had occasioned the greatest skepticism about traditional ways of conceptualizing truth. For Finlay, therefore, Musil's attempt to approach the crisis of the referentiality of narrative as a question of "legitimating praxis" was not just a rhetorical procedure of importance to art; it was also an ethical procedure that sought to construct "a social theory based on a modern project of communication as universal pragmatics" at a significant moment in history (12). This communicative project took up Habermas's question of the "unfinished project of modernity," as Venturelli had done in 1980, but in ways that now conferred foundational significance on Musil's "pragmatic turn" toward new forms of social and ethical behavior. As Finlay argued: "[Musil] problematizes the product and the process of narrating/ writing/inscription, but without neglecting the questions of values and ground" (19).

Finlay's study underscored the significance of Musil's turning away from the classical episteme of knowledge, according to which legitimate communication would no longer be made dependent on the coincidence of knowledge and truth, but would arise from the self-validating aspects of discursive praxis. In a 1990 study, Hans-Joachim Völse also considered self-validating processes in Musil's novel, but from the standpoint of deconstruction in the manner of Jacques Derrida, according to which the absence of originary meaning, strictly speaking, was a precondition of every text. In Völse's view, Musil's category of "Möglichkeitssinn" promoted not only plural perspectives; it also signified plurality based on an incipient absence of origin ("Ursprungslosigkeit"). This meant that "Möglichkeitssinn" sought to bring about a "Gleichberechtigung aller Möglichkeiten, die sich gegenseitig in ihrer historischen Bedingtheit enthüllen" (55). While not disavowing an interest in originary thinking altogether, Völse was nevertheless able to enlist Musil's fiction in the service of the deconstructionist project of "knowledge dissemination" rather than the propagation of any single perspective about knowledge. The result was that Musil could also be seen to defend postwar "critical" thinking in Adorno's sense. In arguing against "Wirklichkeitssinn," Musil sought to avoid the "fanatische Vereinseitigung und Hypostasierung der bestehenden Wirklichkeit" (55) that had befallen totalizing thought, and yet to cultivate a tolerance for the ambivalence and ambiguity that arose from plural perspectives. The organizing principle of "Möglichkeitssinn," he held, was the idea of exactness borrowed from science. To this extent, Musil unfolded "eine kommunikative Form der Wissenslegitimierung [. . .], deren Kernpunkt die Anwendung des wissenschaftlichen Regeldiskurses auf die soziale Pragmatik ist" (256).

For Francesca Pennisi (1990), the ethical dimension of Musil's project centered above all on the issue of order in the novel. This issue had both a formal and a content aspect. The formal aspect was linked to the way Musil set about creatively structuring his narrative. The content aspect dealt with the characters' own understanding of order. Here Pennisi considered positions taken up by General Stumm von Bordwehr and Ulrich (or, in the context of early versions of the novel, Anders/Ulrich). Where Bordwehr was driven by a belief in ontological aspects of order, Anders/Ulrich's understanding of order appeared more functionalist in outlook and was developed, Pennisi contended, under the influence of Mach and Nietzsche. This functional aspect of order represented the key to understanding the overall problem of order in the novel. Pennisi then considered the order of chapters of the novel — an issue that had vexed Musil scholarship throughout the postwar period. In the older dispute in Musil scholarship over Frisé's first postwar edition of the novel, the ordering of chapters had largely been a matter of establishing the "right" chronology by sifting through the mixture of chapter variants from different periods.[10] For Pennisi, by contrast, the order of chapters was really a question of how Musil worked. She demonstrated that Musil wrote experimentally, exploring various conceptual approaches to the same questions, but in ways that did not necessarily attribute greater value to later drafts of chapters and part-chapters. Pennisi thus accorded relatively little significance to the historical-critical principles on which Bausinger's 1964 study and other older assumptions about the genesis of the novel had been based. The progress of Musil's novel, she argued, instead depended on the extent to which Musil was able to bring a problem in the narrative to a sense of ordered conceptual resolution.

The difficulties that prevented Musil from concluding the novel indicated, in Pennisi's judgment, an underlying "paradox of order." Pennisi saw this paradox in Musil's attempt to construe ever more complex and problematic dimensions to reality through the category of "Möglichkeitssinn" on the formal level of the narrative: "Das Paradoxon als Form soll aussagen, daß die Synthese, die das paradoxe Bild gestaltet, unmöglich erfüllbar ist. Sie lebt als Versuch, Aufgabe, Öffnung, Versprechen, ja als Gleichnis" (59).[11] In following an open conception of the narrative, Pennisi asked whether dominant modes of thinking stemmed from surface reality (in which case, war was to be considered in redemptive terms as an "erlösende[r] Gedanke"[12]), or whether, as Schrödinger's model of thermodynamics suggested, thought sought disorder as its ultimate object, in which case order was largely a contingent proposition in the novel. Pennisi favored the second road on this problem. Rejecting an all-too-transparent rationality, Musil's solution to the problem of order was to make order take account of the feeling disposition of individual human beings in the realm of art. The order that Musil envisaged, Pennisi further averred, attempted to construe epiphanic moments of coincidence between feeling and cognitive understanding (151).

Altmann's study of 1992 sought to evaluate what he termed the ontological aspects of the Other Condition, asking whether it constituted "eine zweite *Wirklichkeit* tatsächlichen Wissens," that is, a "Kategorie, deren Wahrheitsgehalt letztlich in der unmittelbaren Erfahrung selbst begründet liegt" (19). This was an important question for ethical approaches, since it assumed that Musil's utopia was meant as a guide for human experience and sought points of real connection with it. Distinguishing between the "normative" structure of Kakanian reality and the "real" reality of the Other Condition, Altmann characterized the ethical thinking Musil promoted in the Other Condition as "ein Denken, das in seiner ästhetischen Orientierung zugleich multiperspektivisch strukturiert ist" (224).

Werner Ego's study under the title *Abschied von der Moral* (1992) was originally presented for examination as a doctoral thesis in the theological faculty of the University of Tübingen in 1989–90. It can be considered one of the most comprehensive analyses of Musil's ethical system and the first such analysis undertaken from a theological point of view (although theology was the focus of the study only in the last chapter). Ego contended that conventional moral positions for Musil were no more than a point of departure for an ethical discussion of infinitely greater complexity. In directing attention away from morality to ethics, Musil attempted to set out an alternative morality that would draw upon reason and emotion in equal measure and at the same time leave behind the more ossified aspects of a rigidly rationalistic, "technical" application of moral positions. Whereas morality was reckoned by Kant to belong to the sphere of practical reason, Ego linked ethics to the more intuitive and less schematic area of aesthetic judgment (from Kant's third *Critique*), which, while not eschewing rational notions altogether, was grounded above all in individual responses to the world. The ethical attitude Musil advocated was expressed in the utopian aspects of the Other Condition, where Ego saw a type of union of the true, the good, and the beautiful. Significantly, this Other Condition, though informed by aesthetic considerations, was in fact shaped by a profoundly confessional and even open religious aspect. It was this confessional quality of belief, Ego argued, that gave the Other Condition its status and efficacy as a new type of ethical outlook on the world.

Ego's study also drew in fruitful ways on the critique of "instrumental reason" outlined in the work of Heidegger, Horkheimer and Adorno, and in French poststructuralism. In sketching Musil's rationalist critique of the knowledge project of the Enlightenment, Ego indicated that Musil's abandonment of conventional morality arose from a sense of disquiet at reason's complicity with power and violence.[13] Ego called the ethical system Musil favored a "Meliorationsmoral," since it was aimed at ameliorating the technical effects of rational thinking while seeking points of contact with the antimetaphysical trajectory of Mach's thinking (to which Musil was known to be sympathetic) (128–51). It was Musil's underlying purpose to counter the secularization in human life evident since Aristotle and particularly apparent since the beginnings of European modernity. Here Musil did not oppose reason as such, but only the science of "economical reason," which Ego defined as the drive to analyze the world in terms of the smallest possible units of comprehension in pursuit of scientific transparency. Instead of knowledge and overtly rational science, therefore, Musil advocated both the passion of belief founded on individual responses to the world and a type of methodical intuition. Ego's study, in this way, uncovered genuine moments of illumination for modern theology in Musil's major novel.

The new interest in Musil's ethical outlook from the late eighties on accorded fundamental importance to Musil's reception of Gestalt theory. As a doctoral student of philosophy and psychology at the University of Berlin, Musil had been exposed to the research environment from which the discovery of "Gestalt formations" as conditioning influences on perception had initially emerged. In his own study of the philosopher Ernst Mach for his dissertation, Musil had investigated the physio-psychological parallelism that directly anticipated Gestalt theory. Discussions with two friends who were later to become Gestalt psychologists, Gustav Johannes von Allesch and Erich von Hornbostel, further added to Musil's knowledge about this new field of research. The basic principles of Gestalt thinking were developed into a coherent theory in two separate schools of research at the University of Berlin and the University of Graz in the period from 1912 to 1920.

Mejovsek's essay of 1987 and Luserke's investigation of possibility and modality, published in the same year, were two studies to register the importance of Gestalt theory for an understanding of Musil's ethical project. Other investigations were subsequently undertaken by Maier-Solgk (1992), Hickman (1992), Kaiser-El-Safti (1993), Berz (1993), Hoffmann (1997), and Loenker (1997). The first comprehensive study of Gestalt theory in Musil was Silvia Bonacchi's full-length study of 1998, which is still the most comprehensive analysis of the subject.

According to Bonacchi, Musil's interest in Gestalt theory arose from a concern about the failure of the empirical sciences to reach true enlightenment on the nature of human life. Despite Nietzsche's invocation to live life to the full in the here-and-now and the dramatic advances of experimental physics in the first decade of the twentieth century in the shape of Einstein's theory of relativity, Musil had been disturbed by the persistent forces of nihilism in his own age and the failure of science to provide insights about the moral dimension of human life. Musil's awareness of this crisis of science and the humanities in his own time emboldened him to apply the advances in empirical methodology suggested by Gestalt theory to human problems, and specifically to the moral and ethical discussion about human action in the realm of art. What particularly suggested Gestalt methodology for art, Bonacchi contended, was the prospect of making sense of the complex layering of experience observable in everyday life. Art, to this extent, paralleled the interest of Gestalt theory in certain modes of complex perception. From 1909 to 1911, Musil explored the complex interaction of emotional and rational impulses that lay behind Gestalt theory in the two early novellas of *Vereinigungen*. In the twenties, Bonacchi argued, Musil's interest in Gestalt theory remained buoyant, and began to underpin an increasing preoccupation with the ideal of a "new human being" — an ideal Musil first explored in essays written at this time (and consciously set out in his first play *Die Schwärmer*). Then, in *Der Mann ohne Eigenschaften*, Gestalt theory became inseparable from Musil's conception of literature and from the moral ideas underlying it. The theory of feeling expounded in the novel by way of lengthy disquisitions of the protagonist, Bonacchi showed, remained indebted to positions derived from the Berlin and Graz schools of Gestalt research, while simultaneously pointing beyond them: "Ulrichs Theorie des Gefühls bettet sich in die Tradition der deskriptiven Psychologie von Franz Brentano, Alexius Meinong, Carl Stumpf, Max Scheler und der Gestalttheorie [. . .]. Zugleich geht Musils Theorie des Gefühls über die deskriptive Psychologie hinaus und mündet in ein umfassendes Menschen- und Weltbild" (341–42).

Astrid Zingel (1999) followed in Venturelli's (1980/88) and Finlay's (1990) footsteps in returning to the question of Musil's "discursive modernity," that is, to the ongoing debate in Musil's novel about the social organization of modern life. Zingel's focus was the relationship between the siblings Ulrich and Agathe. Abandoning the question of incest and judgments about the morality of Ulrich and Agathe's relationship — questions that had preoccupied older scholarship — Zingel saw Agathe not as any imaginary offshoot of Ulrich ("die psychologische Disposition des männlichen Titelhelden" [8]), nor, as Luserke had suggested (1987, 158), as Ulrich's unexplored other self, but rather as a character in her own right. As this fully fleshed-out character, she stimulated and provoked Ulrich, questioning and even undermining his judgments as well as his sense of self. In so doing, she encouraged Ulrich to renounce his "Wissenschaftsseite" and engage directly in life with his whole person. To this extent, the relationship between brother and sister in the novel expressed new ways of envisioning social coexistence in modern society:

> Die Forderung nach einer "Systematik des Zusammenlebens" impliziert die Frage danach, wie Gemeinschaften aussehen müßten, die eine friedliche Koexistenz ermöglichen, Geborgenheit und gleichzeitig Freiheit geben und nicht als Bündelung der Egoismen der einzelnen Mitglieder eine Gefahr für ihre Umgebung darstellen. (100)

Zingel saw significance in the fact that Ulrich and Agathe had been separated from one another before the onset of puberty. They resumed their relationship in a way that allowed for an erotic attachment, which in turn promoted the kind of mutual support typical of sympathetic attachments within the philosophical schools of the ancient Greeks (107–8). The individual and mythic qualities in this relationship, taken together, led in her view to a social utopia that attempted to imagine what might be possible in the coming together of men and women. This utopian project opposed the functional relationships characteristic of Kakanian society. Zingel therefore concluded: "Das Zusammenleben der

Geschwister ist ein Gemeinschaftsprojekt, das der 'Welt des Seinesgleichen' entgegengesetzt wird" (200).

In focusing on the relationship between Ulrich and Agathe, Zingel's study expressed the new interest of feminist criticism in evaluating gender relations in Musil's work. A noteworthy addition to these approaches was a study by Marja Rauch (2000) that made the various "Vereinigungen" depicted in Musil's work a question of importance not simply for gender relations, but also for the ethical trajectory of Musil's project. In a study that examined the novellas of *Vereinigungen* and *Drei Frauen* alongside passages from the third part of *Der Mann ohne Eigenschaften*, Rauch concluded:

> Das Vereinigungsmotiv, das an das Platonische Symposion anknüpft, meint demnach den Versuch, eine erotische Erfahrung mit einem mystischen Einheitsgefühl zu verknüpfen, das zugleich den Ansatz für eine Moral geben könnte, in der das Ich einen neuen Platz fände. (183)

The critique of rational understanding put forward by Nietzsche in the late nineteenth century and by Heidegger in the early twentieth century raised important questions about what rationality systematically excluded, namely "the passions." In Heidegger's view, rational understanding might tell us a considerable amount about the content of our minds and its functional organization, but might not illuminate much about the makeup of the world beyond us, or, indeed, how our body is intuitively tied to that world. Uwe Maier addressed this problem in a 1999 study by investigating Musil's philosophy of feeling. In a far-reaching, sophisticated argument that revealed an acquaintance with skeptical traditions of thought as well as empirical theories of feeling, Maier took a noticeably Weberian line on modernity's crisis by asking how the subject structures her or his existence in a life-world dominated and "disenchanted" by technology.[14] This question became the point of departure for inquiring into the role played by subjective emotions in the structuring of identity. For Maier, feelings evince a level of subjective authenticity (since emotional experience is present only to the subject) and are in some way beyond the reach of epistemological models of understanding. He therefore asked: Does emotion function as a reference point for the subject's experience of reality and provide a valuable way of articulating subjective identity? Or does emotion, in the final analysis, merely tie the subject to practical, and possibly merely mundane, aspects of living? For Maier, a clue to the significance of this "emotional factor" in approaching Musil ("der emotionale Faktor" — Musil's term: cf. *TB II*, 927) was the manner in which subjective feeling had been viewed in social anthropology.

He undertook for this reason an examination of the work of Simmel, Durkheim, and Scheler,[15] who wrote immediately before or at the same time as Musil and, like Musil, became vitally interested in the question of feeling.[16] Maier also accorded significance to the ideas of Ernst Mach, who had advocated a subject-based, emotionally intuitive approach to understanding in the last quarter of the nineteenth century.[17] Maier then set out the phenomenological, anthropological, sociological, and psychological dimensions of Musil's "historical-genetic" approach to feeling. Here he was led by the assumption that, as cognitive understanding develops over time and traditional thinking breaks down, the disposition of feeling becomes an increasingly important faculty in the human being. In following this assumption, he distanced himself from other approaches, in particular that of Gerhard Meisel, who had highlighted scientific aspects in Musil's novel, or, as he put it, "Wissenschaft mit Erkenntnisanspruch" (1991, 7). In rejecting this view of the importance of science, Maier emphasized the ethical direction of Musil's thinking.

A key part of Maier's analysis was the Other Condition, which he interpreted as a genuine dialogue of the emotions with real life. Here bodily sensation played the crucial role: "Der Rückzug auf den Körper als Medium der Gefühle wird zu einer zentralen Strategie, bei der sich das Subjekt noch als 'wahr' erfahren kann" (1999, 96). This centering of responses to the world on actual physical sensations, however, sought to connect contingently "real" behavior with higher forms of ethical "orientation": "Musil und die von ihm geschaffenen Protagonisten suchen nach einer Orientierung, in der sich 'Mehr und Anderes' zum Vorhandenen und Vordergründigen andeutet, ohne den Boden der Tatsachen verlassen zu wollen." (1996, 127) In assessing this approach to life, Maier showed how Musil broke with causality in developing a new ideal of ethical behavior — "das Prinzip der motivierten Schritte." Maier defined this principle as the degree to which the emotional quality of a feeling can arouse an ethical disposition in the subject. Maier demonstrated that this new philosophy of feeling was founded on Musil's deep study of "apperception" (since Kant) and Gestalt theory (since Wertheimer and Köhler). Piaget's notion that the interaction of emotion and cognition played an important role in the growth of the subject was also accorded importance.

Sabine Döring postulated a link between Musil's poetics and his ethics, proclaiming at the start of her 1999 study: "die Erkenntnis des Dichters [ist] Erkenntnis des Ethischen" (10). Her analysis of Musil's philosophy of feeling, around which this assumption about the connectedness of poetry and ethics was forged, represented — despite outward appearances — a departure from earlier studies, such as that of Roth (1972), which had seen connections between scientific and artistic discourses. By contrast, Döring was drawn less to the question of the general influence of scientific discourses and more to specific positions that had been developed in opposition to the comprehensive rationality of scientific thinking — in particular, the tradition of holistic thinking that had grown out of the functionalism of Ernst Mach and Henri Bergson. While the influence of holistic approaches on Musil is well known as a result of the many studies on Gestalt theory, Doering offered fresh perspectives on two less prominent Gestalt theorists, Kurt Lewin and Heinrich Hertz. She also considered the influence on Musil of the Vienna Circle of linguistic philosophy, notably Carnap, Popper, and Wittgenstein. Her argument was built around an analysis of the "Druckfahnen-kapitel" — the chapters Musil took back from the publisher after they had been typeset in 1938 and then reworked until his death in 1942. These twenty chapters, as well as the unpublished variations to them penned by Musil in the last years of his life, Döring contended, contained Musil's most important thoughts about the conceptual aspects of human emotions.

In evaluating the influence of Kurt Lewin's theory of the emotions, Döring showed that Musil had been impressed with Lewin's broad definition of emotion. Lewin had described the process by which a dominant emotion eventually overcomes a range of conflicting lesser emotions. Musil was also drawn to the cognitive quality of the emotions evident in Heinrich Hertz's theories, which suggested an alternative to the rigidly rational understanding of scientific method. Döring's argument took on Nietzschean dimensions by stressing that science (in Nietzsche's words: "the will to truth at any price") was animated by an underlying emotion: "Für Musil kann es keinen nicht-emotionalen menschlichen Zustand geben; vielmehr setzt, anders als gemeinhin angenommen, sogar das wissenschaftliche Erkennen Gefühle voraus" (1999, 94). Döring then linked Musil's theory of emotions to analytical theories of language, that is, theories that assume the priority of language over thought. She found, against Arvon's view of 1970, that Musil not only esteemed the work of the logical positivists; his theory of the emotions also revealed their insistent influence (118–19). Carnap's verificationist theories and Popper's principle of falsifiability played an especially significant role in helping Musil appreciate the role of the emotions in establishing ethical positions. As Döring held in relation to Popper, falsifiability relativizes (even artificializes) truth in the direction of logic and method; falsifiable statements can therefore only claim an indirect link to the world. By contrast, for Musil, the emotions, while arguably deficient in truth content, connected the individual subject with great immediacy to contingent life. The emotions therefore bore on every question about human actions and the possibility of an order of feeling that might issue from them.

Notes

[1] Charles Alteri, "From Expressivist Aesthetics to Expressivist Ethics," in *Literature and the Question of Philosophy*, edited by Anthony J. Cascardi (Baltimore and London: Johns Hopkins UP, 1987), 137.

[2] Ulrich Karthaus, "Musil-Forschung und Musil-Deutung. Ein Literaturbericht," *Deutsche Vierteljahrsschrift für Literaturwissenschaft und Geistesgeschichte* 39, 3 (1965): 441–83.

[3] Luserke differentiated between four modes of possibility ultimately derived from Kant: "the really real," "the really possible," "the possibly real," and "the possibly possible." Cf. Luserke, *Wirklichkeit und Möglichkeit: Modaltheoretische Untersuchungen zum Werk Robert Musils* (Frankfurt am Main: Peter Lang, 1987).

[4] Cf. Arnold Gehlen, "Zeit-Bilder," in *Zur Soziologie und Ästhetik der modernen Malerei* (Frankfurt am Main: Klostermann, 1965²). See also Arnold Gehlen, *Über kulturelle Kristallisation: Studien zur Anthropologie und Soziologie* (Neuwied and Berlin: Luchterhand, 1963).

[5] Michel Foucault, *L'Archéologie du savoir* (Paris: Gallimard, 1969); *The Archaeology of Knowledge*, trans. A. M. Sheridan Smith (New York: Harper and Row, 1972).

[6] Jean-François Lyotard, *La Condition postmoderne: Rapport sur le savoir* (Paris: Minuit, 1970); translated as *The Postmodern Condition: A Report on Knowledge*, trans. Geoff Bennington and Brian Massumi (Minneapolis: U of Minnesota P), 1984.

[7] Martin Menges, a proponent of existential critique, held to precisely such a view when he maintained: "Ich meine in der Tat, daß Ulrich im 'anderen Zustand' u.a. genau das sucht, was ihm weder der Lebensalltag noch das Dasein nach Art der Wissenschaften geben könnte: nämlich Wahrheit — und zwar absolute, nicht-vermittelte, unmittelbare Wahrheit. Er sucht in den mystischen Erlebnissen nicht primär das Glück einer ekstatischen Selbstentgrenzung, sondern 'Wissen' im genauen Sinne des Wortes [. . .]" — Cf. Menges, *Abstrakte Welt und Eigenschaftslosigkeit: Eine Interpretation von Robert Musils "Der Mann ohne Eigenschaften" unter dem Leitbegriff der Abstraktion* (Frankfurt am Main: Peter Lang, 1982), 194–95). A similar outlook was supported by Philip Beard in his article "Clarisse und Moosbrugger vs. Ulrich/Agathe: Der 'andere Zustand' aus neuer Sicht," *Modern Austrian Literature* 9 (3/4, 1976): 114–30.

[8] In particular, those findings of Ingo Seidler ("Das Nietzschebild Robert Musils," *Deutsche Vierteljahrsschrift für Literaturwissenschaft und Geistesgeschichte* 39/3 [1965]: 329–49) and Renate von Heydebrand (*Die Reflexionen Ulrichs in Robert Musils Roman "Der Mann ohne Eigenschaften": Ihr Zusammenhang mit dem zeitgenössischen Denken* [Münster: Aschendorff, 1966]).

[9] "nicht identifizierbar sein, untertauchen im 'Seinesgleichen geschieht' wie ein Partisan der Alterität; leben wir die Figur in einem Buch, sich also zur Fiktion machen, zur Simulation, zum Phantom werden [. . .] die Eigenschaftlosigkeit zum Programm erheben [. . .]." Hartmut Böhme, "Die 'Zeit ohne Eigenschaften' und die 'Neue Übersichtlichkeit.' Robert Musil und die *posthistoire*," in Johann and Josef Strutz, eds., *Kunst, Wissenschaft, und Politik von Robert Musil bis Ingeborg Bachmann* (Munich, Salzburg: Fink, 1986), 316.

[10] Pennisi explained her approach as not reconstructing individual periods of Musil's development as a writer, "das heißt nicht mehr schlicht abstrakt systematisch vorzugehen, sondern den Schwerpunkt auf die Rekonstruktion der Entstehungsgeschichte von Ideen und Motiven quer durch die verschiedenen Phasen zu legen." Pennisi, *Auf der Suche nach Ordnung: Die Entstehungsgeschichte des Ordnungsgedanken bei Robert Musil von den ersten Romanentwürfen bis zum ersten Band von "Mann ohne Eigenschaften,"* (St. Ingbert: Röhrig, 1990), 24. Zingel subsequently endorsed this approach. Astrid Zingel, *Ulrich u. Agathe. Das Thema der Geschwisterliebe in Robert Musils Romanprojekt "Der Mann ohne Eigenschaften."* (St. Ingbert: Röhrig, 1999), 16.

[11] Cf. Arntzen (*Satirischer Stil in Robert Musils "Der Mann ohne Eigenschaften,"* [Bonn: Bouvier, 1960], 4), for whom the constitution of order in Musil becomes "eine unabschließbare Aufgabe."

[12] Note that an earlier title of *Der Mann ohne Eigenschaften* had been "Der Erlöser."

[13] Here the argument may be made that Musil was forced to recognize, as Heidegger was also to recognize in *Der Satz vom Grund,* that rationality is ultimately groundless, which is to say there is no provable objective argument that either empirically or logically precedes it.

[14] "Wie verabeitet das Subjekt diese Situation? Zu welcher Selbstbestimmung findet es in einer von subjektivischen Mächten befreiten und in diesem Sinne 'entzauberten Welt'?" Uwe Maier, *Sinn und Gefühl in der Moderne: Zu Robert Musils Gefühlstheorie und einer Soziologie der Emotionen* (Aachen: Starker Verlag, 1999), 5.

[15] Cf. *TB I*, 918–19: "Wichtig, daß ich mich wohl immer mit Ethik befassen wollte, aber keinen/Zugang wußte, der mir gepaßt hätte. M.a.W. daß ich zu wenig studiert hatte! — denn Scheler hat den Zugang gefunden!" Scheler combined the view that ethics was largely a matter of feeling (from Brentano) with Husserl's phenomenology, and believed that "many ethical values could be intuited from a conscious show or 'immediacy of essences' [*Wesensschau*]": Cf. Michio Imai, "Musil between Mach and Stumpf," in *Ernst Mach's Vienna 1895–1930. Or Phenomenalism as Philosophy of Science,* edited by J. Blackmore, R. Itagaki, and S. Tanaka (Dordrecht, Boston, London: Kluwer, 2001), 201.

[16] Michio Imai wrote: "While it is conceivable that Musil could have read Max Scheler's doctoral dissertation and Habilitationsschrift and even his withdrawn book on logic published in 1903, it seems probable that he could only have noticed the partial similarities in their value-ethical outlook with the publication of Max Scheler's major work which came out from 1913 to 1916." ("Musil between Mach and Stumpf," 2001, 202). Also, William Johnston wrote that Musil blamed rationality for thwarting self-fulfillment (*The Austrian Mind* [Berkeley: U of California P, 1972], 392).

[17] Cf. Uwe Maier: "Auch wenn er an dessen Denken die Leugnung der naturalen Voraussetzungen kritisiert, imponiert ihm Machs Versuch, den klassischen Antagonismus von Geist und Natur zu überwinden" (1999, 136).

6: The Information of Communication

*Was unsre geistige Lage kennzeichnet und
bestimmt, ist aber gerade der nicht mehr zu
bewältigende Reichtum an Inhalten, das
angeschwollene Tatsachenwissen [. . .], dieses
Auseinanderfließen der Erfahrung an der
Oberfläche der Natur, das Unübersehbare,
das Chaos des Nichtwegzuleugnenden. [. . .]
Wir werden daran zugrunde gehn oder als
ein seelisch stärkerer Menschenschlag es überwinden. (GW 8, 1045)*

LITERARY CRITICISM IN THE postwar period has been marked by two
major shifts of emphasis. On the one hand, views resting on the
authority of the author were displaced in the early postwar period by a
wider interest in the social aspects of writing — particularly with respect
to the novel. By the early 1970s, questions focused on the individual and
individual identity had to some extent given way to a concern about the
social whole, and, increasingly, the directions being pursued by that
social whole. This new emphasis on social concerns, however, did not
end all interest in the author, although it certainly appeared to weaken
it. Writers could no longer be trusted as self-conscious authors of individual experience — in fact their self-consciousness was seen as part of
the problem. In the aesthetic discussion of writing in the postwar period,
the self-consciousness of authors was increasingly linked to the issue of
textual production, rather than to the nature of the authorial sensibility
that informed it. For this reason, a second "slippage" — from work of
literature to text, or from the work of art to the art of (literary) work —
took place as the interest in the nature of literary production gained a
foothold in the postwar period. This new point of emphasis also emerged
as an attempt to express the increasingly complex nature of the reading
experience. Texts — especially significant works of literature such as
Musil's major novel — no longer evinced a reliable sense of individual or
social reality, but were shimmeringly perspectival in outlook, delivering
sense and nonsense in equal proportion, and in turn demanding strategies of high complexity in order to approach them. Whether the goal of
deciphering a final sense of truth in such complexly perspectival literature

is realizable has more and more been resolved in the negative in the aesthetic discussion of literature in the postwar period.

The increasingly widespread recognition that texts do not deliver an objective sense of truth has given a new set of goals to the reading experience. This is particularly the case with *Der Mann ohne Eigenschaften*. In ethical criticism, the failure to discover any final truth in Musil's novel actually meant a liberation, since it allowed Musil's writing to be read as a series of experiments that modeled scenarios of moral order in the world. That such order never finally eventuated — or arose, at best, provisionally — only made the search for moral order and a deeper ethical disposition toward the world seem more compelling. Although ethical approaches did not renounce an interest in aesthetic questions altogether, these questions were certainly not viewed with the same sense of urgency. Again, this entailed a type of liberation, since those aspects of communication that had always been accorded prominence in literary criticism could now be seen for what they were — not the vehicles of truth-creation of self-conscious authors, but procedural aspects by which sense is generated discursively in fiction. For this reason, the emergence of ethical criticism in Musil studies in the 1980s was accompanied by a new type of literary response founded on an understanding of the way literature is constituted as a system of communication. Literary texts, from this perspective, were nothing more than a special class of texts that organized communication in notable ways. They concentrated information into knowledge, but also disseminated information — much as Jacques Derrida's notion of deconstruction had suggested. The moments of insight they assembled, therefore, could equally be dissembled and viewed without distortion as particular arrangements of textual sense under the sway of certain dominant ideas. The new accent on communication that arose in the mid to late eighties — Friedrich Kittler's 1985 study *Aufschreibesysteme 1800/1900* marked the arrival of this new approach in the scholarly mainstream — thus sought points of contact with the postmodern discussion of literature, even as it broadened the parameters of this discussion in significant ways.

One of the first works of criticism to take up this new interest in literary communication in the context of Robert Musil was Frithard Scholz's study of 1982. Scholz was not attracted to poststructuralist positions in the first instance, but instead drew on the early systems theory of Niklas Luhmann. Scholz engaged with Luhmann's starting assumption about the way communication had been organized in "old European" society. According to Luhmann, communication had functioned until the eighteenth century in a highly stratified and hierarchical manner on the basis of uncontested and unreflected age-old tradition. From 1800 on, the supports of such tradition, which had been augmented since the early eighteenth century by an idea of the coincidence of social organization and ontological reality, were progressively weakened. The new idea of social communication that began to emerge over the course of the nineteenth and early twentieth centuries was founded on functional notions of the organization of information. In Luhmann's view, the emergence of "functional differentiation," including the vital distinction between "system" and "environment," or "internal" or "self reference" and "external/foreign reference," were crucial components of a form of social organization that marked off modern European society from its older predecessor. As Scholz's study of Luhmann's systems theory now implied, Musil's work was composed against the background of the transition to modern society and reflected this transition in particular ways. Moreover, as Arvon had observed in 1970, Musil's thinking had been enlivened from the beginning by the distinction between causally based ontological understanding and the new functionalist outlook. That — as Arvon also suggested — Musil had not been able to resolve the tension between ontology and functionalism was only further proof that he exactly mirrored the transition from old Europe to modern Europe in his writings.[1]

The discussion of this new idea of information organization was carried further by Pierre Zima and Reinhard Pietsch in the mid to late eighties. Zima focused attention on Musil's criticism of language in an essay that appeared in 1985 and in a longer study on Proust, Kafka, and Musil that appeared in French in 1988. The structures of ambivalence Zima observed were not directed at rediscovering the anguished and socially alienated Musil of existential critique, but rather focused on the way communication in Musil's fiction was rendered "polyphonic" by an internal process of self-reflection. As such, they revealed an interest in how the text as information was internally organized, and, equally, how it was subject to deconstruction. As with Zima's two studies, Reinhard Pietsch's 1988 analysis of "self-implicatory structures" drew on the work of Jacques Derrida to demonstrate the way texts resist readings that aim to distill from them unambiguous meaning. Pietsch showed that terms that have become commonplace in Musil criticism, such as "Nachlaß," "torso," "fragment," and "quotation," registered the novel's awareness of its own self-organization. These "self-implicatory structures" problematized every level of narration in the text: the problem of the author's relationship to the work of art, the difference between strategies of reading and strategies of writing, and the problem of the generation of a literary text through a process of quotation from previous texts. In the case of the descriptor "torso," Pietsch further argued that the phallus, and the moment of creation it suggested, was notably absent from Musil's understanding of art. In this way, Musil's novel set up a sophisticated dialogue of self-reflection that communicated the partial nature of its own structures of communication. This again provided confirmation of earlier findings: the promise of ontologically reliable sense in Musil's novel was undercut by a metatextual reflection in the novel about the problem of the communication in literary writing.

By the early 1990s, Musil criticism in this emerging field of information theory had been drawn to considering a range of new questions. Hans-Dieter Zimmermann (1990) opened up debate about the nature and function of language in an age of technology, Berz (1993) discussed Erich Ludwig von Hornborstel's experiments with acoustic and optical perception and whether Musil's novel could be read as a series of inverted "I-Welten," and Meisel (1991), in view of the new paradigm shift in scientific discourses at the start of the twentieth century, considered Musil's attempt to communicate a new concept of love in the "scientific age." Significantly, Meisel ascribed importance to the activity of poets as agents of knowledge dissemination: "Mit [dem] poetologischen Eingriff in den Strom des Wissens sind die Vorgehensweisen von literarischem Autor und Informatiker nahezu identisch" (290). While this view of the author as "Informatiker" added a new dimension to the author's poetic activity, it also undermined the author's traditional status as an arbiter of taste and a mediator of beauty — notions that had stabilized the role of poets in old European society. Meisel's study was the first comprehensive attempt to dissemble this old notion of the poet's function in society, and, equally, the first to see notions of love and beauty in terms of their functional or information value, rather than as yardsticks by which life as an ontological proposition had to be measured. Moreover, in light of Meisel's insistence on the importance of scientific discourses in Musil's work, love and beauty were immediately made subject to the same conditions of order and disorder that obtained in the wider physical universe, and, with reference to Schrödinger's theory of thermodynamics, particularly subject to the forces of dispersal of information at work in such a universe.

That notions of love and beauty were constituted or could be eroded by the operation of scientific laws already suggested a profound movement away from ethical criticism, which had treated these and other humanistic concepts in terms of their moral value — their capacity to add to or subtract from the value of human life. Value, for ethical criticism, was not a proposition that had any necessary connection with the physical universe, except in the special instance of holistic notions such as Gestalt theory, which provided for a moment of coalescence not entirely open to rational understanding.[2] The radical aspect of Musil's functional poetics in communication theory, by contrast, accorded no priority to notions of value that circulated freely in some kind of ethical domain. Rather, the internal organization of a system or subsystem in a wider social environment emerged by the same process of functional differentiation that held for the evolution of organisms in the natural world. To this extent, the laws that were operative for organic life also held for notions of social organization. This startlingly new idea animated Laurence Dahan-Gaida's short study of 1993/94.[3] Dahan-Gaida sought to apply the physical principles governing thermodynamics to the problem of narration. The predilection for disorder observable in physical systems was also operative, Dahan-Gaida argued, for narrative. Indeed, Musil's unfinished novel had enacted these physical laws in precise ways, since the principle of order in the novel had not been able to establish itself over the disorder it also unleashed, as the very opening image of the novel (a description of the law of thermodynamics in reference to a meteorological system) had already made clear. Dahan-Gaida concluded: "Der immer wieder unterbrochene Faden der Erzählung zerfällt in vielfältige Möglichkeiten, die ohne definitive Auswahl dargestellt werden" (130).

Krommer and Kümmel (1993/94) also undertook a notable attempt to apply information theory to Musil's novel. They drew links between Musil's notion of "Möglichkeitsdenken" and the communication theorist Shannon's information theory. In Shannon's view, the informational content of a particular situation is a function of the amount of free choice available in such a situation. As more possibilities emerge, Shannon had argued, a situation becomes more highly charged, but also more unstable, and is therefore more likely to discharge entropically. What results, Krommer and Kümmel found, is a restatement of the modernist problem by which an event or situation is no longer comprehensible, but merely "interpretable": "je lauter das Rauschen in der Leitung, desto informationshaltiger wird die Verbindung, die allerdings das nicht mehr leistet, was ihren Zweck darstellte: Verstehen zwischen Sender und Empfänger" (159). Krommer and Kümmel further established that Musil's novel was wholly governed by entropic forces. Their analysis of the first chapter of the novel revealed that the human being was the first casualty of entropic processes — from the very outset of the narrative: "Der Mensch kommt erst dann in den Blick, wenn er schon keiner mehr ist, sondern nur noch eine Leiche" (162).

If Krommer and Kümmel had buried the body of subjective aware-ness, Ekkehard Schreiter (1994) applied a conceptual figure from the technical realm ("Verkehr") in order to comprehend the nature of such disembodied experience. His approach was therefore not informed by any notion of ontological reality perceptible to subjects. The "Verkehrs-formen" Schreiter adduced, such as money, mental states, and language, instead represented informational states that evinced — as it were, phe-nomenologically — moments of identity formation in the novel. That identity as a form of coalescence of entities was resisted on the level of narration was an important finding of Schreiter's study. He argued that the chapter variations and fragments Musil had excluded from the novel in the process of writing had nevertheless impinged on the published, "authorized" version. (This idea that the unpublished notes of a particu-lar work excluded by the author under a principle of economy has also been argued — with greater justification — about the economical style of Ernest Hemingway.[4]) Schreiter's study therefore set out to show "wie und mit welchen Mitteln sich *gerade der autorisierte* MoE der Identität des geschlossenen Werkes zu entziehen sucht" (15). Schreiter's study thus upheld earlier findings about the entropic nature of Musil's narration.

Angela Maria Kochs, in her study of 1996, attached great signifi-cance to the open information systems observable in Musil's novel. Musil lived at a time when fundamental insights from science, such as quantum mechanics and the theory of relativity, were changing what was known about the makeup of physical life. In Koch's analysis, Musil's novel re-flected such changes in notable ways. In reconstructing aspects of the historical and philosophical background to the novel, Kochs showed how such complexity emerged from simple beginnings — the world of sev-enteenth- and eighteenth-century Enlightenment values where human beings saw themselves as a type of "divine machine" programmatically embracing the search for freedom and truth. As the European world industrialized and became steadily more complex, statistical analysis and probability theory took on significance as ways to make sense of the emerging paradoxes of modern life. In the preponderance of open sys-tems characterizing modernity, Kochs then argued, chaos theory was of relevance to art as a conceptual model on four main grounds: first, sys-tems based on chaotic forces betrayed verisimilitude (*Selbstähnlichkeit*);[5] second, such systems were self-organizing; third, they grew out of and depended on the conditions that prevailed at inception; and fourth, they were open-ended. Art, from this standpoint, was neither wholly open nor wholly deterministic, but a melding of open-endedness and system (53). Musil's alternative ethics — which Kochs, on a reading of a passage in the diaries, characterized as a type of "pious anarchy" (cf. *TB I*, 487) — could then be understood as this self-organizing chaos in action. It was clearly in evidence, she held, in the story of erotic attachment of the two siblings in the Other Condition: "Die treibende Kraft des Ganzen bildet die informationsschaffende Energie des Eros [. . .], welche nun als Gegenentwurf zur in geschlossenen Systemen herrschenden Macht der Entropie, der selbstähnlichen Anpassung im Gegensatz zur selbstähnlichen Differenzierung, verstanden werden kann" (194). What prevented the energy of the Other Condition from discharging entropically was the quantum notion of complementarity that lay behind Musil's conception of the coming together of the siblings. Complementarity, Kochs argued, suggested a way out of the dualism that had bedeviled the post-Cartesian world: "'Sein oder Nichtsein' ist hier keine Frage mehr. Denn, so weiß auch Musil: 'Es ist immer alles auf einmal da.' Und dies gilt für den Sinn eines jeglichen Seienden genauso wie für die Existenzgrundlage dieses Sinnes selbst" (93). If ontological duality was one of the problems that had dogged "old Europe," as Luhmann had pointed out, chaos theory provided a means of configuring provisional order in the new open systems of conceptual understanding in modern life, where "es ist immer alles auf einmal da": "Als chaotische Anfangsbedingung im Ganzen provoziert der Einzelne potentiell alle Formen von Ereignissen, nimmt er alle möglichen Eigenschaften dynamisch in sich auf und leitet sie weiter. Indem die herkömmliche Sicht des Individuums derart in Frage gestellt wird, wird sie gleichzeitig — in neuer alter Gestalt — unendlich erweitert [. . .]" (243). The perspective of information theory thus gave art and literary activity a new appearance. Literature represented an accommodation with the forces of chaos, a momentary "Konkretion des Irrationalen" (303, 317). *Der Mann ohne Eigenschaften*, accordingly, was a "chaotic novel" whose open-ended, dynamic systems mirrored the steady tension of subject and world, reproducing it macrocosmically, but also changing it at the microcosmic level. Kochs's study asked to be read with a matching sense of "chaotic consciousness" that did not ignore the fact that most of the questions it addressed would be left unresolved (327).

Christoph Hoffmann's study of 1997 was indebted to positions established by Gerhard Meisel (1991) within Musil scholarship and Foucault and Friedrich Kittler outside it. Hoffmann eschewed any reference to aesthetic notions of the text and textual sense in reclassifying Musil's works as

Apparate, in denen Ereignisse nach bestimmten Regeln zusammenge-
bracht und verschaltet werden, einem Apparat zugefallen und übertra-
gen von einem Apparat namens Schriftsteller, der als Medium bestimmt
ist, und hergestellt von einem Schreibapparat, dessen Produktion wie
eine maschinelle Leistung rationalisiert wird. (186)

This view made writing appear less voluntary and more impinged
upon from outside by the preexisting rational discourse systems of the
West. In Hoffmann's view, writing was already always encoded. The
writer was no more than a conduit for the notions of self-organization
within already fully established social systems. Hoffmann therefore set
out an antiutopian, antiromantic story of the writer's craft, according to
which data gleaned from observation was turned into writing: "Ein
Roman wie *Der Mann ohne Eigenschaften* [. . .] kann als Paradefall eines
poetischen Textes gelten, in dem die Arbeit des Autors ganz im Ver-
schalten und Verknoten von Wissensordnungen und Diskurstypen auf-
geht" (230). This already changed the nature of the literary craft. The
writer was less a self-conscious author of reality than a engineer —
perhaps especially so in the case of the technically trained Musil. The
scenarios imagined by writers arose from the technical conditions con-
straining the patterning and reproduction of discourse. This understanding of writing as a self-perpetuating "discourse apparatus" within
tightly controlled experimental conditions also reduced the ambition of
the utopian outlook of literature. This was particularly evident in the case
of the Other Condition. In opposing ethical theories which had ascribed
nonrational value to Musil's literary visions through an application of
Gestalt theory, Hoffmann argued that the Other Condition was rather
to be imagined as "das Andere der Gestalt," which is to say, as a "Ge-
staltinversion" (175).[6] This inverted structure conveyed not more than
the sum of the parts, as Gestalt theory had suggested, but conceivably
exactly that sum or, from a moral point of view, even rather less than it.

Andrea Gnam's study of 1998 broke new ground in Musil scholarship by approaching the issue of conceptual space. Basing her analysis on
the "paradigm shift" in the physical sciences ushered in by the breakdown of the classical space-time continuum at the end of the nineteenth
century, Gnam showed how space was less and less subject to bodily
sensation and more and more dependent on reflective understanding. To
some extent, therefore, space was no longer actually "experienced." It
instead became a "Reflexionsraum," which is to say, an "Ordnungsgefü-
ge, das aus einem Ensemble von Zuordnungen, Begriffen, logischen und
grammatikalischen Beziehungen besteht. [. . .] Der zugrundeliegende
Raumbegriff geht also von einem Geflecht funktionaler Beziehungen aus,

innerhalb derer sich 'Orte' (auf die Sprache bezogen: lexikalische Bedeutungen) beschreiben lassen" (33). Space, in other words, was like the realm it increasingly borrowed from to convey it semantically, namely language. As such, it had to be treated as a type of discursive formation in its own right: "Das zurückgedrängte leibliche Empfinden, das die Entstehung der Sprache begleitet hat, kann allenfalls in der poetischen Sprache, in der Unbestimmtheit der Analogie zum Ausdruck gebracht werden" (35). The question of how this new accelerated space, which disjoined mental from emotional experience, was ordered, suggested, on the one hand, the need to find an alternative to overweening rationality.[7] On the other hand, it led to mysticism. This resulted from the connection between the mystical conception of time and the theory of relativity in Paul Virilio's sense. As Gnam explained it, "Die Zeitdilation in der Relativitätstheorie korrespondiert für Virilio mit dem Eintauchen des Mystikers in eine subjektive Raumzeit" (106). This correspondence could be applied in Gnam's view to Musil's utopia of the Other Condition, where the new mystical experience of the world presupposed a "Verlassen der 'Lokalzeit' beim Übergang in ein anderes mentales Raumsystem" (113).

Albert Kümmel presented in a 2001 study an erudite and allusive examination of Musil's poetological program without falling back on older conceptions of the role of the poet or the work of art. His approach drew upon psychology, epistemology, and metaphysics as well as more modern technical discourses such as Gestalt, systems theory, and thermodynamics in order to postulate an underlying "psychotechnical discourse" (408) in Musil's *Mann ohne Eigenschaften*. Turning away from the textual exegesis of hermeneutic criticism, Kümmel saw Musil's novel as evincing the functionality of a "spiritual machine," that is, as a highly self-aware commentary of the conditions under which the work of art reproduces itself. In other ways Kümmel's study bore the hallmarks of dissertation writing in the age of *posthistoire:* there was no preliminary discussion or "Forschungsbericht" where the author established his position with respect to previous scholarship; instead, the discussion of critical literature was carried out mostly in the footnotes in accordance or at variance with a limited number of predominantly recent critical works. The discussion presupposed a high degree of familiarity with themes and key words in Musil's novel such that little or no narrative contextualization of quoted passages took place; finally, a level of discussion quite removed from the close textual reading of previous eras was established which was chiefly directed at advancing a larger idea about the text.

In Kümmel's case, this larger idea was that of the self-production of art as organized communication — what Kümmel termed the "geistige Organisation" of the text. Such "mental organization" (a notion borrowed from systems theory) occurred to some extent at the expense of its initiator, since the work of art also had to enact the historical circumstances out of which it had arisen and within the terms of which it had gained expression. Kümmel thus examined a range of discursive formations according to which the author did not come across as an initiator or "programmer" of discourses subsequently deployed in his writing, but, on the contrary, as programmed or disciplined by the external discourses that had acted upon him and shaped both his biography as soldier, engineer, and scientist and his conceptual understanding. To highlight the historical nature of this "programming," Kümmel's analysis was accompanied by detailed reference to the emergence of the particular discursive elements that lay behind Musil's organization of the narrative. This approach was especially indebted to Friedrich Kittler's account of the technical conditions that inform literary production in his 1985 book *Aufschreibesysteme*. In this study, Kittler had shown not only that historical circumstances determine how literature is produced, but also pointed to 1800 and 1900 as programmatic moments in the historical generation of "discourse networks," that is, technical formations that constrain as well as promote the conditions of literary production. Applying Kittler's idea about discourse networks to Musil's historical period, Kümmel concluded that the production of literature at and after the turn of the nineteenth to the twentieth century no longer depended upon any unconscious activity of poets and writers of genius, but instead became a "technical" matter, even an "operational procedure" (212).

For Kümmel's approach, the traditional author as an omniscient or overweening creative presence in the text had long since receded. This did not mean, however, that authors ceased to imagine ideal states or to conjure inspirational poetic landscapes. These still existed in Musil's novel, but were embedded, according to Kümmel, in procedures that ironized or otherwise undercut the authority of the text and rendered it highly self-conscious. While previous studies of Musil had noted the existence of what earlier scholarship had investigated under the heading of satire and irony as an underlying negativity and later scholarship understood as dissemination and deconstruction, Musil scholarship had mostly stopped short of dismantling the authority of the author altogether. In Kümmel's analysis, this had occasioned a blindness to the true nature of the Musil's utopian vision, the Other Condition, which had almost exclusively been interpreted in the manner of protest as inherently "other" than the depicted reality of Kakania (428). Therefore, while previous scholarship had declared the rhetorical strategy of Kakania (that is: "seinesgleichen") to be an enemy of ideal communication and therefore of Musil's idyll, "seinesgleichen" in Kümmel's analysis turned out to be the very assumption that made Musil's vision of the Other Condition (and indeed every condition in complex modern societies) possible. Viewing Ulrich as a kind of replicant hunter in the manner of the film *Blade Runner* — that is, as the replicant who hunts replicants without knowing that he himself is a replicant (313) — Kümmel suggested that the iterative quality of "Seinesgleichen geschieht" was the process of duplication that invested all texts as a condition of their textuality. Textual reproduction, accordingly, was an act of "replication" that texts underwent in order to make possible a higher level of discursive complexity. Understood in this way, the text freed itself from the negative dimension of iteration as a procedural copying (defined by a loss of originary presence) to become a positive idea where iteration was a wholly necessary operational procedure promoting new readings and writings of texts. The ideal imagined in the text, therefore, was not any universal value-scheme, but was defined in terms of the quality of its input selection, of its "Hierarchisierung der Ansprüche" (257). The Other Condition was therefore not to be imagined in Kümmel's reading as an alternative vision at odds with reality, but as the completion of the "MoE program," that is, the fulfillment of the novel's promise to construe and reconstrue its own sense of possibility.

Notes

[1] Luhmann refers to this dilemma in his discussion of Kant. Cf. Niklas Luhmann, *Die Gesellschaft der Gesellschaft* (Frankfurt am Main: Suhrkamp, 1998), 977.

[2] Michael Franz, in any case, has announced opposition to the appropriation of Gestalt theory in aesthetic approaches in a more general sense. Cf. Michael Franz, "Die Zweideutigkeiten der Gestalt oder: Taugt 'Gestalt' noch als ästhetischer Grundbegriff?" *Weimarer Beiträge* 41/1 (1995): 5–28.

[3] See also his later study in French, *Musil: Savoir et fiction* (Paris: Presses universitaires de Vincennes, 1994).

[4] Cf. e.g. Gerry Brenner, *Concealments in Hemingway's Works* (Columbus: Ohio State UP, 1983), 11, 17.

[5] Kochs indicates that "Selbstähnlichkeit" doesn't mean an identical likeness, nor exact copies on the micro level of the macro, but rather "'Collagen von Kopien von Collagen'" (*Chaos und Individuum: Robert Musils philosophischer Roman als Vision der Moderne* [Munich: Karl Alber Freiburg, 1996], 263).

[6] Cf. also Ralf Bohn's work on the notion of inversion with respect to Schelling. Bohn held that the "ideality" of art must reclaim its own reality, as it were, from within: "Es ist, am Schluß des transzendentalen Systementwurfs von Schelling projiziert, die Mythologie der zweite Anfang, der als erster zu sprechen beginnt." (*Transversale Inversion: Symptomatologie und Genealogie des Denkens in der Philosophie Robert Musils* [Würzburg: Königshausen & Neumann, 1988], 286).

[7] Gnam cited the following quote from Musil's novel (*MoE*, 1054): "Ringsum tobt die Vernunft in Tausenden von PS. Man trotzt ihr und behauptet, in einem verschlossenen Kästchen eine andre Autorität zu haben. Das ist der Sammelkasten Intuition. Man öffne ihn doch endlich und sehe, was darin ist. Vielleicht ist es eine neue Welt."

Editions of *Der Mann ohne Eigenschaften*

1930. *Der Mann ohne Eigenschaften*. Erstes Buch. Berlin: Rowohlt; 1938, Vienna: Bermann-Fischer.

1932. *Der Mann ohne Eigenschaften*. Zweites Buch. Berlin: Rowohlt; 1938, Vienna: Bermann-Fischer.

1943. *Der Mann ohne Eigenschaften*. Dritter Band. Aus dem Nachlass. Edited by Martha Musil. Lausanne: Imprimerie Centrale.

1952. *Der Mann ohne Eigenschaften*. *Gesammelte Werke in Einzelausgaben*. Vol. 1. Edited by Adolf Frisé. Hamburg: Rowohlt.

1953. *The Man without Qualities*. Vol. 1. Translated by Eithne Wilkins and Ernst Kaiser. London: Secker & Warburg; New York: Coward-McCann.

1955. *The Man without Qualities*. Vol. 2. Translated by Eithne Wilkins and Ernst Kaiser. London: Secker & Warburg; New York: Coward-McCann.

1960. *The Man without Qualities*. Vol. 3. Translated by Eithne Wilkins and Ernst Kaiser. London: Secker & Warburg; New York: Coward-McCann.

1978. *Gesammelte Werke*. 4 vols. Edited by Adolf Frisé. Identical with paperback edition *Gesammelte Werke in neun Bänden*. 9 vols. Reinbek bei Hamburg: Rowohlt.

1992. *Der literarische Nachlass*. CD-ROM. Edited by Friedbert Aspetsberger, Karl Eibl, and Adolf Frisé. Reinbek bei Hamburg: Rowohlt.

Musil Bibliographies

(In chronological order.)

Karthaus, Ulrich. 1965. "Musil-Forschung und Musil-Deutung. Ein Literatur-bericht." *Deutsche Vierteljahrsschrift für Literaturwissenschaft und Geistesge-schichte* 39 (3): 441–83.

Thöming, Jürgen C. 1968a. *Robert-Musil-Biographie.* Bad Homburg v.d.H., Berlin, Zurich: Gehlen. Bibliographien zum Studium der deutschen Sprache und Literatur 4.

———. 1968b. "Kommentierte Auswahlbibliographie zu Robert Musil." *Text+Kritik* 21/22: 61–67. Expanded in 1972 in *Text+Kritik* 21/22 (2nd edition): 73–87.

Goltschnigg, Dietmar. 1972. "Kritische Anmerkungen zur Musil-Forschung." *Österreich in Geschichte und Literatur* 16 (3): 150–62.

Roseberry, Robert L. 1974. *Robert Musil: Ein Forschungsbericht.* Frankfurt am Main: Fischer Athenäum.

Freese, Wolfgang. 1974. "Anmerkungen zu neueren Arbeiten der Musil-Forschung." *German Quarterly* 47: 73–87.

Danner, Karl-Heinz. 1976. "Robert-Musil-Schrifttum 1970–1975." *Modern Austrian Literature* 9 (3/4): 210–39.

King, Lynda J. 1978. "Robert Musil Bibliography 1976/77." *Musil-Forum* 4: 104–16.

Arntzen, Helmut. 1980. *Musil-Kommentar sämtlicher zu Lebzeiten erschienener Schriften außer dem Roman "Der Mann ohne Eigenschaften."* Munich: Win-kler.

Freese, Wolfgang, and Regine Fourie. 1981. "Robert Musil: Ausgaben und neuere Forschung. Ein Bericht." *Acta Germanica* 14: 213–32.

Sihvo, Hannes. 1981/82. "Ein kleiner Streifzug durch die Musil-Forschung." *Jahrbuch für finnisch-deutsche Literaturbeziehungen. Mitteilungen aus der Deutschen Bibliothek.* Vol. 15/16. Helsinki: Deutsche Bibliothek. 35–44.

Arntzen, Helmut. 1982. *Musil-Kommentar zu dem Roman "Der Mann ohne Eigenschaften."* Munich: Winkler. 450–80.

Freese, Wolfgang. 1983. "Zur neueren Musil-Forschung. Ausgaben und Ge-samtdarstellungen." *Text+Kritik* 21/22 (3rd edition): 86–148.

Mae, Michiko. 1983. "Robert-Musil-Bibliographie. Ergänzungsbibliographie 1980–1983." *Musil-Forum* 9 (1/2): 183–220.

Chevalier, Claude, and Jacqueline Magnou. 1987. "Bibliographie chronologique comentée des publications et critiques parues en francais." *Musil-Forum. Wissenschaftliches Beiheft* 3.

Kümmerling, Bettina. 1987. "Robert-Musil-Forschung 1973–1987. Forschungsbericht." *Literatur in Wissenschaft und Unterricht* 20 (4): 540–70.

Welzig, Werner. 1988. "Verwischte Spuren: Zu und aus Anlaß von Helmut Arntzens Musil-Kommentar (*Der Mann ohne Eigenschaften*)." *Germanisch-Romanische Monatsschrift* 38 (3): 343–47.

Corino, Karl. 1990. "Robert Musils Wirkung auf die Weltliteratur." *Musil-Forum* 16 (1–2): 92–102.

Fiala-Fürst, Ingeborg, ed. 1990. "Bibliographie der Rezeption Musils in Polen, Jugoslawien, der Sowjet-Union und der Tschechoslowakei." *Musil-Forum. Wissenschaftliches Beiheft* 4.

———, ed. 1991. "Robert Musil. Internationale Bibliographie der Sekundärliteratur 1984–1991." *Musil-Forum. Wissenschaftliches Beiheft* 5.

Iurlano, Fabrizio, and Aldo Venturelli. 1991/92. "Die Musil-Forschung in Italien 1965–1990." *Musil-Forum* 17/18: 171–205.

Markner, Reinhard. 1991/92. "Einige Ergänzungen zur jüngsten Musil-Bibliographie." *Musil-Forum* 17/18: 245–67.

Rogowski, Christian. 1994. *Distinguished Outsider: Robert Musil and his Critics.* Columbia, SC: Camden House. Studies in German Literature, Linguistics, and Culture: Literary Criticism in Perspective.

Works Consulted

(In chronological order.)

Lukács, Georg. 1933. "Totentanz der Weltanschauungen." In *Literatur und Literaturgeschichte in Österreich*. Edited by Ilona T. Erdélyi. Budapest/ Vienna: Akadémiai Kiadó, 1979. Sondernummer der Zeitschrift Helikon. 297–307.

Kisch, Egon Erwin. 1942. "Auf den Tod Robert Musils." *Freies Deutschland / Alemania Libre* (Mexico) 1 (8): 29. Reprint 1975, Leipzig: Antiquariat der Deutschen Demokratischen Republik.

Lejeune, Robert. 1942. "Robert Musil." *Der Aufbau* 23 (34): 269–71; 23 (35): 276–79; 23 (36): 286–88. Republished 1942 as *Robert Musil: Eine Würdigung*. Zurich: Oprecht. Reprinted 1960 in Dinklage, 409–24.

Riskamm, Karl. 1948. "Robert Musils Leben und Werk." Diss. Vienna.

Anon. [Ernst Kaiser and Eithne Wilkins]. 1949. "Empire in Time and Space." *Times Literary Supplement* 48 (October 28): 689–90.

Maier, Anna. 1949. "Franz Kafka and Robert Musil als Vertreter der ethischen Richtung des modernen Romans." Diss. Vienna.

Csokor, Franz Theodor. 1950/51. "Robert Musil (1880–1942)." *Der Monat* 3 (26): 185–89. Reprinted 1960 under the title "Gedenkrede zu Robert Musils 80. Geburtstag." In Dinklage, 347–56.

Boeninger, Helmut R. 1952. "The Rediscovery of Robert Musil." *Modern Language Forum* 37: 109–19.

Puckett, Hugh W. 1952. "Robert Musil." *Monatshefte* 44: 409–19.

Baumann, Gerhart. 1953. "Robert Musil: Eine Vorstudie." *Germanisch-Romanische Monatsschrift* 34 (3): 292–316.

Kaiser, Ernst, and Eithne Wilkins. 1953. "Foreword." Robert Musil. *The Man without Qualities*. Vol. 1. London: Secker & Warburg; New York: Coward-McCann, iii–xviii.

Mandel, Siegfried. 1953. "The Foibles Dissected." *New York Times Book Review* (June 7): 7.

Bachmann, Ingeborg. 1954. "Ins tausendjährige Reich." *Akzente* 1: 50–53.

Boehlich, Walter. 1954. "Untergang und Erlösung." *Akzente* 1: 35–50.

Braun, Wilhelm. 1954. "Musil's 'Erdensekretariat der Genauigkeit und Seele.' A Clue to the Philosophy of the Hero in *Der Mann ohne Eigenschaften.*" *Monatshefte* 46: 305–16.

Jens, Inge. 1954. "Studien zur Entwicklung der expressionistischen Novelle." Diss. Tübingen. 48–79.

Michel, Karl Markus. 1954. "Die Utopie der Sprache." *Akzente* 1: 23–35.

Otten, Karl. 1955. "Robert Musil, Schwärmer und Rationalist." *Das neue Forum* 4: 273–75.

Rasch, Wolfdietrich. 1955. "Erinnerung an Robert Musil." *Merkur* 9, 148–58. Reprinted 1960 in Dinklage, 364–76.

Schneider, Rolf. 1955. "Tragik des Alleinseins: Der Dichter Robert Musil." *Neue deutsche Literatur* 10 (3): 106–12.

Zak, Eduard. 1955. "Gegen den Strom. Robert Musils *Mann ohne Eigenschaften.*" *Neue deutsche Literatur* 10 (4): 118–36.

Tank, Lothar Kurt. 1955/56. "Robert Musils Tagebücher." *Eckart* 25: 346–48.

Allemann, Beda. 1956. "Musil." *Ironie und Dichtung*. Pfullingen: Neske. 2nd edition, 1969. 177–220.

Berghahn, Wilfried. 1956. "Die essayistische Erzähltechnik Robert Musils. Eine morphologische Untersuchung zur Organisation und Integration des Romans *Der Mann ohne Eigenschaften.*" Diss. Bonn.

Pongs, Hermann. 1956. *Romanschaffen im Umbruch der Zeit*. Tübingen: Verlag der deutschen Hochschullehrerzeitung. 4th edition, 1963. 319–78.

Fischer, Ernst. 1957. "Das Werk Robert Musils: Versuch einer Würdigung." *Sinn und Form* 9 (5): 851–901.

Jens, Walter. 1957. "Der Mensch und die Dinge: Die Revolution der deutschen Prosa — Hofmannsthal, Rilke, Musil, Kafka, Heym." *Statt einer Literaturgeschichte*. Pfullingen: Neske. 59–85. Expanded edition 1978. 113–37.

Kaiser, Ernst. 1957. "*Der Mann ohne Eigenschaften*. Ein Problem der Wirklichkeit." *Merkur* 11 (2): 669–87.

Blanchot, Maurice. 1958. "Robert Musil." *La Nouvelle Revue Francaise* 6 (11): 301–9; 479–90. Reprinted 1959 in Maurice Blanchot, *Le Livre à venir*. Paris: Gallimard. 165–84. 1962 in German in *Der Gesang der Sirenen. Essays zur modernen Literatur*. Trans. by Karl August Horst. Munich: Hanser, 184–206.

Lukács, Georg. 1958. *Wider den mißverstandenen Realismus*. Hamburg: Claasen.

Müller, Gerhard. 1958. "Die drei Utopien Ulrichs in Robert Musils *Mann ohne Eigenschaften.*" Diss. Vienna.

Strelka, Joseph. 1959. "Robert Musil. Der Utopist eines anderen Lebens." In *Kafka, Musil, Broch und die Entwicklung des modernen Romans.* Edited by Joseph Strelka. Vienna: Forum. 36–64.

Arntzen, Helmut. 1960. *Satirischer Stil in Robert Musils "Der Mann ohne Eigenschaften."* Bonn: Bouvier. Abhandlungen zur Kunst-, Musik- und Literaturwissenschaft 9. Second, expanded edition 1970. Third edition 1982.

Bachmann, Ingeborg. 1960. *Frankfurter Vorlesungen: Probleme zeitgenössischer Dichtung.* Reprinted 1980. Munich: Piper. Serie Piper 205.

Baumann, Gerhart. 1960. "Robert Musil. Die Struktur des Geistes und der Geist der Struktur." *Germanische-Romantische Monatsschrift* 41 (10): 420–42.

Csokor, Franz Theodor. 1960. "Gedenkrede zu Robert Musils 80. Geburtstag." In Dinklage, 347–56.

Dinklage, Karl, ed. 1960. *Robert Musil: Leben, Werk, Wirkung.* Reinbek bei Hamburg: Rowohlt.

———. 1960. "Musils Herkunft und Lebensgeschichte." In Dinklage, 187–264.

Fontana, Oskar Maurus. 1960. "Erinnerungen an Robert Musil." In Dinklage, 325–44.

Heintel, Erich. 1960. "Der Mann ohne Eigenschaften und die Tradition." *Wissenschaft und Weltbild* 13: 179–94.

Lejeune, Robert. 1960. "Robert Musil. Eine Würdigung." In Dinklage, 409–24.

Loebenstein, Johannes. 1960. "Das Problem der Erkenntnis in Musils künstlerischem Werk." In Dinklage, 77–131.

Roth, Marie-Louise. 1960. "Robert Musil im Spiegel seines Werkes. Versuch einer inneren Biograpie." In Dinklage, 12–48.

von Allesch, Johannes. 1960. "Robert Musil in der geistigen Bewegung seiner Zeit." In Dinklage, 133–42.

Wotruba, Fritz. 1960. "Erinnerung an Musil." In Dinklage, 400–404.

Sokel, Walter H. 1960/61. "Robert Musils Narrenspiegel." *Neue deutsche Hefte* 7: 199–214. Reprinted 1963 in *Wort in der Zeit* 9 (8/9): 51–64.

Pike, Burton. 1961. *Robert Musil: An Introduction to His Work.* Ithaca, NY: Cornell UP. 2nd edition 1972.

Schöne, Albrecht. 1961. "Zum Gebrauch des Konjunktivs bei Robert Musil." *Euphorion* 55: 196–220. Reprinted 1982 in von Heydebrand, 19–53.

Ziolkowski, Theodore. 1961. "James Joyces Epiphanie und die Überwindung der empirischen Welt in der modernen deutschen Prosa." *Deutsche Vierteljahrsschrift für Literaturwissenschaft und Geistesgeschichte* 35: 594–616.

Frisé, Adolf. 1962. "Angriff auf eine Edition. Einige Hinweise." *Frankfurter Allgemeine Zeitung* 203 (September 3).

Hanke-Tjaden, Irma. 1962. "Der freie Geist und die Politik: zum Problem des Politischen bei Robert Musil." Diss. Freiburg i. Br.

Kaiser, Ernst, and Eithne Wilkins. 1962. *Robert Musil: Eine Einführung in das Werk.* Stuttgart: Kohlhammer.

Kermode, Frank. 1962. "A Short View of Musil." In *Puzzles and Epiphanies.* London: Routledge & Kegan Paul, 91–107.

Rasch, Wolfdietrich. 1962. "Probleme der Musil-Edition I." *Frankfurter Allgemeine Zeitung* 233 (October 6). "Probleme der Musil-Edition II." *Frankfurter Allgemeine Zeitung* 239 (October 13).

Berghahn, Wilfried. 1963. *Robert Musil in Selbstzeugnissen und Bilddokumenten.* Reinbek bei Hamburg: Rowohlt. Rowohlts Monographien 81.

Honold, Helga. 1963. *Die Funktion des Paradoxen bei Robert Musil dargestellt am "Mann ohne Eigenschaften."* Diss. Tübingen.

Pongs, Hermann. 1963. *Das Bild in der Dichtung.* Marburg: N. G. Elwert. 2nd Edition.

Rasch, Wolfdietrich. 1963. "*Der Mann ohne Eigenschaften.* Eine Interpretation." In *Der deutsche Roman: Vom Barock bis zur Gegenwart.* Vol. 2, *Vom Realismus bis zur Gegenwart,* ed. Benno von Wiese. Düsseldorf: Bagel, 1963. Reprinted 1967 in Rasch, 78–134.

Jäßl, Gerolf. 1963. "Mathematik und Mystik in Robert Musils Roman *Der Mann ohne Eigenschaften.*" Diss. Munich.

Bausinger, Wilhelm. 1964. *Robert Musil. "Der Mann ohne Eigenschaften."* Studien zu einer historisch-kritischen Ausgabe. Reinbek bei Hamburg: Rowohlt.

Brosthaus, Heribert. 1964. "Robert Musils 'wahre Antithese.'" *Wirkendes Wort* 14: 120–40.

Baumann, Gerhart. 1965. *Robert Musil: Zur Erkenntnis der Dichtung.* Bern, Munich: Francke.

Bausinger, Wilhelm. 1965. "Robert Musil und die Ablehnung des Expressionismus." *Studi Germanici* N.S. 3: 383–89.

Brosthaus, Heribert. 1965. "Zur Struktur und Entwicklung des 'anderen Zustands' in Robert Musils Roman *Der Mann ohne Eigenschaften.*" *Deutsche Vierteljahrsschrift für Literaturwissenschaft und Geistesgeschichte* 39 (3): 388–440.

Hoffmeister, Werner. 1965. "Die erlebte Rede im Werk Robert Musils." *Studien zur erlebten Rede bei Thomas Mann und Robert Musil.* The Hague: Mouton, 86–159. Studies in German Literature 2.

Irle, Gerhard. 1965. "Der psychiatrische Roman bei Robert Musil." In *Der Psychiatrische Roman.* Stuttgart: Hippokrates. 124–84.

Karthaus, Ulrich. 1965. *Der andere Zustand: Zeitstrukturen im Werke Robert Musils.* Berlin: Erich Schmidt. Philologische Studien und Quellen 25.

Kermode, Frank. 1965. "Preface." Robert Musil. *Tonka and Other Stories.* Trans. by Eithne Wilkins and Ernst Kaiser. London: Secker & Warburg, 7–13.

Kühn, Dieter. 1965. *Analogie und Variation: Zur Analyse von Robert Musils Roman "Der Mann ohne Eigenschaften."* Bonn: Bouvier. Bonner Arbeiten zur deutschen Literatur 13.

Rasch, Wolfdietrich. 1965. "Zur Entstehung von Robert Musils Roman *Der Mann ohne Eigenschaften.*" *Deutsche Vierteljahrsschrift für Literaturwissenschaft und Geistesgeschichte* 39: 350–87. Reprinted 1967 in Rasch, 35–77.

Seidler, Ingo. 1965. "Das Nietzschebild Robert Musils." *Deutsche Vierteljahrsschrift für Literaturwissenschaft und Geistesgeschichte* 39 (3): 329–49.

Bauer, Sybille, and Ingrid Drevermann. 1966. *Studien zu Robert Musil.* Cologne/Graz: Böhlau. Literatur und Leben, Neue Folge 8.

Kowal, Michael. 1966. "Robert Musil: Unread Master." *American German Review* 33 (1): 37–38.

Magris, Claudio. 1966. *Der habsburgische Mythos.* Salzburg: Otto Müller, 278–95.

von Heydebrand, Renate. 1966. *Die Reflexionen Ulrichs in Robert Musils Roman "Der Mann ohne Eigenschaften": Ihr Zusammenhang mit dem zeitgenössischen Denken.* Münster: Aschendorff.

Guntau, Helmut. 1967. *Robert Musil.* Berlin: Colloquium. Köpfe des XX. Jahrhunderts 45.

Nusser, Peter. 1967. *Musils Romantheorie.* The Hague, Paris: Mouton. De proprietatibus litterarum. Series practica 4.

Rasch, Wolfdietrich. 1967. *Über Robert Musils Roman "Der Mann ohne Eigenschaften."* Göttingen: Vandenhoeck & Ruprecht.

Schramm, Ulf. 1967. *Fiktion und Reflexion: Überlegungen zu Musil und Beckett.* Frankfurt am Main: Suhrkamp.

Albertsen, Elisabeth. 1968. *"Ratio" und Mystik im Werk Robert Musils.* Munich: Nymphenburger. Sammlung Dialog 22.

Arntzen, Helmut. 1968a. "Robert Musil und die Parallelaktionen." *Text+Kritik* 21/22: 3–11. Reprinted 1971 under the title "Robert Musil und die Parallelaktionen. (Zum 15. April 1967)." *Literatur im Zeitalter der Information: Aufsätze, Essays, Glossen.* Frankfurt am Main: Athenäum, 93–109. Reprinted in 1972 in *Text+Kritik* 21/22, 2nd edition, 9–22.

———. 1968b. "'Die Reise ins Paradies.'" *Text+Kritik* 21/22: 42–47. Reprinted 1971 under the title "'Die Reise ins Paradies.' Zu dem gleichnamigen Kapitelentwurf in Musils Roman." *Literatur im Zeitalter der Information: Aufsätze, Essays, Glossen.* Frankfurt am Main: Athenäum. 134–47. Reprinted in 1972 in *Text+Kritik* 21/22, 2nd edition, 22–34.

———. 1968c. "Seufzer zur Musilforschung." *Text+Kritik* 21/22: 68–75.

Durzak, Manfred. 1968. "Geistesverwandtschaft und Rivalität: Robert Musil." *Hermann Broch: Der Dichter und seine Zeit.* Stuttgart: Kohlhammer, 114–37.

Kühne, Jörg. 1968. *Das Gleichnis: Studien zur inneren Form von Robert Musils Roman "Der Mann ohne Eigenschaften."* Tübingen: Niemeyer.

Rasch, Wolfdietrich. 1968. "Robert Musils 'Märchen vom Schneider.' Eine Satire auf die Situation des Schriftstellers." *Text+Kritik* 21/22: 39–42. Reprinted in 1972 in *Text+Kritik* 21/22, 2nd edition, 35–39.

Schelling, Ulrich. 1968. *Identität und Wirklichkeit bei Robert Musil.* Zurich, Freiburg i. Br.: Atlantis. Zürcher Beiträge zur deutschen Literatur- und Geistesgeschichte 30.

Wilkins, Eithne. 1968. "Gestalten und Namen im Werk Robert Musils." *Text+Kritik* 21/22: 48–58.

Bachmann, Dieter. 1969. "Robert Musil. 1880–1942." *Essays und Essayismus.* Stuttgart, Berlin, Cologne, Mainz: Kohlhammer, 157–92. Sprache und Literatur 55.

Graf, Günter. 1969. *Studien zur Funktion des ersten Kapitels von Robert Musils Roman "Der Mann ohne Eigenschaften." Ein Beitrag zur Unwahrhaftigkeitsthematik der Gestalten.* Göppingen: Kümmerle. Göppinger Arbeiten zur Germanistik 14.

Reinhardt, Stephan. 1969. *Studien zur Antinomie von Intellekt und Gefühl in Musils Roman "Der Mann ohne Eigenschaften."* Bonn: Bouvier. Abhandlungen zur Kunst, Musik- und Literaturwissenschaft 80.

Seeger, Lothar Georg. 1969. *Die Demaskierung der Lebenslüge: Eine Untersuchung zur Krise der Gesellschaft in Robert Musils "Der Mann ohne Eigenschaften."* Bern/Munich: Francke.

Sera, Manfred. 1969. "Utopie und Parodie in Robert Musils Roman *"Der Mann ohne Eigenschaften"*: *Utopie und Parodie bei Musil, Broch und Thoman Mann.* Bonn: Bouvier, 5–72. Bonner Arbeiten zur deutschen Literatur 19.

Allemann, Beda. 1970. "Ironie als literarisches Prinzip." In *Ironie und Dichtung: Sechs Essays von Beda Allemann, Ernst Zinn, Hans-Egon Hass, Wolfgang Preisendanz, Fritz Martini, Paul Böckmann,* edited by Albert Schaefer, Munich: Beck. 11–37.

Arvon, Henri. 1970. "Robert Musil und der Positivismus." In Dinklage, Albertsen, and Corino, 200–213.

Corino, Karl. 1970. "Robert Musil und Alfred Kerr. Der Dichter und sein Kritiker." In Dinklage, Albertsen, and Corino, 236–83.

Dinklage, Karl, Elisabeth Albertsen, and Karl Corino, eds. 1970. *Robert Musil: Studien zu seinem Werk.* Reinbek bei Hamburg: Rowohlt.

Laermann, Klaus. 1970. *Eigenschaftslosigkeit: Reflexionen zu Musils Roman "Der Mann ohne Eigenschaften."* Stuttgart: Metzler.

Rothe, Wolfgang. 1970. "'Seinesgleichen geschieht.' Musil und die moderne Erzähltradition." In Dinklage, Albertsen, and Corino, 131–69.

Silone, Ignazio. 1970. "Begegnungen mit Musil." In Dinklage, Albertsen, and Corino, 82–85.

Thöming, Jürgen C. 1970. "Der optimistische Pessimismus eines passiven Aktivisten." In Dinklage, Albertsen, and Corino, 214–35.

von Büren, Erhard. 1970. *Zur Bedeutung der Psychologie Im Werk Robert Musils.* Zurich, Freiburg i. Br.: Atlantis. Zürcher Beiträge zur deutschen Literatur- und Geistesgeschichte 37.

Aler, Jan. 1971. "Als Zögling zwischen Maeterlinck und Mach. Robert Musils literarisch-philosophische Anfänge." In *Probleme des Erzählens in der Weltliteratur. Festschrift für Käte Hamburger,* edited by Fritz Martini. Stuttgart: Klett, 234–90.

Cohn, Dorrit. 1971. "Psycho-Analogies: A Means for Rendering Consciousness in Fiction." *Probleme des Erzählens in der Weltliteratur: Festschrift für Käte Hamburger,* ed. Fritz Martini. Stuttgart: Klett, 291–302.

Corino, Karl. 1971. *Robert Musil — Thomas Mann: Ein Dialog.* Pfullingen: Neske.

Hüppauf, Bernd-Rüdiger. 1971. *Von sozialer Utopie zur Mystik: Zu Robert Musils "Der Mann ohne Eigenschaften."* Munich, Salzburg: Fink. *Musil-Studien* 1.

Müller, Gerd. 1971. *Dichtung und Wissenschaft: Studien zu Robert Musils Romanen "Die Verwirrungen des Zöglings Törleß" und "Der Mann ohne Eigenschaften."* Uppsala: Acta Universitatis Upsaliensia, 21–110. Studia Germanistica Upsaliensia 7.

Schaffnit, Hans Wolfgang. 1971. *Mimesis als Problem: Studien zu einem ästhetischen Begriff der Dichtung aus Anlaß Robert Musils.* Berlin: de Gruyter. Quellen und Forschungen zur Sprach- und Kulturgeschichte der germanischen Völker N.F. 36.

Goltschnigg, Dietmar. 1972. "Kritische Anmerkungen zur Musil-Forschung." *Österreich in Geschichte und Literatur* 16 (3): 150–62.

Herwig, Dagmar. 1972. *Der Mensch in der Entfremdung: Studien zur Entfremdungsproblematik anhand des Werkes von Robert Musil.* Munich: List.

Hochstätter, Dietrich. 1972. *Sprache des Möglichen: Stilistischer Perspektivismus in Robert Musils "Der Mann ohne Eigenschaften."* Frankfurt am Main: Athenäum.

Kaiser, Gerhard R. 1972. *Proust, Musil, Joyce: Zum Verhältnis von Literatur und Gesellschaft am Paradigma des Zitats.* Frankfurt am Main: Athenäum. 84–144.

Müller, Götz. 1972. *Ideologiekritik und Metasprache in Robert Musils Roman "Der Mann ohne Eigenschaften."* Munich, Salzburg: Fink. Musil-Studien 2.

Parry, Idris. 1972. "Wave-grain in the Wall." *Animals of Silence: Essays on Art, Nature and Folktale.* London: Oxford UP, 76–84.

Reniers-Servanckx, Annie. 1972. *Robert Musil: Konstanz und Entwicklung von Themen, Motiven und Strukturen in den Dichtungen.* Bonn: Bouvier. Abhandlungen zur Kunst-, Musik- und Literaturwissenschaft 110.

Roth, Marie-Louise. 1972. *Robert Musil: Ethik und Ästhetik.* Munich: List.

Appignanesi, Lisa. 1973. "Robert Musil: Femininity and Completeness." In *Femininity and the Creative Imagination: A Study of Henry James, Robert Musil and Marcel Proust.* London: Vision; New York: Barnes & Noble, 81–156.

Baur, Uwe, and Dietmar Goltschnigg, eds. 1973. *Vom "Törleß" zum "Der Mann ohne Eigenschaften."* Munich, Salzburg: Fink. *Musil-Studien 4.*

Burckhardt, Judith. 1973. *"Der Mann ohne Eigenschaften" von Robert Musil: Oder das Wagnis der Selbstverwirklichung.* Bern: Francke. Basler Studien zur deutschen Sprache und Literatur 48.

Corino, Karl. 1973. "Ödipus oder Orest? Robert Musil und die Psychoanalyse." In Baur und Goltschnigg, 1973, 123–235.

Hönig, Christoph. 1973. "Musils Pläne für einen satirisch-utopischen Experimentalroman: *Land über dem Südpol* oder *Der Stern Ed.*" In Baur und Goltschnigg, 1973, 325–47.

Janik, Allan, and Stephen Toulmin. 1973. *Wittgenstein's Vienna.* New York, London: Touchstone.

Böhme, Hartmut. 1974. *Anomie und Entfremdung: Literatursoziologische Untersuchungen zu den Essays Robert Musils und seinem Roman "Der Mann ohne Eigenschaften."* Kronberg/Taunus: Scriptor. Skripten Literaturwissenschaft 9.

Castex-Rieger, Elisabeth. 1974. "Musil in Frankreich: Verbreitung, kritische Aufnahme, Wirkung." *Literatur und Kritik* 9: 381–89.

Corino, Karl. 1974. *Robert Musils "Vereinigungen."* Munich, Salzburg: Fink. Musil-Studien 5.

Desportes, Yvon. 1974. "Études comparative d'un style et d'une philosophie: une oeuvre de Musil à la lumière de Mach." *Revue d'Allemagne et de pays de langue allemande* VI: 79–90. Reprinted 1982 in German as "Vergleichende Untersuchung eines Stils und einer Philosophie: Ein Werk Musils aus der Sicht Machs." In von Heydebrand, 1982, 281–95.

Freese, Wolfgang. 1974b. "Robert Musil als Realist. Ein Beitrag zur Realismus-Diskussion." *Literatur und Kritik* 9: 514–44.

Goltschnigg, Dietmar. 1974. *Mystische Tradition im Roman Robert Musils: Martin Bubers "Ekstatische Konfessionen" im "Der Mann ohne Eigenschaften."* Heidelberg: Stiehm.

Magris, Claudio. 1974. "Musil und die 'Nähte der Zeichen.'" *Literaturwissenschaftliches Jahrbuch der Görres-Gesellschaft* 15: 189–219. Reprinted 1981 in Freese, 177–93.

Thöming, Jürgen C. 1974. *Zur Rezeption von Musil- und Goethe-Texten: Historizität der ästhetischen Vermittlung von sinnlicher Erkenntnis und Gefühlserlebnissen.* Munich, Salzburg: Fink. *Musil-Studien* 3.

Williams, Cedric Ellis. 1974. "Robert Musil: Vanity Fair." *The Broken Eagle: The Politics of Austrian Literature from Empire to Anschluß.* London: Paul Elek, 148–86.

Schmidt, Jochen. 1975. *Ohne Eigenschaften: Eine Erläuterung zu Musils Grundbegriff.* Tübingen: Niemeyer. Untersuchungen zur deutschen Literaturgeschichte 13.

Schneider, Rolf. 1975. *Die problematisierte Wirklichkeit: Leben und Werk Robert Musils: Versuch einer Interpretation.* Berlin: Volk und Welt.

Schröder-Werle, Renate. 1975. "Zur Vorgeschichte der Musil-Rezeption nach 1945. Hinweise zur Wiederentdeckung." *Musil-Forum* 1: 226–46.

Althaus, Horst. 1976. *Zwischen Monarchie und Republik: Schnitzler, Kafka, Hofmannsthal, Musil.* Munich: Fink.

Beard, Philip. 1976. "Clarisse und Moosbrugger vs. Ulrich/Agathe: der 'andere Zustand' aus neuer Sicht." *Modern Austrian Literature* 9 (3/4): 114–130.

Böhme, Hartmut. 1976. "Theoretische Probleme der Interpretation Robert Musils Roman *Der Mann ohne Eigenschaften.*" *Musil-Forum* 2 (1): 35–70. Reprinted 1982 in von Heydebrand, 120–159.

Fuld, Werner. 1976. "Die Quellen zur Konzeption des 'anderen Zustands' in Robert Musils Roman *Der Mann ohne Eigenschaften.*" *Deutsche Vierteljahrsschrift für Literaturwissenschaft und Geistesgeschichte* 50: 664–82.

Gradischnig, Hertwig. 1976. *Das Bild des Dichters bei Robert Musil.* Munich, Salzburg: Fink. *Musil-Studien* 6.

Hall, Murray G. 1976. "Ein perverser Dichter." *Musil-Forum* 2 (1): 137–38.

Menges, Karl. 1976. "Robert Musil und Edmund Husserl. Über phänomenologische Strukturen im *Mann ohne Eigenschaften.*" *Modern Austrian Literature* 9 (3/4): 131–54.

Strelka, Joseph. 1976. "'Seinesgleichen geschieht' oder Wie lange noch 'erfindet' man Musil-Kritik? Bemerkungen zum gegenwärtigen Stand der Nachlaßbearbeitung und der Editionsarbeiten am Werk Robert Musils." *Modern Austrian Literature* 9 (3/4): 200–209.

Thöming, Jürgen C. 1976. "Musil-Seminar zu Editionsfragen, 19. März 1976, Brüssel." *Musil-Forum* 2 (2): 292–300.

Castex, Elisabeth. 1976/77. "Probleme und Ziele der Forschung am Nachlaß Robert Musils." *Colloquia Germanica* 10 (3): 267–79.

Schröder-Werle, Renate. 1976/77. "Zur Vorgeschichte der Musil-Rezeption nach 1945." *Colloquia Germanica* 10 (3): 247–66.

Barnouw, Dagmar. 1977. "Scepticism as the Literary Mode: David Hume and Robert Musil." *Musil-Forum* 3 (1): 34–56.

Hall, Murray G. 1977a. "Dokumente zur Musil-Rezeption." *Musil-Forum* 3 (1): 57–75.

———. 1977b. "Robert Musil und der Schutzverband deutscher Schriftsteller in Österreich." *Österreich in Geschichte und Literatur* 21: 202–21.

Cohn, Dorrit. 1978. *Transparent Minds: Modes of Representing Consciousness in Fiction*. Princeton, NJ: Princeton UP.

Dawlianidse, David. 1978. "Der offene Romananfang. Am Beispiel von R. Musils Roman *Der Mann ohne Eigenschaften*." *Musil-Forum* 4 (1): 35–59.

Holmes, Alan. 1978. *"Der Mann ohne Eigenschaften": An Examination of the Relationship between the Author, Narrator and Protagonist*. Bonn: Bouvier. Abhandlungen zur Kunst-, Musik- und Literaturwissenschaft 259.

King, Lynda J. 1978. "The Relationship between Clarisse and Nietzsche in Musil's *Der Mann ohne Eigenschaften*." *Musil-Forum* 4 (1): 21–34.

Peters, Frederick G. 1978. *Robert Musil: Master of the Hovering Life. A Study of the Major Fiction*. New York: Columbia UP.

Wiegmann, Hermann. 1978. "Musils Utopiebegriff und seine literaturtheoretischen Konsequenzen." In *Literatur ist Utopie*, edited by Gert Ueding. Vol. 1: Frankfurt am Main: Suhrkamp, 309–34.

Zehl-Romero, Christiane. 1978. "Musils 'letzte Liebesgeschichte.'" *Deutsche Vierteljahrsschrift für Literaturwissenschaft und Geistesgeschichte* 52: 619–34.

Cremerius, Johannes. 1979. "Robert Musil. Das Dilemma eines Schriftstellers vom Typus *poeta ductus* nach Freud." *Psyche* 33 (8): 733–72.

Fuder, Dieter. 1979. *Analogiedenken und anthropologische Differenz: Zu Form und Funktion der poetischen Logik in Robert Musils Roman "Der Mann ohne Eigenschaften."* Munich, Salzburg: Fink. *Musil-Studien* 10.

Henninger, Peter. 1979. "'Wissenschaft' und 'Dichtung' bei Musil und Freud." *Modern Language Notes* 94: 542–68.

Pike, Burton. 1979. "Musil and the City." *Musil-Forum* 5 (1): 68–87.

Rinderknecht, Siegfried. 1979. *Denkphantasie und Reflexionsleidenschaft: Musils Formsynthese im Roman "Der Mann ohne Eigenschaften."* Frankfurt am Main: R. G. Fischer.

Arntzen, Helmut. 1980. *Musil-Kommentar sämtlicher zu Lebzeiten erschienener Schriften außer dem Roman "Der Mann ohne Eigenschaften."* Munich: Winkler.

Aspetsberger, Friedbert. 1980. "Anderer Zustand, Für — In. Musil und einige Zeitgenossen." In *Robert Musil: Untersuchungen,* edited by Uwe Baur and Elisabeth Castex. Königstein, 1980, 46–66. Revised and reprinted 1982 in *Musil in Focus: Papers from a Centenary Symposium,* edited by Lothar Huber and John J. White. University of London: Institute of Germanic Studies, 54–73.

Baur, Uwe, and Elisabeth Castex, eds. 1980. *Robert Musil: Untersuchungen.* Königstein/Taunus: Athenäum.

Frisé, Adolf. 1980. "Unvollendet — Unvollendbar? Überlegungen zum Torso des *Mann ohne Eigenschaften.*" *Musil-Forum* 6 (1): 79–104.

Gumtau, Helmut. 1980. "Robert Musil und die 'Geschichtsbuch-Jahrzehnte.'" *Musil-Forum* 6 (2): 184–206.

Henninger, Peter. 1980. *Der Buchstabe und der Geist: Unbewußte Determinierung im Schreiben Robert Musils.* Frankfurt am Main, Bern, Cirencester: Peter Lang. Europäische Hochschulschriften 359; Literatur & Psychologie 4.

Heyd, Dieter. 1980. *Musil-Lektüre, der Text, das Unbewußte: Psychosemiologische Studien zu Robert Musils theoretischem Werk und zum Roman "Der Mann ohne Eigenschaften."* Frankfurt am Main, Bern, Cirencester: Peter Lang. Europäische Hochschulschriften 368.

Hickman, Hannah. 1980. "Der junge Musil und R. W. Emerson." *Musil-Forum* 6 (1): 3–13.

Kaizik, Jürgen. 1980. *Die Mathematik im Werke Robert Musils.* Vienna: Josef Steiner.

Karthaus, Ulrich. 1980. "War Musil Realist?" *Musil-Forum* 6 (1): 155–27.

Luft, David S. 1980. *Robert Musil and the Crisis of European Culture 1880–1942.* Berkeley, Los Angeles, London: U of California P.

Meister, Monika. 1980a. "Robert Musil als früher Kritiker der 'Kulturindustrie.'" *Musil-Forum* 6: 157–70.

———. 1980b. "Robert Musils Zeitgenossen im Spiegel seiner Kritik." *Maske und Kothurn* 26: 271–85.

Moser, Walter. 1980. "Diskursexperimente im Romantext zu Musils *Der Mann ohne Eigenschaften.*" In Baur und Castex, 1980, 170–97.

Peyret, Jean-François. 1980. "Von jenen, die auszogen, den *Der Mann ohne Eigenschaften* zu verstehen." In Baur und Castex, 1980, 31–45.

Ryan, Judith. 1980. "The Vanishing Subject: Empirical Psychology and the Modern Novel." *Publications of the Modern Language Association of America* 95: 857–69.

Schmitz, Dietmar Bernhard. 1980. "Musils verlegter Weg zum Leser." *Musil-Forum* 6 (2): 213–22. Reprinted 1980 under the title "Musils erschwerter Weg zum Leser." In *Literatur und Kritik* 16 (160): 621–27.

Venturelli, Aldo. 1980. "Die Kunst als fröhliche Wissenschaft. Zum Verhältnis Musils zu Nietzsche." *Nietzsche-Studien* 9: 302–37.

Weissberg, Liliane. 1980. "Versuch einer Sprache des Möglichen. Zum Problem des Erzählens bei Robert Musil." *Deutsche Vierteljahrsschrift für Literaturwissenschaft und Geistesgeschichte* 54 (3): 464–84.

Zeller, Rosmarie. 1980. "Musils Auseinandersetzung mit der realistischen Schreibweise." *Musil-Forum* 6 (1): 128–44.

Böhme, Hartmut. 1981. "Die Suche nach anderem Leben und die Kritik tradierter Ordnung: Robert Musil." In *Sozialgeschichte der deutschen Literatur von 1918 bis zur Gegenwart,* edited by Jan Berg et al. Frankfurt am Main: Fischer, 283–88.

Bohrer, Karl Heinz. 1981. *Plötzlichkeit: Zum Augenblick des ästhetischen Scheins.* Frankfurt am Main: Suhrkamp.

Castex, Elisabeth. 1981. "Zum neuesten Stand der Musil-Editions-Forschung und -Rezeption." *Musil-Forum* 7: 53–64.

Dettmering, Peter. 1981. "Narzißtische Konfiguration in Robert Musils *Der Mann ohne Eigenschaften.*" *Psyche* 35 (12): 1122–35.

Frank, Manfred. 1981. "Erkenntniskritische, ästhetische und mythologische Aspekte der 'Eigenschaftslosigkeit' in Musils Roman." *Revue de Théologie et de Philosophie* 113: 241–57.

Freese, Wolfgang, ed. 1981. *Philologie und Kritik.* Munich, Salzburg: Fink. *Musil-Studien* 7.

Gargani, Aldo. 1981. "Wittgenstein's 'perspicuous representation' and Musil's 'illuminations.'" In *Ethik: Grundlagen, Probleme und Anwendungen,* edited by Edgar Morcher. Vienna: Hölder, Pichler, Tempsky, 508–14. Reprinted 1983 in Strutz, 110–19.

Groeben, Norbert, ed. 1981. *Rezeption und Interpretation: Ein interdisziplinärer Versuch am Beispiel der "Hasenkatastrophe" von Robert Musil.* Tübingen: Narr. Empirische Literaturwissenschaft 5.

Hahnl, Hans Heinz. 1981. "Zu Musils Aktualität." *Musil-Forum* 7 (1/2): 169–73.

Henninger, Peter. 1981. "Über Musils Stil und seine Wahrnehmung (aufgrund einer Textprobe aus dem *Der Mann ohne Eigenschaften*)." *Musil-Forum* 7 (1/2): 29–39.

Karthaus, Ulrich. 1981a. "*Der Mann ohne Eigenschaften* und die Phantasie. Überlegungen im Anschluß an Kant." *Musil-Forum* 7 (1/2): 111–17.

———. 1981b. "Robert Musil und der poetische Realismus." In Freese, 223–45.

Magnou, Jacqueline. 1981. "Zwischen Mach und Freud: Ich-Problematik in den Frühwerken Robert Musils." *Musil-Forum* 7: 131–41.

Marschner, Renate M. 1981. *Utopie der Möglichkeit: Ästhetische Theorie dargestellt am "Mann ohne Eigenschaften" von Robert Musil.* Stuttgart. Stuttgarter Arbeiten zur Germanistik 97.

Mauser, Wolfram. 1981. "Robert Musil." In *Handbuch der deutschen Erzählung,* edited by Karl Konrad Polheim. Düsseldorf: Bagel, 483–90.

Monti, Claudia. 1981. "Musils 'Ratioïd,' oder Wissenschaft als Analogie der Ratio." In Freese, 1981, 195–222. Reprinted 1982 in Farda and Karthaus, 175–96. Reprinted 1983 in Brokoph-Mauch, 205–35.

Olmi, Roberto. 1981. "Musil und Nietzsche." *Musil-Forum* 7: 119–29.

Rocek, Roman. 1981. *"Der Mann ohne Eigenschaften* — Roman ohne Ende?" *Musil-Forum* 7 (1/2): 143–53.

Schlüer, Klaus-Dieter. 1981. "Psychoanalytische Interpretation." In Groeben, 1981, 63–76.

Schönwiese, Ernst. 1981. "Musils Aktualität damals und heute." *Forum* 7 (1/2): 157–61.

Schröder-Werle, Renate. 1981. "Probleme einer künftigen Musil-Edition." Bestandsaufnahme und Lösungsvorschläge." In Freese, 13–52.

Sokel, Walter. 1981. "Robert Musil und die Existenzphilosophie Jean-Paul Sartres: Zum 'existenzphilosophischen Bildungsroman' Musils und Sartres." In *Literaturwissenschaft und Geistesgeschichte: Festschrift für Richard Brinkmann,* edited by Jürgen Brummack et al. Tübingen: Niemeyer.

Strutz, Josef. 1981. *Politik und Literatur in Musils "Mann ohne Eigenschaften."* Königstein/Taunus: Hain. Literatur in der Geschichte, Geschichte in der Literatur 6.

von Heydebrand, Renate. 1981a. "Versuch einer form-analytischen Interpretation." In Groeben, 31–52.

———. 1981b. "Geistesgeschichtliche Argumentation." In Groeben, 52–62.

Arntzen, Helmut. 1982a. *Musil-Kommentar zu dem Roman "Der Mann ohne Eigenschaften."* Munich: Winkler.

———. 1982b. "Ulrich und Agathe — Heilige Gespräche." In Farda and Karthaus, 117–24.

Aspetsberger, Friedbert. 1982. "'Der andere Zustand' in Its Contemporary Context." In Huber and White, 54–73.

Aue, Maximilian. 1982. "Musil und die Romantik. Einige grundsätzliche Überlegungen." In Farda and Karthaus, 125–34.

Beard, Philip H. 1982. "The 'End' of *The Man without Qualities.*" *Musil-Forum* 8: 30–45.

Böhme, Hartmut. 1982. "Der Mangel des Narziß. Über Wunschstrukturen und Leiberfahrungen in Robert Musils *Der Mann ohne Eigenschaften*." In Farda and Karthaus, 45–85.

Düsing, Wolfgang. 1982. *Erinnerung und Identität: Untersuchungen zu einem Erzählproblem bei Musil, Döblin und Doderer*. Munich: Fink.

Eisele, Ulf. 1982. "Ulrichs Mutter ist doch ein Tintenfaß. Zur Literaturproblematik in Musils *Der Mann ohne Eigenschaften*." In von Heydebrand, 160–203. Reprinted 1984 in Ulf Eisele, *Die Struktur des modernen deutschen Romans*. Tübingen: Niemeyer, 114–50.

Farda, Dieter P. 1982. "Einige Bemerkungen zur ästhetischen Konstitutionsproblematik des Romans *Der Mann ohne Eigenschaften* von Robert Musil." In Farda and Karthaus, 19–44.

Farda, Dieter P., and Ulrich Karthaus, eds. 1982. *Sprachästhetische Sinnvermittlung*. Frankfurt am Main, Bern: Peter Lang. Europäische Hochschulschriften 493.

Frisé, Adolf. 1982. "Von einer 'Geschichte dreier Personen' zum *Mann ohne Eigenschaften*. Zur Entstehung von Robert Musils Romanwerk." *Jahrbuch der deutschen Schillergesellschaft* 26: 428–44.

Henninger, Peter. 1982. "Auge und Blick: Notationen zum Sehvorgang in Texten Robert Musils." In Farda and Karthaus, 1982, 86–96.

Huber, Lothar. 1982. "Satire and Irony in Musil's *Der Mann ohne Eigenschaften*." In Huber and White, 99–114.

Huber, Lothar, and John J. White, eds. 1982. *Musil in Focus: Papers from a Centenary Symposium*. London: Institute of Germanic Studies, University of London.

Margwelaschwili, Giwi. 1982. "Die existential-ontologische Thematik in Musils *Der Mann ohne Eigenschaften*." *Musil-Forum* 8: 69–102.

Menges, Martin. 1982. *Abstrakte Welt und Eigenschaftslosigkeit: Eine Interpretation von Robert Musils "Der Mann ohne Eigenschaften" unter dem Leitbegriff der Abstraktion*. Frankfurt am Main, Bern: Peter Lang.

Paulson, Ronald M. 1982. *Robert Musil and the Ineffable: Hieroglyph, Myth, Fairy Tale and Sign*. Stuttgart: Heinz. Stuttgarter Arbeiten zur Germanistik 112.

Scholz, Frithard. 1982. *Freiheit als Indifferenz: Alteuropäische Probleme mit der Systemtheorie Niklas Luhmanns*. Frankfurt am Main: Suhrkamp.

Sokel, Walter H. 1982. "*Robert Musil Mann ohne Eigenschaften* und die Existenzphilosophie." In Farda and Karthaus, 97–102.

Stern, J. P. 1982. "'Reality' in *Der Mann ohne Eigenschaften*." In Huber and White, 74–84.

von Heydebrand, Renate, ed. 1982. *Robert Musil.* Darmstadt: Wissenschaftliche Buchgesellschaft. Wege der Forschung 588.

Zeller, Hans. 1982. "Vitium aut virtus? Philologisches zu Adolf Frisés Musil-Ausgaben, mit prinzipiellen Überlegungen zur Frage des Texteingriffs." *Zeitschrift für deutsche Philologie. Sonderheft: Probleme neugermanistischer Edition* 101: 210–44.

Allemann, Beda. 1983. "Robert Musil und die Zeitgeschichte." In *Literatur und Germanistik nach der Machtübernahme: Colloquium zur 50. Wiederkehr des 30. Januar 1933,* edited by Beda Allemann. Bonn: Bouvier, 90–117.

Böschenstein, Bernhard. 1983. "Historischer Übergang und System der Ambivalenzen: zum *Mann ohne Eigenschaften.*" In Brokoph-Mauch, 181–89.

Brokoph-Mauch, Gudrun, ed. 1983. *Beiträge zur Musil-Kritik.* Bern, Frankfurt am Main: Peter Lang. New Yorker Studien zur neueren deutschen Literaturgeschichte 2. Identical edition in series Europäische Hochschulschriften 596.

Cejpek, Lucas. 1983. *Wahn und Methode: Robert Musils "Der Mann ohne Eigenschaften."* Graz: dbv-Verlag.

Erickson, Susan J. 1983. "Essay/body/fiction: The Repression of an Interpretive Context in an Essay of Robert Musil." *German Quarterly* 56: 580–93.

Frank, Manfred. 1983. "Auf der Suche nach einem Grund. Über den Umschlag von Erkenntniskritik in Mythologie bei Musil." In *Mythos und Moderne: Begriff und Bild einer Rekonstruktion,* edited by Karl Heinz Bohrer. Frankfurt am Main: Suhrkamp, 318–62.

Freese, Wolfgang. 1983. "Zur neueren Musil-Forschung. Ausgaben und Gesamtdarstellungen." *Text+Kritik* 21/22: 86–148.

Fuld, Werner. 1983. "Der Schwierige. Zu Verlagsproblemen Robert Musils." *Text+Kritik* 21/22: 44–62.

Goltschnigg, Dietmar. 1983. "Robert Musil *Der Mann ohne Eigenschaften (1930ff.).*" In *Deutsche Romane des 20. Jahrhunderts,* edited by Paul Michael Lützeler. Königstein/Taunus: Athenäum, 218–35.

Hüppauf, Bernd-Rüdiger. 1983. "Von Wien durch den Krieg nach nirgendwo. Nation und utopisches Denken bei Musil und im Austromarxismus." *Text und Kritik* 21/22: 55–69.

Karthaus, Ulrich. 1983. "War Musil Realist?" In Brokoph-Mauch, 13–24.

Magris, Claudio. 1983. "Hinter dieser Unendlichkeit: die Odyssee des Robert Musil." In Brokoph-Mauch, 49–62.

Meister, Monika. 1983. "Der 'andere Zustand' in der Kunstwirkung." In Brokoph-Mauch, 237–55.

Monti, Claudia. 1983. "Musils 'ratioïd' oder Wissenschaft als Analogie der Ratio." In Brokoph-Mauch, 205–35.

Müller, Götz. 1983. "Isis und Osiris: Die Mythen in Robert Musils Roman *Der Mann ohne Eigenschaften.*" *Zeitschrift für deutsche Philologie* (102): 583–604.

Olmi, Roberto. 1983 "Die Gegenwart Nietzsches." In Brokoph-Mauch, 87–109.

Reis, Gilbert. 1983. *Musils Frage nach der Wirklichkeit.* Königstein/Taunus: Hain.

Roth, Marie-Louise. 1983a. "Essay und Essayismus bei Robert Musil." In *Probleme der Moderne: Studien zur deutschen Literatur von Nietzsche bis Brecht. Festschrift für Walter Sokel,* edited by Benjamin Bennett, Anton Kaes, and William J. Lillyman. Tübingen: Niemeyer. 117–31.

————. 1983b. "Robert Musil als Aphoristiker." In Brokoph-Mauch, 289–320.

Sokel, Walter. 1983. "Agathe und der existenzphilosophische Faktor im *Mann ohne Eigenschaften.*" In Brokoph-Mauch, 111–28.

Strelka, Joseph. 1983. "Robert Musils 'Geschichte aus drei Jahrhunderten.'" In Brokoph-Mauch, 257–62.

Strutz, Josef, ed. 1983a. *Robert Musil und die kulturellen Tendenzen seiner Zeit.* Munich: Fink. *Musil-Studien* 11.

————. 1983b. "Robert Musil und die Politik. Der Mann ohne Eigenschaften als 'Morallaboratorium.'" In Strutz, 1983a, 160–71.

Wallner, Friedrich. 1983. "Musil als Philosoph." In Strutz, 1983a, 93–109.

Beckers, Gustave. 1984. "Strategien dialektischen Humors in Robert Musils Roman *Der Mann ohne Eigenschaften.*" *Musil-Forum* 10: 86–91.

Blasberg, Cornelia. 1984. *Krise und Utopie der Intellektuellen. Kulturkritische Aspekte in Robert Musils Roman "Der Mann ohne Eigenschaften."* Stuttgart: Heinz. Stuttgarter Arbeiten zur Germanistik 140.

Cejpek, Lucas. 1984. "Von der Abwesenheit des Krieges. Friede im *Mann ohne Eigenschaften.*" In Strutz and Strutz, 203–19.

Charriere-Jaquin, Marianne. 1984. "*Der Mann ohne Eigenschaften* als Suche nach einer hermaphroditischen Sprache: Wechselspiel des Konvexen und Konkaven." In Strutz and Strutz, 73–90.

Gargani, Aldo G. 1984. "Philosophy and Metaphor in Musil's Work." In Strutz und Strutz, 44–57.

Hartinger, Ingram. 1984. "Der Besuch im Irrenhaus oder lang ersehnte Annäherung an Latein-Amerika. Zu einem Tagebuchtext Robert Musils." In Strutz and Strutz, 220–39.

Henninger, Peter. 1984. "Verhaltene Phantasien. Robert Musils narrative Gedankenprosa." *Musil-Forum* 10: 120–31.

Hickman, Hannah. 1984. *Robert Musil and the Culture of Vienna.* Beckenham, London, and Sydney: Croom Helm; La Salle, IL: Open Court.

Howald, Stephan. 1984. *Ästhetizismus und ästhetische Literaturkritik*. Munich: Fink. *Musil-Studien* 9.

Moser, Walter. 1984. "The Factual Fiction. The Case of Robert Musil." *Poetics Today* 5: 411–28.

Pott, Hans-Georg. 1984. *Robert Musil*. Munich: Fink.

Reis, Gilbert. 1984. "Eine Brücke ins Imaginäre. Gleichnis und Reflexion in Robert Musils *Mann ohne Eigenschaften*." *Euphorion* 78: 143–59.

Sokel, Walter H. 1984. "Robert Musils Kampf um die Mimesis. Zur Poetologie seiner Anfänge." *Musil-Forum* 10: 238–41.

Strutz, Josef. 1984. "Von der 'biegsamen Dialektik.' Notizen zur Bedeutung Kants, Hegels und Nietzsches für das Werk Musils." In Strutz and Strutz, 11–21.

Strutz, Josef, and Johann Strutz, eds. 1984. *Robert Musil — Literatur, Philosophie, Psychologie*. Munich, Salzburg: Fink. *Musil-Studien* 12.

Vogt, Guntram. 1984. "Robert Musils ambivalentes Verhältnis zur Demokratie." *Exilforschung* 2: 310–38.

Wallner, Friedrich. 1984. "Sehnsucht nach Verweigerung. Musil und Nietzsche." In Strutz and Strutz, 91–109.

Wicht, Gérard. 1984. *"Gott meint die Welt keineswegs wörtlich": Zum Gleichnisbegriff in Robert Musils Roman "Mann ohne Eigenschaften."* Frankfurt am Main, Bern, New York: Peter Lang. Europäische Hochschulschriften 792.

Willemsen, Roger. 1984a. *Das Existenzrecht der Dichtung: Zur Rekonstruktion einer systematischen Literaturtheorie im Werk Robert Musils*. Munich: Fink.

———. 1984b. "Die sentimentale Gesellschaft. Zur Begründung einer aktivistischen Literaturtheorie im Werk Robert Musils und Robert Müllers." *Deutsche Vierteljahrsschrift für Literaturwissenschaft und Geistesgeschichte* 58 (2): 289–316.

———. 1984c. "Über die Möglichkeit eines Musil-Kommentars." *Göttingische Gelehrte Anzeigen* 236 (3/4): 231–49.

Alt, Peter-André. 1985. *Ironie und Krise: Erzählen als Form ästhetischer Wahrnehmung in Thomas Manns "Zauberberg" und Robert Musils "Mann ohne Eigenschaften."* Frankfurt am Main, Bern, New York: Peter Lang. Europäische Hochschulschriften 722.

Arntzen, Helmut. 1985. *Roger Willemsen: Eine Fallstudie*. Münster: Sonderdruck im Selbstverlag.

Baltz-Balzberg, Regina. 1985. "Antidekadenzmoral bei Musil und Nietzsche." In Strutz and Strutz, 204–26.

Cometti, Jean-Pierre. 1985. "Psychoanalyse und Erzählung." In Strutz and Strutz, 153–65.

Dinklage, Karl. 1985. "Ende der *Schwärmer* — Ende des *Mann ohne Eigenschaften*." In Strutz and Strutz, 227–43.

Moser, Manfred. 1985. "Erinnerung, blitzartiger Einfall und — natürlich — die Ironie." In Strutz and Strutz, 110–42.

Schmidt, Jochen. 1985. "Robert Musil: die Genie-Moral eines Mannes ohne Eigenschaften; der 'potentielle Mensch' als der schöpferische Mensch." In *Die Geschichte des Genie-Gedankens in der deutschen Literatur, Philosophie und Politik*, vol. 2. Darmstadt: Wissenschaftliche Buchgesellschaft. 278–98.

Strutz, Johann, and Josef Strutz, eds. 1985. *Robert Musil: Theater, Bildung, Kritik*. Munich, Salzburg: Fink.

Willemsen, Roger. 1985. *Robert Musil: Vom intelletuellen Eros*. Munich, Zurich: Piper.

Zima, Peter V. 1985. "Robert Musils Sprachkritik. Ambivalenz, Polyphonie und Dekonstruktion." In Strutz and Strutz, 185–203. *Musil-Studien* 13.

Böhme, Hartmut. 1986. "Die 'Zeit ohne Eigenschaften' und die 'Neue Unübersichtlichkeit.' Robert Musil und die *posthistoire*" In Strutz and Strutz, 9–33.

Chiarini, Paolo, ed. 1986. Musil, *Nostro Contemporaneo*. Rome: Istituto Italiano di Studi Germanici.

Dowden, Stephen. 1986. "The Cloud of Polonius: Rewriting Reality in Robert Musil's *Mann ohne Eigenschaften*." In *Sympathy for the Abyss: A Study in the Novel of German Modernism: Kafka, Broch, Musil and Thomas Mann*. Tübingen: Niemeyer. 57–93. Studien zur deutschen Literatur 90.

Goltschnigg, Dietmar. 1986. "Die Rolle des geisteskranken Verbrechers in Robert Musils Erzählung 'Die Vollendung der Liebe' und im *Mann ohne Eigenschaften*." In Chiarini, 103–16.

Heftrich, Eckhard. 1986. *Musil: Eine Einführung*. Munich, Zurich: Artemis.

Kim, Rae-Hyeon. 1986. *Robert Musil: Poetologische Reflexionen zur Geschichtlichkeit der Literatur*. Bonn: Bouvier. Literatur und Reflexion 4.

Strutz, Johann, and Josef Strutz, eds. 1986. *Kunst, Wissenschaft und Politik von Robert Musil bis Ingeborg Bachmann*. Munich, Salzburg: Fink. *Musil-Studien* 14.

Vogt, Guntram. 1986. "Robert Musil. Politik als Methode. Zum Kontext von Kunst, Wissenschaft, Politik." In Strutz and Strutz, 146–64.

Willemsen, Roger. 1986. "Dionysisches Sprechen. Zur Theorie einer Sprache der Erregung bei Musil und Nietzsche." *Deutsche Vierteljahrsschrift für Literaturwissenschaft und Geistesgeschichte* 60 (1): 104–35.

Classen, Albrecht. 1987. "Robert Musil: *Mann ohne Eigenschaften*: Der antizipatorische Charakter des ersten Buches." *Carleton Germanic Papers*. Ottawa: Carleton University. Vol. 15. 1–16.

Cometti, Jean-Pierre. 1987. "Es gibt Geschichte und Geschichten." *Musil-Studien* (13): 164–81.

Dresler-Brumme, Charlotte. 1987. *Nietzsches Philosophie in Musils Roman "Mann ohne Eigenschaften."* Frankfurt am Main: Athenäum. Literatur in der Geschichte, Geschichte in der Literatur 13.

Frisé, Adolf. 1987. *Plädoyer für Robert Musil.* Reinbek bei Hamburg: Rowohlt.

Horn, Peter. 1987. "'Wenn ich den Sinn wüßte, so brauchte ich dir wohl nicht erst zu erzählen.'" *Euphorion* 81 (4): 391–413.

Jakob, Michael. 1987. "Von der 'Frau ohne Eigenschaften' zum *Mann ohne Eigenschaften.* Anmerkungen zu Clarisse." In Strutz, 1987a, 116–33.

Lethen, Helmut. 1987. "Eckfenster der Moderne. Wahrnehmungsexperimente bei Musil und E. T. A. Hoffmann." In Strutz, 1987a, 195–229.

Luserke, Matthias. 1987. *Wirklichkeit und Möglichkeit: Modaltheoretische Untersuchungen zum Werk Robert Musils.* Frankfurt am Main, Bern, New York: Peter Lang. Europäische Hochschulschriften 1000.

Mejovsek, Gabriele. 1987. "Das Modell der Gestalt als Prinzip 'anfänglichen Denkens' bei Musils Versuch der Erstellung eines 'beweglichen Gleichgewichts.'" In Strutz, 1987a, 273–92.

Middell, Elke. 1987. "Robert Musils *Mann ohne Eigenschaften.* Annäherungen." *Weimarer Beiträge* 33: 981–1003.

Moser, Walter. 1987. "Zwischen Wissenschaft und Literatur. Zu Robert Musils Essayismus." In *Verabschiedung der (Post-)Moderne? Eine interdisziplinäre Debatte,* edited by Gérard Raulet and Jacques Le Rider. Tübingen: Narr, 167–96.

Payne, Philip. 1987. *Robert Musil's Works, 1906–1924: A Critical Introduction.* Frankfurt am Main, Bern, New York: Peter Lang. Europäische Hochschulschriften 961.

Pfeiffer, Peter C. 1987. "Nicht Fisch und nicht Fleisch. Robert Musils Reaktion auf den Nationalsozialismus." In Strutz, 1987a, 145–63.

Pott, Hans-Georg. 1987. "Musil und das Problem einer Ethik nach Freud." In Strutz, 1987a, 44–59.

Reis, Gilbert. 1987. "Perspektivische Verkürzungen des Verstandes. Wirklichkeitsdarstellung unter dem Gesichtspunkt der Subjektivität." *Euphorion* 81 (2): 119–30.

Schaunig-Baltz-Balzberg, Regina. 1987. "Musils 'Rezept: Organisation.' Zur Klagenfurter Nachlaß-Forschung unter Karl Dinklage." In Strutz, 1987a, 16–26.

Strutz, Josef, ed. 1987a. *Robert Musils "Kakanien" — Subjekt und Geschichte: Festschrift für Karl Dinklage zum 80. Geburtstag.* Munich, Salzburg: Fink. *Musil-Studien* 15.

———. 1987b. "'Die Welt vom sechsten Schöpfungstag': Sigmund Freuds Begriff des 'Todestriebs' und Musils 'Stilleben'-Konzept im Mann ohne Eigenschaften." In Strutz, 1987a, 230–43.

Wallner, Friedrich. 1987. "Das Konzept einer Philosophie als Dichtung und einer Dichtung als Philosophie." In Strutz, 1987a, 134–44.

Cejpek, Lucas. 1987/88. "Geschichte als Literatur. Zu einer Philosophie der Geschichten. Robert Musils *Mann ohne Eigenschaften.*" *Musil-Forum* 13/14: 113–24.

Alt, Peter-André. 1988. "Allegorische Formen in Robert Musils Erzählungen." *Jahrbuch der deutschen Schillergesellschaft* 32: 314–43.

Bohn, Ralf. 1988. *Transversale Inversion: Symptomatologie und Genealogie des Denkens in der Philosophie Robert Musils.* Würzburg: Königshausen & Neumann. Epistemata: Reihe Literaturwissenschaft 33.

Cellbrot, Hartmut. 1988. *Die Bewegung des Sinnes: Zur Phänomenologie Robert Musils im Hinblick auf Edmund Husserl.* Munich: Fink. *Musil-Studien* 17.

Corino, Karl. 1988. *Robert Musil — Leben und Werk in Bildern und Texten.* Reinbek bei Hamburg: Rowohlt.

Farda, Dieter P. 1988. *mundus pluralis: Robert Musils Roman "Mann ohne Eigenschaften" im Wechselspiel von Reflexion und Phantasie.* Heidelberg: Carl Winter.

Frank, Manfred. 1988. "Remythisierte Erkenntniskritik (Robert Musil)." In *Gott im Exil: Vorlesungen über die Neue Mythologie.* Part II. Frankfurt am Main: Suhrkamp, 315–32.

Payne, Philip. 1988. *Robert Musil's "The Man without Qualities": A Critical Study.* Cambridge, New York, Melbourne: Cambridge UP.

Pietsch, Reinhard. 1988. *Fragmente und Schrift: Selbstimplikative Strukturen bei Robert Musil.* Frankfurt am Main, Bern, New York: Peter Lang. Europäische Hochschulschriften 1082.

Renner, Rolf Günter. 1988. "Postmoderne Perspektiven im Text der klassischen Moderne: Robert Musil." In *Die postmoderne Konstellation: Theorie, Text und Kunst im Ausgang der Moderne.* Freiburg: Rombach, 124–44.

Ryan, Judith. 1988. "Validating the Possible: Thoughts and Things in James, Rilke and Musil." *Comparative Literature* 40 (4): 305–17.

Schiller, Dieter. 1988. "Die Grenze der Kultur gegen die Politik. Zu Robert Musils Rede auf dem Pariser Kongreß 1935." *Zeitschrift für Germanistik* 2: 274–90.

Sokel, Walter H. 1988. "*Der Mann ohne Eigenschaften* und das achtzehnte Jahrhundert." In *Das neuzeitliche Ich in der Literatur des 18. und 20. Jahrhunderts,* edited by Ulrich Fülleborn and Manfred Engel. Munich: Fink, 293–305.

Strutz, Josef. 1988. "Unzutreffend." *Kleine Zeitung* (Klagenfurt) (August 28): 41.

Venturelli, Aldo. 1988. *Robert Musil und das Projekt der Moderne.* Frankfurt am Main, Bern, New York: Peter Lang. Europäische Hochschulschriften 1039.

Welzig, Werner. 1988. "Verwischte Spuren: Zu und aus Anlaß von Helmut Arntzens Musil-Kommentar (Der Mann ohne Eigenschaften)." *Germanisch-Romanische Monatsschrift* 38 (3): 343–47.

Wilkins, Sophie. 1988. "Einige Notizen zum Fall der Übersetzerin der Knopf-Auflage des *Mann ohne Eigenschaften.*" In Daigger and Militzer, 1988, 75–90.

Zima, Pierre. 1988. *L'Ambivalence romanesque: Proust, Kafka, Musil.* Frankfurt am Main: Peter Lang.

Bangerter, Lowell A. 1989. *Robert Musil.* New York: Continuum.

Brooks, Daniel Josef. 1989. "Aesthetic Nietzscheanism in *Mann ohne Eigenschaften.*" *Musil-Forum* 15: 94–112.

Hall, Murray G. 1989. "Der Preis der Stadt Wien." *Musil-Forum* 15: 166–70.

Magris, Claudio. 1989. "Die Odyssee des Robert Musil." *Merkur* 33: 139–55.

Moser, Manfred. 1989. "Ing. Dr. phil. Robert Musil: Ein Soldat erzählt." In *Arsenale der Seele: Literatur- und Medienanalyse seit 1870,* edited by Friedrich A. Kittler and Georg Christoph Tholen. Munich: Fink, 97–115.

Pekar, Thomas. 1989. *Die Sprache der Liebe bei Robert Musil.* Munich: Fink. *Musil-Studienk 19.*

Venturelli, Aldo. 1989. "Die Erfindung der Geschichte. Musils Auffassung der Geschichte in *Mann ohne Eigenschaften.*" In *Die österreichische Literatur: Ihr Profil von der Jahrhundertwende bis zur Gegenwart (1880–1980),* edited by Herbert Zeman. Vol. 2. Graz: Akademische Druck- und Verlangsanstalt. 1037–50.

Wagner-Egelhaaf. Martina. 1989. *Mystik der Moderne: Die visionäre Ästhetik der deutschen Literatur im 20. Jahrhundert.* Stuttgart: Metzler.

Corino, Karl. 1990. "Robert Musils Wirkung auf die Weltliteratur." *Musil-Forum* 16 (1–2): 92–102.

Diersch, Manfred. 1990. "Draußen, Drinnen und Ich. Ernst Machs 'Spiegel der Erkenntnis' als Anregung für österreichische Erzählkunst des 20. Jahrhunderts." In Strutz and Kiss, 29–42.

Finlay, Marike. 1990. *The Potential of Modern Discourse: Musil, Peirce, and Perturbation.* Bloomington, Indianapolis: Indiana UP.

Gutjahr, Ortrud. 1990. "'. . . Den Eingang ins Paradies finden': Inzest als Motiv und Struktur im Roman Robert Musils und Ingeborg Bachmanns." In Strutz and Kiss, 139–58.

Hassler-Rütti, Ruth. 1990. *Wirklichkeit und Wahn in Robert Musils Roman "Mann ohne Eigenschaften."* Frankfurt am Main, Bern, New York: Peter Lang. Europäische Hochschulschriften 1189.

Le Rider, Jacques. 1990. *Das Ende der Illusion: Die Wiener Moderne und die Krisen der Identität.* Vienna: Österreichischer Bundesverlag.

Longuet-Marx, Anne. 1990. "Proust, Musil — Ethiken des Schreibens." In Strutz and Kiss, 53–66.

Nadermann, Peter. 1990. *Schreiben als anderes Leben: Eine Untersuchung zu Robert Musils "Mann ohne Eigenschaften."* Frankfurt am Main, Bern, New York, Paris: Peter Lang. Bochumer Schriften zur deutschen Literatur 17.

Pennisi, Francesca. 1990. *Auf der Suche nach Ordnung: Die Entstehungsgeschichte des Ordnungsgedanken bei Robert Musil von den ersten Romanentwürfen bis zum ersten Band von "Mann ohne Eigenschaften."* St. Ingbert: Röhrig.

Pfeiffer, Peter C. 1990. *Aphorismus und Romanstruktur: Zu Robert Musils "Der Mann ohne Eigenschaften."* Bonn: Bouvier. Bonner Arbeiten zur deutschen Literatur 46.

Schärer, Hans-Rudolf. 1990. *Narzißmus und Utopismus: Eine literaturpsychologische Untersuchung zu Musils "Der Mann ohne Eigenschaften."* Munich: Fink. Musil-Studien 20.

Strutz, Josef, and Endre Kiss, eds. 1990. *Genauigkeit und Seele: Zur österreichischen Literatur seit dem Fin de siécle.* Munich, Salzburg: Fink. Musil-Studien 18.

Tewilt, Gerd-Theo. 1990. *Zustand der Dichtung: Interpretationen zur Sprachlichkeit des "anderen Zustands" in Robert Musils "Der Mann ohne Eigenschaften."* Münster: Aschendorff. Literatur als Sprache. Literaturtheorie — Interpretation — Sprachkritik 7.

Völse, Hans-Joachim. 1990. *Im Labyrinth des Wissens: Zu Robert Musils Roman "Der Mann ohne Eigenschaften."* Wiesbaden: Deutscher Universitätsverlag.

Zimmermann, Hans-Dieter. 1990. "Die zwei Bäume der Erkenntnis: Rationalität und Intuition bei Robert Musil und Max Weber." *Sprache-im-technischen-Zeitalter* 28: 29–34.

Düsing, Wolfgang. 1991. "Goethe in ironischer Beleuchtung. Zur Klassik-Rezeption in *Musils Der Mann ohne Eigenschaften.*" *Jahrbuch der deutschen Schillergesellschaft* 35: 257–74.

Frisé, Adolf. 1991. "Mißdeutungen und Fehlschlüsse. Wie Robert Musil bisweilen von der Kritik gesehen wird." In *"die in dem alten Haus der Sprache wohnen": Festschrift für Helmut Arntzen,* edited by Eckehard Czucka, Thomas Althaus, and Burkhard Spinnen. Münster: Aschendorff, 365–75.

Hickman, Hannah, ed. 1991. *Robert Musil and the Literary Landscape of His Time*. Salford, England: Department of Modern Languages, University of Salford.

Honnef-Becker, Irmgard. 1991. *"Ulrich lächelte": Techniken der Relativierung in Robert Musils Roman "Der Mann ohne Eigenschaften."* Frankfurt am Main, Bern, New York, Paris: Peter Lang. Trierer Studien zur Literatur 20.

Huber, Lothar. 1991. "Nietzsches 'freier Geist' und das Repertoire der deutschen Literatur um 1910: Zu Ideologie und Struktur von Musils Novelle 'Die Vollendung der Liebe.'" In Hickman, 35–52.

Hüppauf, Bernd. 1991. "Musil in Paris. Robert Musils Rede auf dem Kongreß zur Verteidigung der Kultur (1935) im Zusammenhang seines Werkes." *Zeitschrift für Germanistik. Neue Folge* 1 (1): 55–69.

Lahme-Gronostraj, Hildegard. 1991. *Einbildung und Erkenntnis bei Robert Musil und im Verständnis der "Nachbarmacht" Psychoanalyse.* Würzburg: Königshausen & Neumann. Epistemata: Reihe Literaturwissenschaft 65.

Lavin, Carmen. 1991. "Patterns of Expectation in Musil's *Der Mann ohne Eigenschaften*." In Hickman, 172–89.

Maier-Solgk, Frank. 1991. "Musil und die problematische Politik: Zum Verhältnis von Literatur und Politik bei Robert Musil, insbesondere zu einer Auseinandersetzung mit Carl Schmitt." *Orbis Literarum* (46): 340–63.

Meisel, Gerhard. 1991. *Liebe im Zeitalter der Wissenschaft vom Menschen: Das Prosawerk Robert Musils.* Opladen: Westdeutscher Verlag.

Petersen, Jürgen H. 1991. *Der deutsche Roman der Moderne: Grundlegung — Typologie — Entwicklung.* Stuttgart: Metzler, 114–31.

Renner, Rolf Günter. 1991. "Transformatives Erzählen. Musils Grenzgang im *Mann ohne Eigenschaften*." *Germanic Review* 66 (2): 70–80.

Ryan, Judith. 1991. *The Vanishing Subject: Early Psychology and Literary Modernism.* Chicago: U of Chicago P.

Wagner-Egelhaaf, Martina. 1991. "'Anders ich' oder: Vom Leben im Text. Robert Musils Tagebuch-Heft 33." *Deutsche Vierteljahrsschrift für Literaturwissenschaft und Geistesgeschichte* 64 (1): 152–73.

Webber, Andrew J. 1991. "The Beholding Eye: Visual Compulsion in Musil's Works." In Hickman, 94–111.

Zeller, Rosemarie. 1991. "Robert Musil und das Theater seiner Zeit." In Hickman, 134–50.

Altmann, Volker. 1992. *Totalität und Perspektive: Zum Wirklichkeitsbegriff Robert Musils im "Mann ohne Eigenschaften."* Frankfurt am Main, Bern, New York, Paris, Vienna: Peter Lang. Literaturhistorische Untersuchungen 19.

Bonacchi, Silvia. 1992. "Robert Musils Studienjahre in Berlin 1903–1908." *Musil-Forum. Beilage* 1: 1–58.

Brokoph-Mauch, Gudrun, ed. 1992. *Robert Musil: Essayismus und Ironie*. Tübingen: Francke. Edition Orpheus 6.

Cejpek, Lucas, ed. 1992. *Nach Musil: Denkformen*. Vienna, Berlin: Turia & Kant.

Dreis, Gabriele. 1992. *"Ruhelose Gestaltlosigkeit des Daseins": Pädagogische Studien zum "Rousseauismus" im Werk Robert Musils*. Munich: Fink. *Musil-Studien* 23.

Ego, Werner. 1992. *Abschied von der Moral: Eine Rekonstruktion der Ethik Robert Musils*. Freiburg, Vienna: Universitätsverlag/Verlag Herder. Studien zur theologischen Ethik 40.

Harrison, Thomas. 1992. *Essayism: Conrad, Musil, and Pirandello*. Baltimore, London: John Hopkins UP.

Hickman, Hannah. 1992. "Freud, Musil and Gestalt Psychology." *Austrian Studies* (3): 95–108.

Kampits, Peter. 1992. "Musil und Wittgenstein." In Brokoph-Mauch, 1992, 153–60.

Kyora, Sabine. 1992. *Psychoanalyse und Prosa im 20. Jahrhundert*. Stuttgart: Metzler, 162–238.

Maier-Solgk, Frank. 1992. *Sinn für Geschichte: Ästhetische Subjektivität und historiologische Reflexion bei Robert Musil*. Munich: Fink. Musil-Studien 22.

Vietta, Silvio. 1992. "Musils *Der Mann ohne Eigenschaften.*" In *Die literarische Moderne: Eine problemgeschichtliche Darstellung der deutschsprachigen Literatur von Hölderlin bis Thomas Bernhard*. Stuttgart: Metzler, 89–103.

Berz, Peter. 1993. "I-Welten." In Pott, 171–92.

Bouveresse, Jacques. 1993. *L'Homme probable: Robert Musil, le hasard, la moyenne et l'escargot de l'histoire*. Combas: Editions de l'éclat.

Deutsch, Sibylle. 1993. *Der Philosoph als Dichter: Robert Musils Theorie des Erzählens*. St. Ingbert: Röhrig. Beiträge zur Robert-Musil-Forschung und zur neueren österreichischen Literatur 5.

Honold, Alexander. 1993. "Die verwahrte und entsprungene Zeit. Paul Kellers *Ferien vom Ich* und die Zeitdarstellung im Werk Robert Musils." *Deutsche Vierteljahrsschrift für Literaturwissenschaft und Geistesgeschichte* 67 (3): 302–21.

Kaiser-El-Safti, Margret. 1993. "Robert Musil und die Psychologie seiner Zeit." In Pott, 126–69.

Krommer, Axel, and Albert Kümmel. 1993. "Pendelbewegungen des Sinns. Vorschlag einer informations- und chaostheoretischen Bewertung des *Mann ohne Eigenschaften.*" *Rapial* 3 (3): 2–11.

Pott, Hans-Georg, ed. 1993. *Robert Musil: Dichter — Essayist — Wissenschaftler*. Munich: Fink. Musil-Studien 8.

Rzehak, Wolfgang. 1993. *Musil und Nietzsche: Beziehungen der Erkenntnisperspektiven.* Frankfurt am Main: Peter Lang.

Dahan-Gaida, Laurence. 1993/4. "Die Wärmetheorie bei Robert Musil." *Musil-Forum* (19/20): 117–31.

Fourie, Regine. 1993/94: "Musil als Realist?" *Musil-Forum* (19/20): 132–43

Honold, Alexander. 1993/94. "Der Tanz auf dem Vulkan. Kakanien und der Erste Weltkrieg." *Musil-Forum* 19/20: 144–57.

Krommer, Axel and Albert Kümmel. 1993/94. "Ordnung verlangt nach Zerrissenwerden. Skizze einer informationstheoretischen Deutung des *Mann ohne Eigenschaften.*" *Musil-Forum* (19/20): 158–64.

Dahan-Gaida, Laurence. 1994. *Musil: Savoir et fiction.* Paris: Presses universitaires de Vincennes.

Hehner, Cay. 1994. *Erkenntnis und Freiheit: Der Mann ohne Eigenschaften als "Übergangswesen."* Munich: Wilhelm Fink. Musil-Studien 24.

Schraml, Wolfgang. 1994. *Relativismus und Anthropologie: Studien zum Werk Robert Musils und zur Literatur der 20iger Jahre.* Munich: Eberhard Verlag. Grenzen & Horizonte.

Schreiter, Ekkehard. 1994. *Verkehr bei Robert Musil: Identität der Form und Formen der Identität im "Mann ohne Eigenschaften."* Opladen: Westdeutscher Verlag. Kulturwissenschaftliche Studien zur deutschen Literatur.

Honold, Alexander. 1995. *Die Stadt und der Krieg: Raum- und Zeitkonstruktion in Robert Musils Roman "Der Mann ohne Eigenschaften."* Munich: Wilhelm Fink. Musil-Studien 25.

Luserke, Matthias. 1995. *Robert Musil.* Stuttgart/Weimar: J. B. Metzler. Sammlung Metzler 289.

Mackowiak, Klaus. 1995. *Genauigkeit und Seele: Robert Musils Kunstauffassung als Kritik der instrumentellen Vernunft.* Marburg: Tectum Verlag.

Mehigan, Tim. 1995. "Moral und Verbrechen. Einige Gedanken über Robert Musils intellektuelle Position." *Wirkendes Wort* 45 (2): 227–40.

Kochs, Angela Maria. 1996. *Chaos und Individuum: Robert Musils philosophischer Roman als Vision der Moderne.* Munich: Karl Alber Freiburg.

Precht, Richard David. 1996. *Die gleitende Logik der Seele: Ästhetische Selbstreflexivität in Robert Musils "Der Mann ohne Eigenschaften."* Stuttgart: M and P.

Haslmayr, Harald. 1997. *Die Zeit ohne Eigenschaften: Geschichtsphilosophie und Modernebegriff im Werk Robert Musils.* Vienna, Cologne, Weimar: Böhlau. Literatur in der Geschichte. Geschichte in der Literatur 44.

Hoffmann, Christoph. 1997. *"Der Dichter am Apparat": Medientechnik, Experimentalpsychologie und Texte Robert Musils 1899–1942.* Munich: Wilhelm Fink. Musil-Studien 26.

Loenker, Fred. 1997. "'Die Landschaft nicht im Wagen suchen.' Der frühe Musil und die Psychologie." *Scientia poetica* 1997 (1): 183–205.

Mehigan, Tim. 1997a. "Robert Musil, Ernst Mach und das Problem der Kausalität." *Deutsche Vierteljahrsschrift für Literaturwissenschaft und Geistesgeschichte* 71 (2): 264–87.

———. 1997b. "Violent Orders in Robert Musils *Der Mann ohne Eigenschaften* und Thomas Bernhard's *Kalkwerk*." In *War, Violence and the Modern Condition*, edited by Bernd Hüppauf. New York: Walter de Gruyter. European Cultures: Studies in Literature and the Arts, 300–316.

Schoene, Anja Elisabeth. 1997. *"Ach, wäre fern, was ich liebe!": Studien zur Inzestthematik in der Literatur der Jahrhundertwende (von Ibsen bis Musil)*. Würzburg: Königshausen und Neumann.

Schwartz, Agata. 1997. *Utopie, Utopismus und Dystopie in "Der Mann ohne Eigenschaften."* Frankfurt am Main, Berlin, Bern, New York, Paris, Vienna: Peter Lang.

Bonacchi, Silvia. 1998. *Die Gestalt der Dichtung. Der Einfluß der Gestalttheorie auf das Werk Robert Musils*. Bern, Berlin, Frankfurt am Main, New York, Paris, Vienna: Peter Lang. Musiliana 4.

Bringazi, Friedrich. 1998. *Robert Musil und die Mythen der Nation: Nationalismus als Ausdruck subjektiver Identitätsdefekte*. Frankfurt am Main, Berlin, Bern, New York, Paris, Vienna: Peter Lang.

Gnam, Andrea. 1998. *Die Bewältigung der Geschwindigkeit: Robert Musils Roman "Der Mann ohne Eigenschaften" und Walter Benjamins Spätwerk*. Munich: Wilhelm Fink.

Hartwig, Ina. 1998. *Sexuelle Poetik: Proust, Musil, Genet, Jelinek*. Frankfurt am Main: Fischer.

Bolterer, Alice. 1999. *Rahmen und Riss: Robert Musil und die Moderne*. Vienna: Editions Praesens.

Döring, Sabine. 1999. *Ästhetische Erfahrung als ethische Erkenntnis*. Paderborn: Mentis.

Maier, Uwe M. 1999. *Sinn und Gefühl in der Moderne: Zu Robert Musils Gefühlstheorie und einer Soziologie der Emotionen*. Aachen: Shaker Verlag.

Mehigan, Tim. 1999. "Robert Musil." In *Reclams Romanlexikon. Band 3: 20. Jahrhundert I*, edited by Frank Rainer Max and Christine Ruhrberg. Stuttgart: Reclam. Universal-Bibliothek 18003. 323–32.

Zingel, Astrid. 1999. *Ulrich u. Agathe: Das Thema der Geschwisterliebe in Robert Musils Romanprojekt "Der Mann ohne Eigenschaften."* St. Ingbert: Röhrig.

Hadjuk, Stefan. 2000. *Die Figur des Erhabenen. Robert Musils ästhetische Transgression der Moderne*. Würzburg: Königshausen und Neumann. Epistemata: Würzburger wissenschaftliche Schriften, Reihe Literaturwissenschaft 338.

Jonsson, Stefan. 2000. *Subject without Nation: Robert Musil and the History of Modern Identity.* Durham/London: Duke UP. Post-Contemporary Interventions.

Rauch, Marja. 2000. *Vereinigungen: Frauenfiguren und Identität in Robert Musils Prosawerk.* Würzburg: Königshausen and Neumann. Epistemata: Würzburger wissenschaftliche Schriften. Reihe Literaturwissenschaft 310.

Coetzee, J. M. 2001. "Robert Musil's *Diaries.*" In *Stranger Shores. Essays 1986–1999.* London: Secker and Warburg, 104–22.

Imai, Michio. 2001. "Musil between Mach and Stumpf." In *Ernst Mach's Vienna 1895–1930: Or Phenomenalism as Philosophy of Science,* edited by J. Blackmore, R. Itagaki, and S. Tanaka. Dordrecht, Boston, London: Kluwer. Boston Studies in the Philosophy of Science 218, 187–210.

Kümmel, Albert. 2001. *Das MoE-Programm: Eine Studie über geistige Organisation.* Munich: Wilhelm Fink. Musil-Studien 29.

Mehigan, Tim. 2001. *Robert Musil.* Stuttgart: Reclam. Universal-Bibliothek 17628.

Pieper, Hans-Joachim. 2002. *Musils Philosophie: Essayismus und Dichtung im Spannungsfeld der Theorien Nietzsches und Machs.* Würzburg: Königshausen und Neumann.

Taschner, Rudolf. 2002. *Musil, Gödel, Wittgenstein und das Unendliche.* Vienna: Picus Verlag. Wiener Vorlesungen im Rathaus 87.

Index